BASIC TEXTS IN COUNSELLING AND PSYCHOTHERAPY

Series editor: Stephen Frosh

This series introduces readers to the theory and practice of counselling and psychotherapy across a wide range of topic areas. The books appeal to anyone wishing to use counselling and psychotherapeutic skills and are particularly relevant to workers in health, education, social work and related settings. The books are unusual in being rooted in psychodynamic and systemic ideas, yet being written at an accessible, readable and introductory level. Each text offers theoretical background and guidance for practice, with creative use of clinical examples.

Published

Jenny Altschuler
COUNSELLING AND PSYCHOTHERAPY FOR FAMILIES IN TIMES OF ILLNESS AND DEATH 2nd Edition

Bill Barnes, Sheila Ernst and Keith Hyde
AN INTRODUCTION TO GROUPWORK

Stephen Briggs
WORKING WITH ADOLESCENTS AND YOUNG ADULTS 2nd Edition

Alex Coren
SHORT-TERM PSYCHOTHERAPY 2nd Edition

Jim Crawley and Jan Grant
COUPLE THERAPY

Emilia Dowling and Gill Gorell Barnes
WORKING WITH CHILDREN AND PARENTS THROUGH SEPARATION AND DIVORCE

Loretta Franklin
AN INTRODUCTION TO WORKPLACE COUNSELLING

Gill Gorell Barnes
FAMILY THERAPY IN CHANGING TIMES 2nd Edition

Fran Hedges
AN INTRODUCTION TO SYSTEMATIC THERAPY WITH INDIVIDUALS

Fran Hedges
REFLEXIVITY IN THERAPEUTIC PRACTICE

John Hills
INTRODUCTION TO SYSTEMIC AND FAMILY THERAPY

Sally Hodges
COUNSELLING ADULTS WITH LEARNING DISABILITIES

Linda Hopper
COUNSELLING AND PSYCHOTHERAPY WITH CHILDREN AND ADOLESCENTS

Sue Kegerreis
PSYCHODYNAMIC COUNSELLING WITH CHILDREN AND YOUNG PEOPLE

continued overleaf...

Geraldine Shipton
WORKING WITH EATING DISORDERS

Gerrilyn Smith
WORKING WITH TRAUMA

Laurence Spurling
AN INTRODUCTION TO PSYCHODYNAMIC COUNSELLING 2nd Edition

Paul Terry
COUNSELLING AND PSYCHOTHERAPY WITH OLDER PEOPLE 2nd Edition

Jan Wiener and Mannie Sher
COUNSELLING AND PSYCHOTHERAPY IN PRIMARY HEALTH CARE

Shula Wilson
DISABILITY, COUNSELLING AND PSYCHOTHERAPY

Steven Walker
CULTURALLY COMPETENT THERAPY

Jenny Walters
WORKING WITH FATHERS

Jessica Yakeley
WORKING WITH VIOLENCE

Invitation to authors
The Series Editor welcomes proposals for new books within the Basic Texts in Counselling and Psychotherapy series. These should be sent to Stephen Frosh at the School of Psychology, Birkbeck College, Malet Street, London, WC1E 7HX (e-mail s.frosh@bbk.ac.uk)

Basic Texts in Counselling and Psychotherapy
Series Standing Order ISBN 0–333–69330–2
(outside North America only)

You can receive future titles in this series as they are published by placing a standing order. Please contact your bookseller or, in the case of difficulty, write to us at the address below with your name and address, the title of the series and the ISBN quoted above. Customer Services Department, Macmillan Distribution Ltd Houndmills, Basingstoke, Hampshire RG21 6XS, England

INTRODUCTION TO SYSTEMIC AND FAMILY THERAPY

A User's Guide

JOHN HILLS

Family Therapist, Tavistock Clinic

First published 2013 by
PALGRAVE MACMILLAN

Palgrave Macmillan in the UK is an imprint of Macmillan Publishers Limited, registered in England, company number 785998, of Houndmills, Basingstoke, Hampshire RG21 6XS.

Palgrave Macmillan in the US is a division of St Martin's Press LLC, 175 Fifth Avenue, New York, NY 10010.

Palgrave Macmillan is the global academic imprint of the above companies and has companies and representatives throughout the world.

Palgrave® and Macmillan® are registered trademarks in the United States, the United Kingdom, Europe and other countries
ISBN 978-0-230-22444-5   ISBN 978-1-137-01560-0 (eBook)

DOI 10.1007/978-1-137-01560-0

This book is printed on paper suitable for recycling and made from fully managed and sustained forest sources. Logging, pulping and manufacturing   processes are expected to conform to the environmental regulations of the country of origin.

A catalogue record for this book is available from the British Library.

Library of Congress Cataloging-in-Publication Data

Hills, John.
    Introduction to systemic and family therapy/by John Hills
      p. ; cm.
    Includes bibliographical references.

    I. Title.
    [DNLM: 1. Family Therapy—methods. WM 430.5.F2]

    616.89'156—dc23
                                    2012024724

10 9   8 7   6   5   4   3   2   1
22 21 20 19 18 17 16 15 14 13

To Joan Picton and Jack Hills, who brought me into this world of wonders and stood with me at the times I faltered

CONTENTS

CONTENTS

ACKNOWLEDGEMENTS

My own experiential learning developed over four decades, so there are many individuals to thank. I hope most know privately who they are and if I haven't cited them here it does not mean they are not in my mind.

From my immediate locality in Canterbury and the Kent and Medway Partnership NHS Trust, where much of the work in this book first developed, and continues to do so, I am especially grateful to my psychoanalytical colleague Ali McLewin. Eileen Bill, Elaine Lee and Trisha Sinclair were also part of the adult mental health services at Laurel House, Canterbury, foolhardy enough to join our forays into the family crucible as a reflecting team.

Alison Culverwell and Elizabeth Field of the Older Adult Psychological Services at St Martin's Hospital, Canterbury had the vision to introduce family systemic work with a patient group with whom it is rarely used. That team is a special joy to work with: one feels validated by good managers who achieve that rare integration of high managerial and clinical skills.

My former team colleagues at the Adult Psychotherapy Clinic at Cossington Road, Canterbury, provided me with many different psychotherapy perspectives over my 20 years there, a working environment offering humour, and support to those 'troubled in mind'. I owe a great deal to colleagues Brendan Flynn, Ania Liro, Lesley Middleditch and Dirk Stikker at the Mount Zeehan Unit, Canterbury, who over nine years helped co-evolve a family-based systemic service for the alcohol-dependent. After winning the Mental Health Team of the Year 2008 award from the *Nursing Journal*, the team was rewarded with the closure of the unit 18 months later, and have all gone their separate ways.

I have already acknowledged many of the influences the Tavistock Clinic, London, has had on my development in the tribute book to my supervisor John Byng-Hall, whose thinking on family scripts is presented here. David Campbell, who tutored on the systemic psychotherapy course at the Tavistock for many years, was instrumental in the publisher's approach to me to write this book. I hope this faith has not been misplaced. Barbara Dale, who trained with me in the early 1980s, was a key figure in achieving recognition for systemic psychotherapy as a discipline in this highly conservative institution. She was a great advocate of the importance of the 'intuitive leap', an approach I apply to much of my work as a result. Both died recently, and their loss makes their influence more keenly recalled. My teaching colleagues at the Tavistock Clinic on the Introductory and Intermediate Systemic Training courses (Sharon Bond, Kate Daniels, Ruth Erskine, Carol Halliwell, Vince Hesketh, Kate Pelissier and Jane Dutton) helped create a free open climate of learning that came from a deep respect for systemic ideas and appreciation of difference.

Thanks to David Challender and Mary Godden for our very different conversations in supervision; to John Whitwell, Head of Therapy of ISP Childcare and the exceptional group of psychotherapists employed there over the years, and to Mandy Stevens, who helped with the typescript. To valued colleagues and friends Sara and John Barratt, Andrew and Marigemma Rocco Briggs, Nick Child, Maureen and Hugh Crago, Una Freeston, Martin Garsed, Jürgen Hargens, Rose Kent, Polly Klinefelter, Sebastian Kraemer, Rob Leiper, Jim and Anni Neal, Peter Smith, the two Thom(p)sons, Malcolm and Mary Louise, I owe much in helping me identify that the serious need not be dealt with solemnly. Thanks to Brian Cade, who took over as editor of that 'bucking bronco', *Context* magazine, and the lively inventiveness of the AFT Publishing group and the former 'Thinking Families' section of *Context* that included a genogram on which my guide was partly based. The Association of Family Therapy, and its dynamic administrator Sue Kennedy, its Executive and Board, are models of how an organisation should be run and helping this particular modality punch above its weight.

To all at the Friends Meeting House in Canterbury I owe many peaceful hours of contemplative silence beside the still waters of the River Stour; whilst to the other five members of the Kamikaze Blues Band and our long-suffering partners I have valued the many hours of our driving if voluminous sound.

To Hayley and William, for allowing our work be put into the public domain, and to the Cockburn family for permission to freely use the material from *Henry's Demons*. My thanks to all my patients who, as John Bowlby said of his, worked hard to educate me. I hope they learned as much from me as I did from them.

I'm truly grateful to Stephen Frosh, who commissioned this book, and to Catherine Gray, from Palgrave Macmillan, who painstakingly stuck by me with valuable advice and guidance in the difficult process of bringing it into life.

Finally, to those closest to me, the whole network of my family, without whose embodiment of 'goodness and love unfailing' this book could not have been written with conviction. For Kate, my loving and equal life-traveller who has patiently shared my attention with these pages for several years and whose love I return. She helped unstintingly with editing the proofs. She and our children Joel, Kirsten and Lauren; their partners Marie-Laure and Simone and grandchildren Noa, Mario, Adele and Dora are living reminders of the many and deep pleasures that can flow from being in a family, as well as the momentary *sturm und drang* gone through to hold it secure.

Alas, this is not a recipe book for happy family life, if such was ever possible to write. My hope is that it points to ways in which skilfully directed therapeutic work can reveal and work with the obstacles to well-being.

The perennial, optimistic disposition of a therapist can always spot openings for change, but I shall resist these and leave the text to stand or fall as it will.

INTRODUCTION

The background of the book

This book is intended as an introductory guide to anyone seeking to work with whole families. Its title incorporates four elements: family, systemic, therapy and user's guide. There are many professions, in social work, mediation and mental health, across the age range, to palliative care, and family intervention services in the voluntary and statutory sectors, already working with whole families. The more radical idea of treating not just the problems presented by individuals but working with whole sets of personal relationship networks which form their context has gained professional and political acknowledgement. Such an approach, seeking to appraïse and consult the total system of family and their assisting professional relationships, has grown in the 60 or so years since it first began to emerge in the UK, the USA and parts of Europe. It is now a transcultural approach increasingly embedded in the interventional repertoire of many different societies.

Looking across the whole relational environment in which an individual difficulty is embedded offers greater potential for change in the professional task, though it demands greater and different management skills. The earliest book written on the approach, *Family Group Therapy*, remains a useful description, but it has become cross-fertilized in the intervening years with more complex analyses of social and personal differences of gender, race, sexual orientation, culture, class and disability. Indeed, the idea of 'family' has little normative validity. There are many different ideas of 'family', not least defined by those who see themselves as composing one.

The other huge paradigm shift brought into the mix has been the growing influence of systemic and ecological thinking. This thinking, derived from science and technology, has presented us with a schema of interlocking environments, from the cosmological to the closely personal and micro-cellular. The depth and breadth of such perspectives are only now beginning to reveal their revolutionary potential for a new understanding. Previously impregnable boundaries of discrete knowledge are being broken down in many domains for a much more integrative world view. Such fluidity can be disconcerting, dispensing as it seems to do with the certainties of established truths and beliefs. The basic assumptions of psychotherapy, individual casework and group work have been perturbed by a quietly disruptive newcomer using an eco-systemic approach, with a growing evidence of effective outcomes in the USA and the UK. This systemic paradigm is not unlike a chameleon blending in with the many different disciplines it joins in seeking a connected understanding. It is not contained in the boundary of science and technology but crosses into the aesthetics of poetry, spirituality and mysticism in its search for connection to our world. As the seventeenth-century metaphysician Thomas Traherne put it: 'You never enjoy the world aright, till the sea itself floweth in your veins, till you are clothed with the heavens, and crowned with the stars: and perceive your self to be the sole heir of the whole world: and more than so, because men are in it who are everyone sole heirs as well as you' (2002:4).

However, though many of the ideas and approaches of this family systemic paradigm excite the newcomer as much as the veteran, they are not always easy to get hold of, far less to incorporate into effective confident practice. Its chameleon-like properties enable it to blend with the diverse uses it is put to by its advocates, none of which seem to have much convergence. Similarly, 'the family' is a kaleidoscope of many shapes and sizes, with no common shape or identity. This makes methodological demands on the practitioner, and the natural desire for a 'one-size-fits-all' application frequently ends in failure, aggravating an already distressed system.

The third element of the book's title, 'therapy', is best left undefined for the present apart from acknowledging that it contains certain key aspirations: the relief of suffering, reduction of conflict, better understanding and relational communication, and improved problem-solving and well-being. This will be frequently revisited in the text.

The book seeks to be a 'user's guide'. This may need a little clarification, for the term is usually associated with 'user-friendliness'. The text certainly endeavours to be that, with full summaries at the end of each chapter and a glossary. However, it invites you to reflect as fully and deeply on the structure of your own experience, your beliefs, the feelings you avoid or embrace and the relationships that have been enhancing, inspirational or disruptively painful. A key belief to most effective forms of therapy and intervention is that the more available you are to your own experience and to engaging with others the more substantial will be your range and effectiveness. This ability, like all arts and skills, emerges with directed, disciplined practice. The communal, live work of family systemic therapy where trust, empathy and openness inform the spirit of working together is a powerful and unique element of this form of practice.

An experiential perspective is to directly engage with lived existence and others who share our world, as Traherne suggests. This approach, advocated in this book, is not a comfortable one, since it offers no refuge behind philosophical propositions (however enjoyable the disputation of these may be); nor scientific theories, which may help to construct and explain the order of things; nor theological beliefs, which seem to describe who is favoured in the here and now and the hereafter. The paramount feature of experientialism is personal and asks what the world means to you; how you deal with all its pains and pleasures, desires and woes; loves and losses; how you determine the guiding aspects to your life and, more importantly, how you act on them.

Experientialism involves an awareness of the human condition, the given experiences around which we must shape our own stances, attitudes and responses. The message of this book is thus a paradox of inclusivity: we have our own unique set of circumstances, our personal condition from which we make what we can of a world to which we sometimes may not fully feel connected or understand. We also share with the rest of humanity at least four elements of experience: the fact of death, isolation, the search for meaning amidst absurdity and our freedom. From these darker materials we may also discover the profound significance of attachment, care and the pleasures of being moved by the beautiful. Such an existential context, the total world in which we have our being, our ontological self, will be revisited from time to time in the book. These ideas can seem forbidding at first, though they form the basis of self-discovery, learning and navigation through psychic and relational distress. Exercises will be given at certain stages to guide your own experiential discovery. It is important in all casework, mediation and therapy to have access to an effective mentor, whether as supervisor or personal therapist. Such a person is a guide through the difficult terrain of an experiential way of working with others. You will also bring to this relationship your own unique experience of family life, from its initial nurturance to its current dynamic.

Our experiential world of interlinking systems

Opening ourselves fully to an awareness of the awesome grandeur of the heavens, it requires little knowledge of science to grasp the view of George Ellis, mathematician and Professor of Systems at Cape Town University, that a tiny variation of physics would be needed for our world not to exist at all. Whilst physicists believe they have identified the Higgs Boson 'God' particle, the basic unit of all matter, the vast, opposing energies in the cosmos are very finely calibrated in the creation of sustainable existence. From the experiential response to the universe's grand scale and its 'non-possibility', to the personal ordinariness of daily rituals, a pattern of organization, of systems, is always present. We can discern this in our everyday existence.

You get up for work and take a shower, whose water is fed from sources many miles away. You clean your teeth with your usual method of brushing. Your breakfast, devoured in haste, is usually bought at the local supermarket that sources supplies via global networks. It is raining; everyone has taken to their cars so traffic is heavy; but no matter, for you have your own system for just such eventualities, and by using back roads and short-cuts you get to the office, though others have had the same idea and so some of the congestion has spilled over into these side roads.

You want to reach the office early this morning to please the manager because she has indicated she is going in early too. It won't harm your promotional chances to be seen to be enthusiastic. After all, you are in a chain of authority, and have your responsibilities within this hierarchy. Your manager is 'the other' to whom you will have to account.

There are a host of new emails on screen reminding you of work throughput and productivity targets that shape and organize what you do and how you do it. It is early and the manager has not yet arrived. The office is too cold – the central heating has not been adjusted to the end of British Summer Time – you shiver and are uncomfortable. You go to the central- heating thermostat and adjust the temperature.

Your mobile rings. It's your partner. Could you get a birthday card for your grandfather, which you forgot at the weekend? Here very different systems converge, communicating information and relationship: the mobile phone with its network and the network of personal and family relationship. Finally, checking the data on the bank's computer, you discover your shares are in freefall. They are your main form of savings for your long-planned house move. A quick call to your partner to arrange their immediate sale is vital. The stock market in the East is taking a hammering; panic is growing everywhere. Mortgage interest rates will rise. The house move and your pension and retirement plans may have to be revised if this goes on. Already the government has decided that you will not be able to retire at the age you thought you would. You feel momentary envy for those on benefits or who have already retired; they may not have much, you muse, but at least they are secure. Two economic systems impinge on each other: housing costs and retirement plans resonate differently with these changes. Systems in panic reverberate to produce personal panic.

Your mobile rings again: this time it's your mother, in that commanding tone of voice that you dislike, reminding you not to forget your grandfather's birthday, 'as you always manage to do'. You feel irritated and want to bite back, but remember she is recovering from a serious illness, so you soften and ask how she is. She sounds close to tears, so you don't quite know what to say next, and wish she would not bother you at this hour of the day with emotional stuff you don't want to deal with. You tell her you love her and not to worry, you already have it in hand. She says it's a good thing she has a strong faith because she knows she will come through and returns your expression of affection with an injunction not to give any more thought to your neglectful employers because they will never value you properly. You smile quietly to yourself, thank her for calling and say you must get on. Meanwhile you can see on the computer screen that your shares have taken another tumble.

This contrived scenario describes just how complex and richly conjoined the systems of our world are, from the work/organizational, the family/relational, the communicational/informational, economic/social/transportational/environmental. We can see how interactional and relational the world is. Changes in certain parts of our interactional world can produce a chain reaction that leads to widespread adjustments in others. Somewhere beyond the activities of the parts is the working-out of an invisible whole that we might try to anticipate in our response, or leave spontaneously to be. This is the exercise of our freedom to choose, but we never quite know the outcome of the process.

Each person's response to different changes in different systems varies according to their position in that system and how they wish to 'play the system' to secure the outcomes and intentions that are important to them and that they think they can achieve. However, as the saying goes, 'You can't easily buck the system', whether to avoid traffic at peak periods in changeable weather, work for long in a cold office, control your finances, or work at your own pace. Everything requires adaptation and improvisation, reconciling and navigating the claims of competing systems. 'Nets' and 'webs', those metaphors of connecting processes, are also constrainers and containers.

This way of thinking may be, as I suggested earlier, harnessed for the pursuit of human well-being. It makes available through awareness and process-mapping all manner of possibilities. Systemic thought has huge practical applications and implications for many ways of thinking about human relationships, particularly for thinking/talking differently in the personal areas of human experience: distress, suffering, conflict and intimacy. It is in the specific relationship work of mental health and well-being that the application of systemic thought to counselling and psychotherapy has the greatest scope to demonstrate its transformational potential.

We have seen the informal system of dodging traffic jams is set alongside the complexity of traffic signals that permit their maximum flow. Both are systems (one, formal and structured, the other personal and improvisational) based on experiment, but they operate differently (one with some rigidity and the other with flexibility).

An extraordinary creation: the ecology of existence

In 1968 the National Aeronautics and Space Administration (NASA) published a view of our planet from the surface of the moon. In the picture, entitled 'Earthrise', the Earth stands out from utter darkness as a blue-and-white luminescent 'marble' adrift in an infinite ocean bereft of light. We look at our planetary home, alone in a vast cosmos of cold and empty space, and cannot but be struck by awe at its desolation and terrifying beauty. How have we survived through the aeons in the face of the forces of the universe? How have our intelligence and consciousness evolved to enable us to witness their miracle and mystery? With increased knowledge, what do we have to do to be proper custodians of our planet against our collective threats and depredations?

Until comparatively recently we had been able to look out to the cosmos and speculate, but we could not see ourselves from the perspective of the heavens. The camera has changed all this, and the real and symbolic importance of the universe cannot be understated. Here is the visual evidence, if any were needed, that we are part of a global community and planetary ecosystem; earth is our common home, our secure base. Identified in the Greek myth as the earth goddess Gaia (Lovelock, 1979), our planet and its teeming, vast, interwoven planetary organisms, life systems and their forces which sustain creation are wondrous, even sacred, whatever your world-view.

Creation's world of spectacular marvels is the cosmological base from which all philosophical, spiritual and systemic thought, the human relational world, family life and their therapeutic energies and assumptions begin. We can see ourselves, our home on earth, focusing down like a Google-mapping exercise to our particular community, street and house or away into the frozen, dark spaces of the cosmos. As children we used to play a game, a kind of cosmic location game: 'I'm Charlie Brown, 47 Dartmoor Road, Copnor, Portsmouth, Hampshire ...' through to '... Solar System, Outer Space, and the Whole Wide Universe.' *In Portrait of an Artist as a Young Man*, James Joyce's alter ego Stephen Dedalus plays a similar game on the flyleaf of his geography book (Joyce, 1972). This game, which existed way before GoogleWorld, provided a visual means of moving freely in the imagination between these different spatial contexts, each child struggling to outdo the other in elaboration. We had a defining place, an ontological context and consequent identity somewhere in the vast scheme of things. Our lives span both space and time, giving us what we might call our ontological identity.

Whatever metaphor is used, whether 'lifeboat', 'spacecraft', 'holding environment', 'life support' or 'home', in the midst of such cosmic nothingness, we and all we hold dear are sustained in the world in which we exist. The threats to it are innumerable: we know it relies on a delicate balance of energies and forces, its homeostasis; we know too that we may be citizens of particular cultures, social groupings, communities and nation-states, but we are also members of a vast and diverse human family. The first Islamic astronaut Sultan din al Arabi reported his first view of the world: 'The first day or so we pointed to our own countries ... by the fifth day we were aware of only one earth' (Poole, 2008: 00). Our collective view of the human species may be of a fragmented, rapacious and disputatious family. However, it is also one connected by ties of genetics, global location, trade links, migration and a capacity, if we cultivate it, to enter into one another's consciousness and experience, and see the world from that perspective. Psychotherapy and the creative arts give us the tools and sensibility, while ethics and politics give us the ideas to do so. Taken together in systemic thought (the patterning of organization), they give us the means to a powerful integrated world view, one that has the potential to deliver permanent change.

We know there are dual processes at work in all of nature, especially human nature, to create a sustainable balance between creation and destruction, growth and decay. As custodians and witnesses of our world it would seem tragic to allow this wondrous planetary ecosystem to decay into some unsustainable life form. Yet it could happen; our collective destructive capacities continue to put our planet and our life-support systems at risk.

We surely need more universal application of ecological thinking, not just to preserve the sustainable integrity of the earth but also sustainability in human relationships; to seek out an ethic from the cultural heritage of our whole species that which makes this possible and gives us the tools to understand and manage our own natures better. As the Swiss psychiatrist and analyst Carl Jung put to John Freeman in a BBC interview in 1959 with a chilling intensity: 'We need more psychology, we need more understanding of human nature because the only real danger that exists is Man himself ... His psyche should be studied because we are the origin of all coming evil' (Freeman, 1959).

Systemic thinking provides a powerful methodology to work at changing aspects of our own nature by changing the relational context in which we exist. Human systems are the link between the diverse members of the human family; systems are the linkages with the natural world and the physics of the cosmos. If we are to make our global environment sustainable for future generations, it is surely imperative to make the micro-environment in which we nurture future generations equally sustainable. Some of the ideas and practice in this book are a modest attempt to offer options of how that could happen.

The organization of the book

Looking at the contents list, you will see that the book starts directly with practice in Chapters 1 and 2. The guiding ideas and principles follow in Chapters 3, 4, 5 and 6 and we then return to their application in Chapters 7, 8 and 9. This may be confusing at first, for when we construct a jigsaw, it is more usual to look at the whole picture and then try fitting the particular pieces together. However, the process of jigsaw building is also circular, as one moves constantly between assembly and template. You are encouraged to do the same here. There is a Glossary at the very end of the book of the main terms and concepts emboldened in the text, which you can refer to as you go when an idea is not clear from its context.

From the initial chapters you may begin to get a feel of the direct experience of work with a family (as if you won't have had already!); the engagement with their distress; their sense of the 'impossibility' of their situation; and how, from the collaboration with colleagues with inquiring, clear and curious minds, you avoid taking on the 'heat' of others' distress with its risk of associative suffering and paralysis (often referred to as 'secondary' or 'vicarious traumatisation'). Others' distress can seep into the lives and consciousness of those around them, especially those seeking to provide amelioration.

I have preferred to use the conventional term 'patient', derived from the Latin *patior* (meaning 'to suffer' or 'to bear'). This is not from any identification with the 'medical model' but to emphasise the existential perspective of an experiential approach. Suffering is one of the givens of the human condition; we are all patients at some time, in some state or another. Pain in its many forms and manifestations may be both unpleasant and undesirable but is often the ground from which art, spiritual discovery and psychotherapy emerge. In its everyday form, the transformation that suffering can bring about to our attitudes and beliefs is commonly witnessed in the resilience, courage, determination, understanding and forgiveness within a community. The notion of the 'wounded healer' is not a fanciful one. The experience of 'woundedness' frequently provides the energising, healing resourcefulness in and around the person wounded. The term 'patient' is decidedly good enough.

With four exceptions, all the case narratives described use fiction-alised names, and personal details are slightly altered to disguise their identity. The work described, however, is as it was. The exceptions are William Gilroy, Hayley Andrews, Paul Wagg and the Cockburn family, whose accounts are already in the public domain. I wish you a fruitful journey of discovery through the family life processes which I have tried to capture in this text.

1

USING THE GENOGRAM AND CONVENING THE FAMILY

The 'Catch-22' of not working with families

The given of any family and **systemic** approach is a belief in the value of gathering members of a **family system** together to look at what is going on and what difficulties are getting in the way of more fully using family strengths. This is a difficult belief to put into practice, yet, without it, none of the techniques and ideas attached to a systemic approach make much sense. There is a 'Catch-22' to adopting such a change, as follows:

> If the families we work with were functional then they would have found their own solutions. The families we work with haven't found their solutions, so they cannot be functional. Best not touch the severe dysfunctionality of the whole family system; we'll just treat the individuals.

Nothing could be further from the truth. However, many tentative attempts to work with whole families founder early on, often for clear reasons: family members resist working in one another's company; they believe the disruptiveness and difficulty are located in particular individuals who they want 'fixed'; professional systems are not organised to absorb the full onslaught of family dynamics within their agencies, or within their informational recording systems; there is high anxiety about possibly worsening a volatile situation, leading to domestic violence and abuse; and not everyone is in a family anyway.

There are a host of such arguments for following Freud's treatment method and keeping family members firmly outside the door of the consultation room. Jay Haley wrote a richly ironic paper summarising the reasons for keeping to individual work (Haley, 1975).

Exercise 1.1: The challenge of working with families

Alone or with a colleague, list at least 20 reasons why it is inadvisable and difficult to think about working with whole or parts of families in your work setting. Try to find as many reasons to the contrary, and the kind of resources you would need to practise in this way.

If you have convinced yourself against the wisdom of working this way you should discard this book and redirect your training else-where, perhaps to cognitive behavioural therapy!

In a little-known paper given to the Association of Family Caseworkers in 1969, entitled 'Intervention in Social Situations' and more recently reprinted as 'Situation, Situation, Situation' in *Context* magazine, R.D. Laing says perceptively:

> This situation [a case just described] is one of many which have the characteristic: no one in the situation knows what the situation is. If one stays in such a situation just a little, say for 90 minutes, we get more and more lost and confused, disorientated .... We can never assume that the people in the situation know what the situation is. A corollary to this is: the situation has to be discovered. (Laing, 2002: 5)

This is very often a family's experience of itself. It takes an outside perspective to help a family reveal its whole situation to itself. There is a paradox about closeness; the more involved you are in a situation the less clearly you see it, especially when there are many versions of how it can be seen and described. We can better construct the 'whole situa-tion' from a remote position; however, social situations engaged experi-entially and close to are more kaleidoscopic and elusive. Any casual observer of a case conference will see that many perspectives can be held. My earliest piece of research for an MA dissertation was to survey how a team of six probation officers set about writing a court report and making a recommendation based on a particular case history. It will come as no surprise that there were six different narratives of the offender's life and as many different sentence recommendations.

Laing was concerned as to how social interactional processes ascribed and maintained definitions of 'mental illness' and how the family's personal constructions, whether well-informed or 'folk narratives', contributed to the experience. He thought it important to be able to see the 'whole' situation accurately, so he endeavoured not to align with any particular family subgroup or prejudgement about a family's **experiential** phenomenon of mental illness.

A key element in family and systemic work which enables both the therapist and the family to get as accurate a description of the 'whole situation' as possible through their individual interactional repertoires, beliefs and feelings is to map these through the device of the **genogram**. It is a means of joining with the family in an open conversation, by providing a containing structure for the initial exploration. The process is co-operative and circular, a joint odyssey of discovery from the flow of feedback and experience. Following the therapists' interested curiosity, family members begin to discover different aspects of the family story and awareness of one another and their shared situation.

About this approach of experiential **phenomenology** Laing wrote: 'Its study is the relation between experience and experience; its true field is **inter-experience** ... I cannot experience your experience. You cannot experience my experience. We are both invisible ...' (Laing, 1967: 16). **Dialogue**, especially around the genogram, is a means of making different experiences visible.

This technique is best begun with yourself and, if you have never practised it before, best tried out on your own family. However, if you do the latter it is best to confine the exploration to gathering information about events, circumstances and relationships. Be wary of venturing into the subjectivity of interpreted experience, except in the exercise that follows about you. Think of it as a journalistic or historical inquiry with the family, certainly not therapy. Your family may be keen or apprehensive in any case, in seeing it as therapy for them. In any event, resist or reassure, depending on their attitudes. Be interested and curious, but keep the exploration as plain and uncontentious as you can.

You never just 'do' a genogram. It is a task without limit or time. Genograms are not mysterious – in essence they are family trees – but they are deeply symbolic as holistic, cultural, contextual maps of whole family systems and the persons within them. Unlike a genome, which maps the strands of DNA and is finite, a genogram has an infinitesimal series of informational branches to help the family describe where and how they locate themselves socially, relationally, existentially, emotionally, and in terms of belief and values. It helps them, as well as the inquiring therapist, to see how they are organised and how much of that organisation – that scripting – is the product of the past or kept alive in the present. A **family script** is the totality of their interactive, living experience with one another based on remembrances, attitudinal beliefs, emotional responses, behaviour, relationship structure, role models and narratives. We shall return to an analysis of scripts more fully in Chapter 8 and in the Glossary at the back of the book.

Exercise 1.2: Constructing your own genogram

Ideally, it is best to work with a trusted and informed colleague who can pose questions that stimulate dialogue and reflection between you. However, you could start it on your own and discuss it with a systemically informed supervisor or therapist. In any event, it is best to keep personal journal notes of the connections, associations and further questions that come to mind as you work. Take a large piece of paper, such as a flip chart, and, using the symbols in the Appendix, draw out the main scaffolding of your family relationships at the present time.

The genogram should cover at least three generations, four if you include any current 'family of creation'. Include all ages, births and deaths, so all the family *dramatis personae* are included. You might want to include significant other relationships to you, such as informal family members or close friends who may have provided refuge at times when family relationships were taxing, pets, or interests that did likewise. Don't overload it, but think carefully about the relationships of real value to you and include these. This is the basic framework. From here there are a number of dimensions you might want to explore. You need not do all, and certainly not at the same time. You can revisit these as you develop your ideas through the book.

Look closely at the changes and transitions in terms of losses, separations, moves and migration, health and employment issues and life events. Write down or describe to your genogram consultant the impact these events had on the family and who had been most affected. How did you know about this? We shall call this existential backdrop the **circumstantial script**, the family story of circumstance.

Note down the stories and explanations about the experiential impact of these events. Were they inferred, spoken about, or noted from changed behaviour or attitudes in relationships? How have these communicated experiences shaped your beliefs? This is the **assumptive script**, the beliefs about living, change, suffering, resilience and possibility.

Think about the values and the communication of those values through the different cultural backgrounds of family members. Did

→

---

they help position you in relation to your particular differences and that of your social **context**, and if so, how? How were any personal differences of identity, beliefs and values responded to in the family? The bases of these are the family gender, class, faith, non-faith, ethnic and sexual orientation beliefs. This is the **assumptive identity script.**

Looking again at the basic relationship scaffolding of your family tree, mark in and describe the closeness and distance in relationships; the attachments and detachments; the configuration of dominance and non-dominance and sub-system alliances in the family. How were these communicated? How were decisions taken, and difficulties and changes negotiated? Who was involved in them? What was the quality of those decisions? This is **the structural problem-solving script.** Think about how these different dimensions were communicated directly through remembered or contemporary conversations and stories. This is the **delivered script.**

The silences of participants are also part of the delivered script since we 'cannot not communicate' (Watzlawick, Beavin & Jackson, 1967: 51). Think about the silences and the unspoken expressions in the family. What did you take them to mean about the unlived life or the personal differences which were not voiced? Where did they usually come from, and what happened to them in the family transactions? How did you deal with them and communicate about them? What happened if you did? This is the **subscript** – the nuanced, sometimes defensive/sometimes aggressive unexpressed stratum of family experience.

It is not so important to remember the script headings at this stage as the content and family processes. It helps to give you an idea of how versatile the genogram is as a containing structure for examining family experience, a window into the life of your own family that will equip you better to assist families to look more fully at the phenomenology of their lives.

Convening a family meeting

The next step is to find systemically informed colleagues, who are perhaps undergoing training, and a systemically registered supervisor (or one who is completing their supervision training), and join with them as a collaborative team. When beginning to engage families you definitely need the support of your agency manager, the basic accommodation for a reasonably large family with room for you and a co-therapist, and a small team if there are enough of you. You should seek out a systemically trained supervisor and use any recordings made in supervision so you can examine how you manage the process between yourself and the family. You will obviously need to obtain the whole family's consent for this.

It is best to convene as many of the family as you can and, occasionally, other significant people they might nominate. It is best if you do this by telephone, introducing yourself and checking their awareness of and consent to the referral. It is important to explain how you work and to make it clear it is not about attributing blame (usually their apprehension), but rather having an open conversation with as many people as possible to build a clearer picture and look for ways forward. This should be rehearsed through role play and difficult responses enacted to help build a confident and clear dialogue about your aims and intentions. Reassurance should be given that confidentiality is paramount, and how this works in a shared context of openness; you should touch briefly on the exceptions to it. It helps to give reassurance about your role responsibility and rules in managing the whole situation which avoid it getting out of hand.

You will have set down a marker about concern for the well-being of all the group. You might ask your initial informant who they think is most or least likely to be uneasy with the process. It might be necessary to help the informant with some ideas as to how they could discuss the meeting with the others. You might report from previous experience how families respond to the method, their apprehensions and their endorsements.

It is essential to assist referrers to prepare the family for referral, and it can be helpful to invite potential referrers to observe your work so that their knowledge is based on first-hand experience. A copy of the leaflet for families explaining the service could be sent to referrers and they should be invited to ask elucidating questions about the service. Remember the cardinal principle of systemic work is in using relational networks to their full potential, not just working with 'difficulties in themselves'.

Exercise 1.3: Making families welcome

Take a recent referral to your agency. Think carefully about who has made the referral and what they think about it. Imagine if you were to establish a family-centred service how you would want them to present this to the family and how you might write a leaflet of introduction about the service for the family.

The telephone call is followed by letters to the whole family, addressing each member personally and repeating the basic reasons for having an open meeting. It is good practice to enclose a leaflet about the service. There is an example of a general one on the AFT website (www.AFT.org.uk) that can be downloaded and used as a template for the specific service you are providing. Working together to adapt the leaflet for one that covers your needs using your language and ideas is a valuable task of solidifying the team ethos. A service can be provided by a single worker, but without considerable experience this can be risky in both providing safe containment for parts of a family system and following the myriad exchanges attentively.

Family systemic practice has matured well beyond the time when patients would be sent away if only a part of the family attended. A 'minimum sufficient system' of two is required to ensure a basic inter-relational dialogue. However, many experiential techniques, notably from Gestalt Therapy, demonstrate how the internalised presence of 'the other(s)' is an active ingredient in a relationship, even if the other is physically absent. Using a **systemic phenomenological** approach (see Chapter 7), all family members are present in the work if absent from the room.

Family members who are initially reluctant or resistant to attend should be respected and their response understood as natural. A survey of members conducted several years ago by the UK Association for Family Therapy showed that only 3 per cent acknowledged they had brought their own families into therapy. If practitioners show this level of unease, it is hardly surprising that the general population will act any differently. An active experiential belief in the method, built up in developing your practice, gives a secure base from which to inform, encourage and persuade the referred patient family group to suspend their natural reticence and try it out. If some family members begin the work, others often join in later usually out of curiosity.

The first meeting: setting the scene

It is important to have a sufficiently large, soundproof room, with comfortable, attractive seating. If there is a one-way screen and a visual recording link this should be flagged up at the point of referral and mentioned in the leaflet sent to the family. The same is true for the presence of a reflecting team.

A team, one-way screen and video are not essential requirements for good systemic working. In the past, there has been a tendency to make a fetish ritual of their use, as if no effective or 'pure' work could otherwise be possible. However, for training in collaborative teamwork, observation, service development and experimentation under conditions of skilled live supervision, they are necessary. Together they form the key theatre of operations – indeed, the secure base – that holds and develops the craft of systemic working.

Where the full set-up is available, it helps to settle everyone by offering to demonstrate the facilities and introduce the members of the team beforehand. Children are usually fascinated by the one-way mirror and want to explore it. Humour is ever the essential tool for helping everyone relax. You will find your own ways. One such is to ask the children if they know the children's story *Alice through the Looking Glass* as it will help them understand just how 'weird' and 'strange' the whole set-up is. Getting permission to film a session is a potentially difficult negotiation, but experiencing the benefit of reviewing your work and looking closely at the process makes for a more confident request. This is a necessary part of systemic training, so you will have overcome the common reluctance at seeing yourself work in a negative light. Playful, teasing humour can help: 'Don't worry, these sessions never turn up on youTube. However, if you want them to I'm sure we can arrange it!' As with all use of humour, it must be finely judged. You may get a feel for a family's capacity for humour, with its implied social trust, from the initial telephone contact.

In the same vein, it is important to develop an ease with the ordinary language of everyday social life and not to feel restricted by your professional role. Your professional authority comes from a different presence. Jay Haley (1976), among others, stressed the importance of this in making direct and early connection with families. They may have had a host of difficult communications with professionals in the past and will view your work warily, anxious lest they be misunderstood.

This will also ease the way into 'problem talk', the reason the family has responded to your invitation. With so many present, there are often family anxieties about where the 'problem talk' may lead, by exposing the whole system rather than confining it to a distressed individual (often a shared, unspoken worry in the team). There is an innate concern that the professionals will see less benevolent elements of the family experience beneath the struggle to maintain aspects of care and unity, or that hoped-for solutions may not materialise or even exist. After all, in the Greek myth, Pandora's box, once opened, led to mayhem (although at the bottom of it lay 'hope').

By improvising the scenario of a family coming to therapy for the first time, the team will better understand and anticipate the unspoken worries in the family. Just as a knitter tests the tension required to knit a garment and adjust the size of the needles accordingly, so the therapist/team anticipates the family's tension at the outset and adjusts the pace and style of the meeting.

The genogram should be introduced as an essential aid for the therapists getting to know the family better, as well as stressing its benefits to the family. Humour-wise, it may be useful to draw the family's attention to TV programmes such as 'Who Do You Think You Are?' where celebrities trace their ancestry and their stories through their family trees and emerge with a different perspective. Such work can also be carried out, and often is, in the family home. The unfamiliarity of the setting is offset by a more rapid engagement. The family's 'home advantage' is valuable so long as it does not prove a distraction to getting down to the work. Responsibility for preventing this rests with the therapeutic leadership.

The genogram

When working with a family, the room should have a white board or a flip chart (the latter can be taken to a home-based session). You may choose your own symbols, though the universal shorthand above is easy to learn. The therapist-led genogram is the predominant approach until more confidence is gained in the technique. Later, families may be helped to take their own initiative. Coloured stones or different objects can be used on flat flip charts with family members choosing the objects that represent for them a person in the family. You can then invite them to give the reasons guiding their choice. A further variation is to have a large collection of familial figures of the kind used in sand tray-based psychotherapy (e.g. Lego figures or figures from popular films and television series, such as *Star Wars or In the Night Garden*). Each family member can be invited to explain their choice and its associations (e.g. Darth Vader as father/grandfather). These variations are most suitable where children and adolescents are in the session. However, they should not be discounted for use with older adults, though toys with suitable generational reference are obviously important.

Most people in human services work will know of and have used a genogram; many will have worked on their own. There is no limit to the number of times you can revisit the roots of every family's story or your own. As with your own genogram, draw out the family tree across four generations, carefully noting who is seen as being in the family and who is not. Discuss the main stories that are part of the family tradition to explain changes, discontinuities, losses, migrations, characters and characteristics of significant family members. This is the basic framework of the family traditions and scripts. It should make you curious and may open up all manner of questions about events that do not receive much family attention. Sometimes you may be aware of a 'family fog' and wonder what that might conceal. Your own genogram work will sensitise you in developing the dialogue.

Though it should be emphasised that there is no correct way to draw a genogram except your own way, it is usually best to go through the intergenerational picture 'once over lightly', so you have the main structure in place. In larger families with many comings and goings and complex shifts of membership this may take some time and more than one sheet of paper. Decisions about the size of the family; responses to births, deaths, events and life changes; and perceptions of the characteristics of past and present family members are all essential parts of the family's shared storytelling and social history keeping. This is the family's oral tradition of the circumstantial script that may have got submerged in the present difficulties and the many distractions and stresses of modern life. This tradition though is alive and awaiting revival. It helps to provide a different level of experience to the present struggles and generally gives the family, however fractured their current relationships, a sense of the continuity of living and being a part of this particular family.

Contrariwise, such narrative-sharing can release feelings about the emptiness and disconnection of present life, though this is often an unspoken driver of any sustained interpersonal tension. As you follow the narrative listen out for repeating patterns, recurring themes and areas associated with estrangement and anxiety. It is one of the many strengths of live therapeutic work that the method helps the family feel more available to itself.

You may soon have a sense of simple but remarkable family patterns emerging (family size, incidence of male and female children and age of starting a family, etc.). Pointing these out with curiosity, one often finds that they are connected with some family folklore and belief. They are important for building alliances and lead to the discussion of more personal connections, especially recurring patterns of anniversaries when events seem to repeat themselves across generational life with a surprising coincidence. Over time you will train yourself like an ancient prospector to look for such connections and patterns.

It is important to make a few forays into feeling states and disclosed experiences. Sometimes family members are prepared for this, and understand therapy as a cathartic, freeing experience and so need little or no prompting. The therapist, with an understanding of their role as a steering presence, gently corrects the direction of the session to balance strength of feeling. This may be done by quietly acknowledging the intensity of distress and moving to a different theme or asking other members of the family who seem to be unmoved for their perspective.

Occasional and briefly sketched self-disclosure by the therapists or team members who have encountered similar experiences can be very freeing for a family struggling to find a better understanding of a difficulty. However, the service is for the benefit of the patient family, not the therapist-system, who have other contexts to explore their experiential material.

The first session is essentially one of discovery for family and therapist systems. It identifies key themes and inducts the family system into the experience of therapy. Near the end of session, brief reflection from the conjoint therapists, reflection team or lone therapist should gather together adversities and virtues of the family's script into an account which the family can acknowledge and feel that they have been heard. Conveying experientially to the family core values of respect, understanding and care, the family usually responds to the invitation to return and is open to negotiation about how many sessions would be most useful. A balance must be struck between affirming the importance of their free choice and encouraging them to 'sit with' the doubt and anxiety the work might arouse.

Once such an initial engagement has been made and the main genogram outline is in place, the work of developing the therapists' thinking takes place at the end of one session and at the beginning of the next. There is a deepening of curiosity about the major family themes and their cross-connections. These can be explored with the family next time. An abundance of possibilities and questions may arise but their relevance to the presented difficulty by the family must be held in mind to 'ground' the experience for the family. Such themes will be described in Chapter 3.

Key ideas to hold in mind and watch out for

1. Engage openly and genuinely with each family member present to create a presence of respectful listening and interest, informed questioning with gentle challenges to clarify.
2. Create a climate of confidence in the abilities of all family members in working together towards hoped-for solutions, though without guarantees.

3. Create a climate of trust and confidence in the method – as with any skill or accomplishment it is best achieved experientially, working and learning together, rehearsing through the dramatised improvisation of role play

4. Many families come with a natural reticence to trusting their collective experience to inquiring minds, often doing so out of desperation. Where they are compelled to do so, as part of a parenting risk assessment, the reluctance is even stronger and anxieties more acute. However, in this context, whilst the work should be informed by family systemic thinking, it has different immediate goals to those of therapy. An active scepticism about accepting and acknowledging personal responsibility for harm or neglect, intermixed with a freely associating curiosity, needs to be part of the assessors' position and methodology.

5. Confidence and authority can be gained by working with non-referred families, as some training courses offer. Observation of families, in and out clinical settings, offers a baseline for gaining experience in task explanation and the collaborative, storytelling dialogue around genogram work.

6. The therapists and team need to work towards a position of comfortable, confident authority based on a command of method and technique. This will model open, collaborative group relations as a system for the family, especially where authority seems to be diffused and ineffective.

7. Whatever information or perspective about another is being highlighted through attention to one family member, it is usually best checked out with them, and certainly children or the less active participants. For example: Did they know this from X previously? How true was it? Did it come as a surprise?

Therapist to Jim: You seemed very upset, Jim, by what Monica had to say then. Can you tell us what part you disagreed with?
[Jim states reaction]
Therapist to Jim: It did also seem that she was saying ... [offering a less emotive summary of the same point]. Do you think there's any part of that you find fair comment, or even true? The principle of an interactional 'call and response' should pervade the work continuously. This is the circularity of the systemic phenomenological method (see Chapter 7), and any intense feelings that may arise are held through reflected listening.

8. Not every member of the family will have equal personal knowledge about the others (there's no reason they should, all human groups have important internal alliances of confidentiality). Adult sexual relationships are best engaged separately, though hints will emerge from others. It often comes as a revelation to family members, e.g. adults, that children know more about the adults than the adults think they would or should know; adults also know less about one another's history or family stories than they think they do. It is an important principle never to assume knowledge without enquiry.

9. Where news of family secrets and shameful episodes emerges it should be managed with care and sensitivity, and by seeking an adult to explain the situation to the child. Sometimes the therapists can best help by conveying the reported experience dispassionately and the emotions involved, in a detoxified way. This may open up a whole family dialogue. Once, conjointly conducting a family session of adults centred on a 45-year-old depressed woman, she began disclosing her adolescent sexual abuse by her father; then her younger sister did the same; her older brother reported violent assaults from his father as a child and the mother then reported having been raped as a young woman by the father's best friend. They gathered each year at their father's grave to honour his memory. After this session of discovery, they all decided they could not do so again.

    Where shame is associated with the secrecy there is usually some indication from family members through a reticence to venture into the area. It is usually best to 'flag it up' to families early on when introducing the work by saying something such as: 'Most, if not all, families have some kind of secrets from one another and you will no doubt have your own. You will want to keep these private from one another and it's not our task to change your mind about this. However, the cost of keeping them to yourself is often worse than the distress you might feel bringing them into the open.' However, situations where disclosure of clear harm, violence and abuse occur need to be handled with reference to other systems responsible for personal protection and safety, and the reasons given.

10. Everyone in the family has a Janus-like position as observer/actor. 'Spect-actors' was the term the Latin American community dramatist Augusto Boal (1992) coined for this duality of player–spectator. They are witnesses, observers of one another, forming an understanding and a perception of the other which is often a rich source

of knowledge. The genogram leader can use this resource of proximate commentator where the subject of his curiosity (sometimes the identified patient) is struggling to express a thought or a feeling. This is the operational realisation of Robert Burns's famous plea: 'Wad some power the giftie gee us / To see airselves as others see us.'

Therapist: Jim, how do you think Monica is feeling about what seems like a difficulty in your relationship with each other?

Jim: Well she just closes down, won't talk to me and gets angry with the children.

Monica: Sometimes, I suppose. Jim just doesn't help, the way he goads me.

Therapist: So you close down. Monica, and you. Jim, provoke.

Jim: I suppose we do, put like that.

Monica: It's true.

Therapist: So how come you can agree with what I've just put back to you, mostly using your own descriptions, but you can't hear that from each other?

Jim: Hmm, I suppose that's why we're here.

11. The ownership of ideas and experience (their inter-experience) is held within the family and not subject to the therapist's interpretations, certainly in the earlier stages. The systemic-phenomenological method seeks clarity of personal description and is not necessarily concerned with explanation, justification, ascription or causation. As they describe, the family members may sometimes start to reinterpret for themselves. However, reflective feedback and therapeutic **reframing** certainly help to reinterpret their situation and thereby reappraise what it means for them.

12. At all stages the genogram leader must be able to see and join with the many different perspectives and accounts. This is why it is essential to have explored your own family heritage, for the insufficiently examined default position from which you operate can prove seriously limiting. Your own role and gender identifications, culturally organised values and beliefs, and emotional repertoire all have their experiential basis here. Without a degree of self-awareness they covertly organise selective attention during genogram work. The 'play's the thing', as Hamlet rightly deduced, to capture his mother and uncle's guilt through the staged **enactment** of a parallel dramatic story. Your family drama, past and current, is 'the thing' to which you will unfailingly respond as

both strength and weakness. It is circular: the more you are open to your own experience, the more you will be open to others'; the more open to others', the more to your own.

13.   It is essential to experience regular personal work, either on your own genogram with a colleague, psychotherapist, counsellor or supervisor, and sometimes in conjunction with your own family. As with other forms of psychotherapy, to enrich your own understanding and the process, it is necessary to be the subject and consumer of it. Such opportunities for self-discovery are enriching and lifelong, shared by those who understand the growth that comes from accomplished attachment to their disciplines and human relationships.

14.   With problem-centred behaviour, it is essential to track the circumstances/context in which it exhibits itself as well as the exceptions when it does not. The 'call and response' both to the problem, the 'problem holder' and their interacting systems are essential to inquire about and understand. This may include wider systems (e.g. schools or other services) and may involve network conversations with their representatives.

15.   This may offer 'strategies of the absurd' on which to base an intervention. Problems with behaviour are usually accompanied by strong negative affect such as a sense of failure, guilt, irritation, embarrassment, anger and helplessness that hinder communication, finding respite or resolution. It is always helpful to acknowledge the emotions around the difficulty, whilst tracking around the presented difficult behaviour, searching for other unvoiced tensions.

> *Therapist* (to teenager): Lisa, we've all just heard about how difficult it is when members of the family have heard you have cut yourself. Some say they feel angry, some sad for you, others at a loss to know what to do. Did you know they feel all these different ways? Sometimes I imagine it must make you feel worse and like cutting yourself some more.
>
> *Therapist* (to the family): Does Lisa's behaviour in cutting when she feels stressed have echoes for anyone else in the family, or from family stories in which anyone else felt the same way?

It may help to enlarge the joint quest for understanding and may also bring up some unresolved 'gestalt' from somewhere within the collective family experience.

This question may well raise some unexpected responses, followed by the therapist's further interest and curiosity. Brian Cade, Jay Haley and a number of other strategic therapists have some very playful ways of challenging Lisa's difficulties by using the family and task requirements of the absurd.

These, then, are the general guidelines to setting the scene for using the genogram.

Summary

- The importance of getting into a mindset of 'whole-situation' thinking and the phenomenology of 'inter-experience' are stressed.
- An exercise is described for constructing your own genogram, which enables you to adopt this different mindset, including the main symbols and self-directed questions which facilitate this.
- The elements of the family script are outlined and explained.
- Guidance is given on ways of convening a minimum sufficient system of the family and explaining the working method.
- Ways of introducing the equipment of a therapy room and the presence of a team to the family are explained.
- Creative ways of using a genogram with a family are explored.
- 15 principles of good practice to optimise the therapeutic process are described and amplified.

2

A FAMILY SESSION OBSERVED

Teamworking in the reflecting process

Luigi Pirandello's postmodern drama *Six Characters in Search of an Author* (1923; Pirandello, 1993) has a family group disrupting the rehearsal of a play by Pirandello in order to play themselves, independently of their author's creation. The exasperated producer, shaking with rage, cries out, 'You can't have one character coming on like you're doing, trampling over the others, taking over the play. Everything needs to be balanced and in harmony' (1993: 46).This could just as well be a cry from every family therapist facing a family playing themselves by playing out their dynamics in front of the therapist.

So how does systemic psychotherapy look and work experientially? To help demonstrate this, I have adapted a recent family meeting when the 'Green' family was assessed for therapeutic work. I have blended a number of elements from other sessions of working with other families and a reflecting team. This means, unlike Pirandello's characters, that they will at times be more co-operative than they may want to be since they are taking some of their authorship from me. The work with the family on whom the Greens are based has been completed. They were very much themselves, and their resolutions of the series of severe crises that beset them very much their own. The two main approaches for working with whole-family systems that have a clear methodology, assumptions and techniques are the structural model of Salvador Minuchin, and the systemic-phenomenological model of the Milan Associates. There are other important approaches that will be discussed later, but these are the most coherent, well-explained approaches and underpin much of the work described in this book.

My colleague, Ali McLewin (a psychoanalytically trained psychother-apist) and I developed a model that connected these two family approaches with the experiential assumptions from psychoanalytic thinking. We did this in an NHS adult mental health clinic, over six years, developing a family therapy-based service for adults and older adults. Whole families are invited to attend, as with child referrals, though this is not as common a practice as in child and adolescent serv-ices. We selected and trained a reflection team from mental health workers whose task, like that of the chorus in classical Greek drama, was to provide an experiential commentary on the unfolding dialogue and levels of script. Their commentary provided an additional yet different perspective for the family and the working alliance with the family. Traditionally called reflecting teams in family therapy literature, their role evolved from auxiliaries to the therapist's oracular reflections to open commentators on the whole therapy process (Milan Associates, 1978; Papp, 1982; Andersen, 1987). Not all family psychotherapists have been enamoured of this way of working, however. Carl Whitaker remarked: 'When you're behind a screen you are thinking but not deeply experiencing' (1984: 7). In other forms of psychotherapy there are echoes of this role of auxiliaries with Freud's two medical contem-poraries in Vienna – Jacob L. Moreno and Alfred Adler. Both used 'the community of understanding others' in their therapeutic work; Moreno in *Psychodrama* (1987) and Adler in his founding work in the Child Guidance Services in Vienna in 1922 (1956: 393). Systemic-based family therapy has always contained a communitarian aspect, encouraging and providing multiple voices of difference; in some ways it might be considered as a temporary, therapeutic 'extended family'.

The reflecting teams we established were drawn from all disciplines and levels of experience in adult mental health services who wished to work in this way. We provided a short introductory training in systemic thinking, using genograms, role play and revision teaching about the central issues of attachment, loss and bereavement. They observed us working for a time. We then encouraged them to use their own obser-vations and trust in their professional and life experiences to reflect helpfully in an unrehearsed, open dialogue in the presence of the family. The effects on staff have not always been comfortable (Slator, 2010). However, the responses reflecting teams receive from the family are often remarkably moving and mobilizing in their content and effects (Stikker, 2005; Flynn, 2010). I have included an example of such a reflection at the end of the imagined session.

The Green family genogram looks like this (see the Appendix for more on genograms).

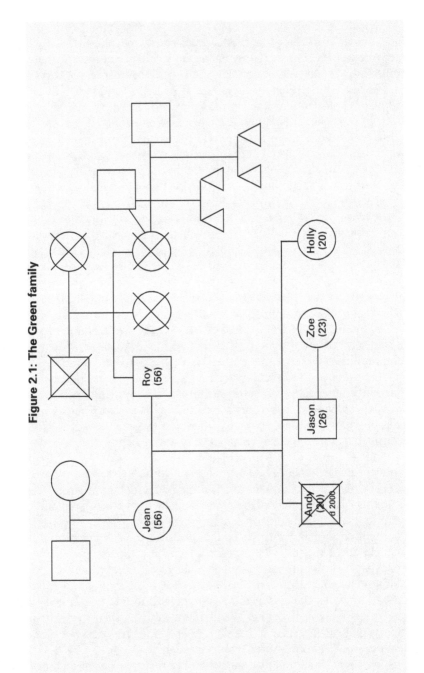

Figure 2.1: The Green family

CASE STUDY 2.1: HOLLY GREEN

Holly Green (20) had recently been discharged from an NHS psychiatric hospital in south-east England, where she had been a patient suffering from suicidal depression, self-harm and phobic anxiety. This had been her third hospitalization. She had been receiving individual psychotherapy while in hospital and the family had attended family psychotherapy sessions at the unit, located many miles from their home.

Individual therapy had continued in the community following Holly's discharge. This was due to finish shortly, and her therapist Kate Black had requested an assessment for systemic family therapy. Kate was concerned at what she described as an intense, close, mutually identifying relationship between Holly and her mother, Jean Green (56). Jean suffers from chronic anxiety and bipolar disorder for which she had been hospitalized on many occasions throughout Holly's childhood. She is receiving regular support from the community psychiatric services. Roy Green (56) is an IT specialist whose work is based in London, 70 miles away, where he commutes daily. They have a son, Jason (28), who is married with a child and living locally. Their elder son, Andy, committed suicide by overdosing eight years previously. He had also been hospitalized for depression. As a family system, it was activated by adult mental health crises whose central subjects were Holly, Jean and, in the past, Andy. Both Roy and Jason were active in their support and care, particularly Roy, but did not display any signs of mental health distress.

The family members are actively practising Christians and have been so since the children were young. Though Holly does not attend church regularly, she frequently prays for strength to conquer her troubled, intrusive thoughts of self-destruction and worthlessness and for her mother's good mental health. Most of the background information came from an individual psychotherapist who had been seeing Holly on her own and felt family psychotherapy would be an important complement, a collaborative situation we often endorse.

Stage 1: Preparing heart and mind to engage the family

Before starting a session such as this we would seek to engage as many of the family members as possible and speak with the referrer. Then, following the principles of a phenomenological perspective (Laing & Esterson, 1964; Valle & King, 1978; Spinelli, 1989 – described in Chapter 7), we would air any presumptions (literally pre-assumptions) from this information. Using a lightly sketched genogram based on the information provided, we would speculate about the experiential stresses and tensions, explicit and covert, that might exist, and how they might be perturbing the family system. We also start to think about how and with whom we might best form initial alliances to help guide the dialogue most fruitfully after the groundwork of engaging with each family member.

This gathering of early information to hypothesize about the organizational processes of the family and reactions to stressful changes tends to follow the pattern described early on by the Milan Associates (1980). The Milan group was clear that the developed hypotheses were not fixed assumptions but speculative ideas directing the therapist's inquiries. In this way they sought to apply a method of scientific enquiry to their thinking. Therapy, however, is not an exact (or exactly a) science, any more than drama is, though it may share many of the basic procedures of science in perceiving connections and consequences and seeking evidential bases for suppositions. Therapy, too, is experimental but it deals in the empiricism of personal experience. 'Experimental' used to mean 'experiential' three and a half centuries ago, but has given way to science's definition of the word. The changed meaning can be seen from its usage by the Quaker, George Fox (1652): 'This I know experimentally', which in modern English means 'This I know to be true from experience' (Ambler, 2001: 11).

Knowledge of the family-circumstantial script and the distressing changes on relationships, beliefs and reactions is an invisible experiential template for therapy. Often impossible to be examined or fully understood by the family, the capacity of past distress to be repeated in the family script is immense (Byng-Hall, 1995). This is a family-systemic version of the philosopher George Santayana's dictum, 'Those who cannot remember the past are condemned to repeat it' (1905: 284) Suffering and tragedy thread their way through the **human condition** and human experience. The dramatic arts create a safe containing theatre in which the toxic elements can be expressed, examined and both set down and set aside, rather as in a dream. Like all art, they hold a mirror up to reality, as does the mirror screen in a therapy suite to the family and the work of the therapeutic team. Each is mirrored physically and metaphorically through the process of reflection.

However, not all tensions are located in the past. Negotiating change in the here and now and the momentum of the life cycle is also an essential template. We work to understand the family's experiential landscape and to empathize with individuals in the family and the family as a whole; to listen closely and attentively to the dialogue of the adversities as well as the strengths hidden and unused in the family experience; how we might negotiate areas of tension and frame our questions accordingly; and when and how we might acknowledge the non-problematic areas of their experience. To accomplish all, or any of this, a relationship of trust and openness has first to be developed within the team.

We do not attribute blame or responsibility to families or family members. They often arrive with that particular skill already finely honed. Blame is simple but deflects from deeper analysis and is often a natural recourse for the frustration, anxiety and helplessness which arise in the 'pressure cooker' of family life. For a number of years family therapy was burdened by the attribution 'parent-blamers' (especially mothers), a charge levelled by anxious families and more orthodox practitioners who were eager to disparage the use of this alternative therapeutic model. Family therapists were partly responsible historically for the 'tag', for at the time some bizarre interventions were issued in the name of change.

A shared view developed in the team (whether its members were parents or not) was that raising a family and remaining a committed, involved member of it is a complex and taxing life task, and an inexact, imperfect process. Where key family members live separately this does not alter the task or the family's accomplishment, but can make it more exacting. Family experience is error-activated and any corrective processes may initially be more exacting and stressful (Byng-Hall, 1995). The rewards are proportionately greater, however, with improved understanding, acceptance and depth to relationships through an improved ability to give and receive intimacy and care. The pre-session meeting is an opportunity to check the therapeutic experiences the family or individual members may have had previously. These need to be enquired about early on since they act as a guide to the therapy team in anticipating and avoiding some of these other interventions' pitfalls, as well as capitalizing on their benefits.

A sense of security comes from the family knowing that the team has a coherent view of what it is about and confidence in realistic reflections which prize the well-being of persons and the system. The team must establish this secure base for itself in order for the family to feel safe exploring. The formation of this working alliance with the individuals and the whole system has many names: 'therapeutic alliance', 'therapeutic relationship' and 'therapeutic coalition'. It should seek to communicate an understanding that the family matters at some level to each member, even when it becomes clear that the family relational structure is breaking down. The pain of disappointment is often present in the family subscript even when it is denied.

Carl Whitaker, in characteristic style, recommended conjoint-led therapy: 'If therapy is parenting, it's best done by two. Two of you are less apt to become part of the delusional system which you know nothing about ... be careful not to be the single parent, you become somebody's partner in their delusional system' (1984: 6–7). We found it most beneficial to work with two therapists in the room, ideally in a male–female pairing. This best facilitates gender alliances, effective use of **empathy** and reciprocity of identification between team and family members and helps rebalance any embedded mistrust of one gender. This was especially important with Holly and Jean Green, since both disclosed a history of childhood sexual abuse with an older man, a family friend. Trusting one man in an authority role with the intimacies of one's life story is potentially distressing, though the context of co-therapy means there is less direct personal exposure. Cross-gendered working, as with teamwork, allows for a greater richness of empathic identification and alliance formation, though this is not necessarily along same-gender lines. This, like all therapy, is not an invariant principle, for it is impossible to have universal empathy, a therapeutic sensibility that has to be cultivated through practice. It is, however, a goal of optimizing therapeutic effect, for empathy is still at 'the heart of therapy' (Perry, 1993: 73–4).

It is a common theme in systemic therapy that much of the distress in families, as in all human groups, arises from fixed beliefs and apprehensions that make for rigid assumptive scripts, so restricting other possibilities, open dialogue and different truths. When these become apparent, the therapeutic work is to find influential ideas that help to loosen fixed truths, using a variety of techniques.

Empathic sensibility: its importance and its struggles

Therapeutic work is a hybrid activity, both a science and an art; it engages elements of the logical thought of the left side of the brain but tends much more to right-brain activity, recognized in neuroscience for its intuitive, symbolic, imaginative and mystical abilities. Both are important and equal ways of knowing. Empathy or attunement are the terms used to describe the fundamental transcultural and transpersonal property of the human imagination to seek to enter fully the experience of the 'different other'. This remarkable innate ability, unless seriously impaired by damaging experiences, develops through relationships. This capacity of the psyche contains the central energy of healing, repair and understanding. From this comes the potential redemptive transformation of the person, relationship and situation. What may be 'deemed', that is, seen as, fixed and inevitable, can be 're-deemed', that is, reappraised, given a different meaning and can thus become a different experience. Empathy is connective, able to make new links that make for a different comprehending; it is the wholehearted openness to noticing and joining with the others' difference. In families, it is noticing what is left unsaid as much as what is said. The person-centred psychotherapist, Carl Rogers, described it in the individual context thus:

> It involves being sensitive, moment to moment, to the changing felt meanings which flow in this other person, to the fear or rage or tenderness or confusion or whatever hurt s/he is experiencing. It means temporarily living in his or her life, moving about in it delicately without making judgments, sensing meanings of which s/he is scarcely aware, but not trying to uncover feelings of which the person is totally unaware, since this would be too threatening. (Rogers, 1980: 142)

Whilst this skill is important for individual work, it needs modifying for systemic-based family work. However, empathy can be used multi-directionally, as a recent Rogerian approach to family systems work describes (O'Leary, 2011). The imaginative sensibility of empathy, so vital to the interpretative skills of all performance art, is also a key attribute of Irvin Yalom's exceptional guide, *The Gift of Therapy* (2002).

All forms of psychotherapy, and the 'corrective emotional experience' they offer, are variations of a 're-parenting' process: the repair of the ontological and attachment root damage of the person's self-experience. The characters in a family are often frail, damaged, flawed, victimized and victimizing, imperious, demanding, controlling, distressed and distressing, disabling, heroic or compassionate. It is sometimes difficult to connect with anything appealing or redeeming in the experiences that individuals and families, bring. This is a further reason for teamwork. They may not seem remotely likeable, let alone engaging to work with, yet in families there is almost always a fresh voice, still sufficiently untouched by the emotional wreckage around them, to be able to release a new spirit. You can witness elements of this process towards the end of Edward Albee's play *Who's Afraid of Virginia Woolf?* The character Martha castigates the 'vile' state of her marriage and reveals how her fantasy child, Sonny Jim, provided life and hope in the bleak relationship (Albee, 1962).

Systemic therapy provides a space where families should neither feel on show nor misused. They should be able to disclose themselves to one another, as well as to the therapy team, without pretence or defensiveness, in their own time and in their own way. This is a huge challenge, given long-standing defensive boundaries. However, it can sometimes be their first experience of talking in such ways, ways that may surprise and encourage them. Danger and apprehension in family members is understood and identified by the therapists and can be responded to directly or obliquely by changing the emotional climate of the session, whilst recognizing the discomfort occasioned.

Exercise 2.1: Questions to understand the Greens' experience

Before meeting the Greens, try some free-associative thinking of your own on the basis of the information you have already received. There is a series of connecting distressing and tragic experiences. Think up and write down questions that invite both open and quantifying descriptions of self-experience and other experience and differences and connections between these: Do you feel better or worse than your mother? Who do you think in the family seems to be least vulnerable/most vulnerable to the series of distresses you have been going through? What do they do to show you they are managing? Think of how you might reach the family's more difficult material by way of talking about the ordinary, inviting everyone to participate; think too of how you would word questions to encourage extending and deepening the descriptions given; think of how you would look for unrecognized and unacknowledged resourcefulness; think how you might use imagined responses to shape your own responses and further curiosity; think of at least one statement of compassionate understanding you could make to the family as a whole and to each individual member; and think about the issues that seem difficult to raise and any unhelpful judgements you find yourself making (work to set these aside and concentrate on engaging the family and their experiences).

Stage 2: The family arrives

So the Greens arrive. The team's 'head' is full of questions. The momentous effect of Andy's death by suicide has been at the centre of the team's attention. There was speculation about the family processes that led up to it as well as the ways the family as a system reorganized itself afterwards. May it have caused relief to some? Was it believed that it gave relief to Andy? Was it intentional? Who heard about it first, how was it communicated? How did it split relationships, or did it emerge from splits? How is this related to Holly's depression? How far has this momentous event been explored in previous therapy? How resilient are the family as a result of their previous therapy? How resistant are they? Did the experience cause discomfort, with or without benefit? How far can they tell us the story of the therapeutic journey so far? How comfortable will the family be discussing suicide? How comfortable will the team feel discussing it? What else might be the family's strengths and worries unconnected with this event? Despite its severe nature, we should not make it the organizing focus. What about the seeming close-ness of Holly's relationship with her mother, which Kate Black identi-fied as an obstacle to the effectiveness of her work? What differences or similarities were there between the mother's and the daughter's experi-ence of sexual abuse? How did each happen? Have they ever discussed this? What feelings are attached to these different experiences?

The therapists want to get a feel for the family first and establish some comfort and confidence with each other in conversation. The family will be left to choose their different stories and recount them at their own pace, while the therapists will listen for openings and invita-tions to deepen the dialogue. The team's questions may challenge the family's defensive structure, which could be fragile and threaten the gains already made during Holly's hospitalization. For the moment, these potential preoccupations are set aside. They are mostly of too great intimacy and may not be explored at all if there is no alliance.

Each member is warmly greeted and usually offered a handshake. Rarely is this declined and, when it is, an explanation is offered of a personal or cultural kind. A 20-year-old patient had a phobia about touching, and apologized, explaining her difficulty. This behaviour had a severe long-term paralyzing effect on the parents and gave the team immediate experiential information.

Family members would then be invited to nominate the name or title by which they wish to be addressed by the team. However, this may come later in a session, once a stronger alliance of acceptance and trust has been formed, and until then formal titles may be best. Immediate talk is of the difficulties caused by roadworks en route to the clinic. We commiserate with them. Canterbury city is getting increasingly congested and gridlocked; we join them in a communal irritation about this.

We tell them that they probably know that systemic family work is a rather different but useful method of helping and to reassure them, we may quote some research findings that support this view. We gauge their reaction. If it is their first experience of family therapy, we may say some-thing like: 'People often think they know one another best in families and yet can still treat each other as if they are being constantly misunderstood.' We are watching to see each member's response to this generalized assertion which seeks to set them at their ease and signal that we are on the side of family understanding, not just personal. From these responses the therapists may already have an initial sense about who the potential allies are and who is least convinced about the value of the meeting. Since engagement works to reduce estrangement, it is always important to invite doubt and scepticism into the dialogue. The Green family members all seem apprehensive but entrust themselves to the developing involvement.

> 'We have been asked to meet with you for the next hour and a quarter to see if there are ways we might be helpful to you and Holly.'

It is always important to acknowledge the primary status of the designated patient as the reason for attending, even though, as the session continues, this may seem less and less relevant. The 'patient role' vanishes and there is another (or a set of relationships) in its place. Carl Whitaker described this as the 'revolving patient'. Like a revolving door, whoever occupies the compartment of attention going in or out can change. This is often a feature of a highly distressed family.

Here is another paradox; 'the patient' is also 'not the patient'. This is not to say all the family is 'sick' or that the 'sick' one is somehow 'scapegoated' to protect the others, or even that 'sickness' is a helpful construct. It is a derivative of the medical 'language game' of diagnosis. The shift to the experiential language of suffering and distress must be done gradually, especially in heavily institutionalized situations. Early forays into a different 'language game' give the family access to a different, less clinically saturated language in which to convey their experience. Within a systemic-phenomenological framework, 'life distress' is the human condition default, intolerable in most of its forms, though all families share some aspects of it. The psychiatric 'belt and braces' diagnostic definition of mental suffering provides support, structure and relief. It is an error of judgement to undermine this scaffolding. However, it is an equal error of judgement to confuse the scaffolding for the building within it.

Therapists also revolve, and with 'evenly-suspended attention' (Freud, 1912: 242) focus on a particular person, relationship or system but only so long as it seems fruitful, and they are then are free to shift their attention elsewhere, usually with a question arising from the dialogue or a whole-system reflection.

'Have they had family therapy before?' 'Yes we have,' answers Father. They all look at each other quizzically, as if to say, 'Shall I or you tell them more?' 'Did it help?' 'Well, a bit, but I felt they criticized us for Holly's condition,' adds Father, acting as spokesperson for the whole family. An amber warning light flashes – not to do more of the same and fall into the same pattern of implicit blame, however much the father may have misinterpreted the other team's intentions.

'So, Holly, what would you want to come out of our work with you and your family, if we could achieve it, because it sounds as if your parents felt blamed by our other colleagues for how you are?' One colleague invites Holly's thoughts. Holly declares emphatically that she wants to get back into her life again and wants her parents to be less worried for her and her for them. This seems a more constructive theme of concern than that of responsibility so it is lodged in the mind of the therapist and more might be made of it later, when the opportunity presents itself.

Salvador Minuchin prefers the term 'tracking' to describe information-gathering on a particular theme from all family members. For this, the therapist must not hold a fixed attachment to individual distress or to an explanatory story about it, for to do so would disrupt the flow of systemic connections (being preoccupied with a 'part', albeit a whole person, and not the wider family, the 'whole'). A response provides an expression of experiential meaning and attitude in the same way that free association does for a psychoanalytic therapist. Free association operates just as much in a wider family system. The family psychotherapist and team are present to respond to the clues and cued to help develop richer and different associations without 'fear or favour' to any one person in the system.

Such a form of therapy demands particular attention and concentration; teamworking is essential until the method is fully learned. Free association with family members is another way of thinking about circular questioning, in guiding the 'call and response' of information flow. In responding empathically you freely associate possible meanings and connections. However, being a group, it is like prisoners being released from their cells to mix socially when there may be old scores to settle. Opening up a family dialogue is an invitation to free expression which can invite 'payback' time.

The therapists are now presented with a number of options. To enquire of the mother whether she wants anything different, or of the father what he thinks Holly means or whether this is what he wants too: *'So what worry for whom do you think Holly means, Mr Green?'* (At this stage the therapist has not sought permission to ask the father by what name he wishes to be called, but this will happen as the therapeutic alliance with him begins to form.) He gives a bland, noncommittal answer:

> *'Er, she has been very unwell, you know, and we want her to continue to recover as she is going along just now.'*
> *'And you, Jean?'*
> *'Well, I think Holly means she wishes she could stop worrying about me, because sometimes I have felt like killing myself. I want her to live her own life.'*

So, unexpectedly, the picture changes. Mother moves on to the vacant patient seat as father is helping Holly vacate it. We are invited to see a shared identification, a relationship proximity which may be termed 'enmeshment' (Minuchin, 1974), 'insecure attachment' (Bowlby, 1988), 'parentification' (Böszörményi-Nagy & Spark, 1973) or a mutual 'protection racket' (Whiffen, 1981). This is information about distress, relationship alignment and exclusion: is Roy the excluded one in a triangle? Is this gender-based? How might this fit with the elder son's suicide in event order? So the therapist might want to ally with the father. Better if the female therapist can do this, since it may carry the assumption that manoeuvring across gender lines is possible. Equally, a male therapist would strengthen Mr Green's sense of having a potential ally in the family work. This is not essential but it is important to recognize the implications and possibilities in using any available differences creatively and freely:

> *'So do you feel left out, stuck "on the edge", Mr Green, or is it a "male thing" of not owning up to feeling like that?'*

It might be better, then, to start by asking, first of all, the more personal:

> *'Do you mind if we call you Roy, or would you prefer "Mr Green"?'*

Or, given his assent:

> *'How have you coped with so much distress around you, Roy, from the womenfolk in the family?'*
> Roy: 'Yes, it's been very hard, sometimes, but I have my faith, which gives me a lot of support, and the church community.'

Again, here is an account of strength, supportive alliance and wider systemic networks. The associations for the therapist are many, and as with all systemic work it can be taken in many directions, but it is better to stick to one:

> *Therapist* (to Holly and Jean): 'Your dad (looking at Holly) and husband (to Jean) has just told us he gets a lot of comfort from your church. Does it have the same effect for you?'
>
> *Jean*: 'It has kept me from going over the edge many times, particularly since Andy ... (said with feeling but without tears, faltering for a moment) but it is very important for Roy and I, thank God for that and for sustaining me.'
>
> *Therapist* (to Holly): 'And what about you, Holly? It does sound like a lifeline for your parents.'
>
> *Holly*: 'It means more to my parents, I wish I could believe like they do, but I don't. My therapist Kate, Dr Black, keeps telling me I am stronger than I give myself credit for.'
>
> *Therapist*: 'But you don't believe her, or don't think she means it?'
>
> *Holly*: 'Oh I do, but (hesitantly) sometimes my life just feels like a hopeless mess. I don't want to get up some mornings.'
>
> *Therapist*: 'Hmm, that sounds pretty bleak and desolate. But it also sounds as if you do get up and battle on with it, despite feeling as you do.'

The therapists now have a picture of the stresses and distresses in the family as well as the strengths. They are starting to feel an alliance with the family. Clearly the earlier family therapy in Holly's psychiatric unit has helped bring painful experiences into the open so the family has begun to reflect openly with each other, although they are not fully where they want to be. They seem to challenge us to push them further, though this will be checked out with them towards the end of this session, when we discuss working with them further.

The therapists are using their curiosity freely and openly. Curiosity is a basic attitude to discovery and learning, which has echoes of the wonderment with which a child begins to engage with the world. For Alfred Adler (1956), 'social interest' was a basic tool of imaginative empathy. But there is also a sense of evenly weighted attention and careful listening to every experience and its differences. The different accounts, with their unique beliefs and associated feelings, are noted, and given equal time. The therapist joins the dialogue by introducing descriptive words like 'on the edge', to seek to capture the lived experience more fully and move away from the deadening language of mental health typology. Respect is given to the member's acceptance of the description of being on the 'edge'. Where the father locates himself is not yet apparent.

It might be time to affirm the family's own strengths. The language of psychopathology and diagnosis may be comforting at times for some, in providing a clear structure, but it also re-enforces experiences of inferiority, inadequacy, instability and alienation, of being an outcast. It is a language of the dead end, an experiential cul-de-sac, not a language of a more animated, fully lived experience. It is full of the institutionalized language of 'dissing' – i.e. dys-function, dis-order, dis-ease and disenfranchisement – and away from the more natural language of experience. As the early anti-psychiatry movement made clear, diagnostic language 'doubly indemnifies' the problematical 'bad experience', compounding it by the addition of socially constricting and excommunicating language. A person's self-experience, however problematic, becomes a classification, 'closing down' the subjective description of that experience. However, this is not to make light of the terrible imprisonment that is mental distress. *Henry's Demons* is a salutary reminder that changing personal suffering is not achieved by the simple trick of changing the language game. The possibility of well-being that comes from maintaining a balance between the opposite energies – the destructive, life-annihilating tendencies and those life-creating and care-affirming ones – is an extremely difficult one, involving as it does tendencies of the will, thinking and feeling. Nathan Ackerman wrote:

> Often the sense of tension and danger mounts in family interview process. The therapist must steer a path between Scylla and Charybdis. He must move between the extremes of rigid avoidance of the dangers of closeness and the uncontrolled explosion of hostile conflict that tends toward panic and disorganization. (1962: 35)

So the therapists might now attempt a conversation in front of the Greens or invite the team in, like an ancient Greek chorus, to reflect:

> *First respondent*: 'I don't think any of us hasn't felt deeply moved by what we have heard and how the family has gone through terrible suffering that would defeat many others.'
> *Second respondent*: 'Yes, from what we have heard already the Greens are really battling with difficult, empty feelings that can feel destructive at their worst and a feeling of ... well, why bother, there seems so little to hold on to but more confusion and distress.'

Third respondent: 'Sure, all this is so, and yet there is a feeling I also get that it is faith – spiritual faith, as well as faith in each other – that, however tough it gets, is pulling them through. Of course, we don't know so far how much Andy's loss has affected them, though Jean has hinted at it.'

First respondent: 'The family does seem very open in working with us and are very straightforward and honest in what they say about each other and in front of one another. They don't hold back on how it is, which, frankly, sounds like a kind of hell.'

Second respondent: 'They certainly don't lack courage. I hope they'll feel able to stay in this work with us a little longer so we get a fuller picture of not just what they've gone thorough, but ... er, as you were saying, about where they get their strength from.'

Third respondent: 'Yes, you see I feel quite hopeful the family can come through this. When I was nursing on psychiatric wards I did see a lot of recovery and the family certainly played an important part in that, often without realizing it. I hope they will stay working with us, because we will with them.'

At this stage the team will leave. They have directed the conversation to one another; the family overhears in a reversal of the theatrical convention, where the characters in the drama are not privy to what the chorus says. The therapists will then turn to the family and ask:

'Any thoughts on that? Is that how you are experiencing our work together so far?'

Roy: 'Well they're right, it's painful, like baring your soul, but we know it will be helpful. It has been for Holly in the past when we tried it before.'

Jean: 'Anything is better than how I feel sometimes and Holly is the one who counts. We just want to see her well.'

Holly: 'Yeah, I hate having to put Mum and Dad through this. They've already been through enough without me adding to it. But I cannot think of anything otherwise. My therapist wants me to end in three session's time and rely on everyone coming here.'

Therapist: 'And what do you think about that?'

Holly: 'Well I don't want to, but I can see why she's saying it.'

The therapists now switch attention to Jean:

Therapist: 'You were telling us, Jean, you have seemed close to the edge, and seem to understand what Holly has been going through.'

41

Jean: 'Yes I do (hesitates) ... you see, I suffer from bipolar disorder. That's what I've been told, anyway. I also have what a psychiatrist called a borderline personality disorder. I have suffered it for years. I got very bad postnatal depression after Andy was born, you see.'

Therapist: 'What does having been described as having a borderline personality disorder mean to you Jean?'

Jean: 'Well, that I just feel on the edge, as if I cannot do anything. I looked it up recently on Google and a lot of it seemed to fit. I don't really, sort of, own my life. Sometimes, there's these thoughts that keep telling me to finish it all. I wish I was not like that. I do get a lot of support from the Mental Health Team.'

Therapist (to Roy and Holly): 'How has Jean's living on the edge affected you, Roy, and you, Holly?'

Roy: 'Well, like I said before, I try to remain calm and strong for everyone.'

Holly: 'I absolutely hate it. I wish I could do something. Instead, I am unwell myself and feel the same way sometimes which doesn't help Mum. I don't know how he does it (gestures to father) ... Dad, I mean. How he manages to stay so calm and so on. He's like a rock. I wish I was like it a bit more.'

Again, all sorts of responses and tentative connections come to the minds of the therapists. It is at an early stage of the meeting and already the family – highly charged and attuned to living in crisis – have revealed a great deal about the extent of their distress. Therapy seeks to express, contain and offer hope of relief from the personal, relational and systemic experience of suffering. Care and sensitivity in the dialogue is important, since the family has already lost one member through suicide. However, this does not mean it cannot be spoken and thought about in its implication for each of their lives. The Greens, like many other families on the edge, keep each other going and hoping. Reflection offers a meaning or belief to embed in the family's individual and collective mind which, like a slowly dissolving medicine, may work to reconfigure elements of their experience beneficially. Sometimes it needs to be repeated in different forms to strengthen its influence. There is usually the systemic disjunction between cognition, affect, and volition in persons and systems: 'I/we know this is not good and right for me/us, but I/we feel I/we must do it anyway to release me/us from the tension and bad feeling I/we have'.

Since therapeutic healing and persuasion are closely interlinked (Frank, 1961), it is open to the therapists to reflect aloud about the systemic connections between thinking, feeling and willing to influence the whole experience. Ways of thinking about this might be:

Therapist (to Holly and Jean): 'Well, that's certainly a puzzle for you both, and interesting. Do you think, Jean that Holly gets unwell in some odd way as her method of caring for you? She almost distracts you; she takes your mind off your troubles and on to caring for her. It's a difficult way of going about it, we guess, but still Holly's thinking could make a lot of sense.'

Jean: 'Well, we have thought of this. It could be true. (To Holly) What do you think?'

Therapist (interrupting): 'It would be interesting to hear this, Holly. We are not offering this as an explanation, but a strong feeling you may have for wanting to get your mother better, feeling helpless to know what to do, yet protecting her even from bad feelings around Andy's death.'

This is said in part to prevent moving into a discourse of explanatory science. Explanations are useful, and sometimes medicalized ones are highly valuable as psycho-educational information. However, they run the risk of closing down further exploration and, once the explanation has run out of its ability to satisfy or console, its shelf-life. It is much more about experiential truth, the lived experience the whole connecting discourse of heart, mind and will which constitutes the complex system of the person.

Holly: 'I do love my mother, and worry a lot about her. It is a bit of a drastic way of going about it though, isn't it?'

Therapist: 'Well, perhaps not. Don't people make a lot of sacrifices for love, especially in families?'

Reflections from other systemic approaches

In their early years, the Milan Associate systemic psychotherapists might have used a greater edge of certainty of connection which also contains a paradoxical twist to the meaning of the behaviour. Their intervention might have gone something like this:

'Holly, we believe you are sacrificing yourself to save your mother from any more distress and pain. You are protecting her, and we think this is a worthy idea, and we think you and the family will choose to give it up when you feel ready.'

Salvador Minuchin, the pioneer of structural family therapy, might have offered the following reframe, with its directness and request to enact an unscripted dialogue:

> *'Holly, you are destroying your life by taking care of your mother. She is a strong person and, anyway, has your father to look after her.' 'Don't you, sir?' 'You are standing on your mother's shoulders, or perhaps she is standing on yours. You don't need to do this to her.' 'Roy, I want you to discuss this with your daughter now and help her see your place is to look after Jean. See if you can persuade her to step aside. I shall listen and hear how you get on.'*

In each of these ways, the therapist or the team is using directional authority. This is not to humiliate the family but to provide it with openings to discuss, react, object or concur, reflect and reorganize. A therapist perturbs a system. This is the dialectical process which forms part of therapeutic dialogue and uses the rhetoric skills of the therapist as persuader.

The therapist and the team enter the dialogue in many ways, but first need to let the family's characters and their perspectives get inside their experience. The family is searching for an authority, but discover, as the therapists and team gently pass responsibility back to them, that there is no one – only themselves - directing the meaning of their lives and their possibilities. Family systemic therapy in action is always a joint enterprise of co-scripting between the therapists and the family. There are many dialogues and script possibilities. Existence creates endless circumstances and situations which require a human response. The aspiring family therapist is encouraged to study plays and watch dramas, especially those centred on family life, since these manufacture many of the basic processes the therapist engages.

So, it is near the end of the first session. The therapists think the family is committed to work, partly because they feel they have no other safe alternative with Kate Black's withdrawal of therapeutic support. She has identified Holly's tendency to dependency as an issue and this seems to have been accepted by family members. This life pattern has transferred directly from Jean to Kate. Holly does not dissent from this observation, but just feels paralysed and infantilized by this attachment relationship in which, a structural therapist might suggest paradoxically, she has become her mother's mother.

We invite the family to meet with us again. Ten therapy sessions are proposed to the Greens, and then together we will see where we are. Why ten? This is a median but not absolute number set as a goal. Family dialogue goes on between sessions, but creating a focus for this requires the live encounter. Absent or deceased members of the family cast can have their beliefs and feelings represented. This makes the family/systemic-based approach a very different way of working. In the working mind of the therapists, the whole system is always present.

So, the therapists might say:

> 'We feel we have made a good start with you and we have a sense of the depth of your pain and struggle. In families it is not just the person who obviously suffers but everyone else who cares for that person. We don't know about Jason, but we are sure you know some of how he regards this situation. With your agreement, we would like to work together at least 10 times, hopefully finding a time that suits us both. Kate Black has already indicated she thinks you two Jean and Holly were too close and depended on each other too much. This is something we want to think about with you all a bit more next time. It feels hard for you to cut the umbilical cord (both nod) and we guess Roy, you may have some worries about what might happen to you if these ties were to be eased away. Anyway, what do you think?' (All look at each other.)
>
> *Jean*: 'Yes, I would like to come back.'
> *Holly*: 'Yes that's OK.' (Hesitantly, and looks slightly forlorn)
> *Therapist*: 'Roy?'
> Roy: 'I'll go along with what the others want.'
> *Therapists*: 'Fine. Two weeks' time at 2pm?'

So the process is under way. The therapist and family are configured as a new system. The therapist's reflected observations, like carefully placed acupuncture needles, are designed to stimulate the family's reflective process, not to define a cause or give an explanation. It may be important to identify a goal, but it is a mistake to believe this is the means of securing change and one can therefore push too hard for it. Change cannot be prescribed, though 'no change' can be and this is done to heighten the system's awareness of its slumbering enchantment with the rigidity and fear of unexamined belief.

We can see a number of possibilities and difficulties. The therapist is like an author seeking to challenge her 'characters' to emerge more fully into a different foreground, to transform excommunicated experience into a communicated one.

Summary

- A 'live' family session with the Greens is presented and examined.
- The formation and training of a reflecting teamwork are described.
- The first stage of preparing the 'hearts and minds' of experiential engagement is discussed.
- An exercise is given to prepare your own thinking.
- The first stage of preparing the 'hearts and minds' of experiential engagement is discussed.
- Commentary is provided on the assumptions and intentions behind the therapist's questions and reflections.
- Examples of team reflection are given.
- Example reflections from the Milan and structural approaches are given.
- A contract for further sessions is negotiated with the Greens.

3

ESSENTIAL IDEAS IN SYSTEMIC THOUGHT AND PRACTICE

The gentle pervasion of systemic thinking

The term 'systemic' and the processes it describes have entered our language to the point of almost becoming commonplace. In the early 1970s, the term was linked with 'family therapy', particularly through Salvador Minuchin's use of it in his structural analysis of families in the groundbreaking book *Families and Family Therapy* (1974). He was heavily influenced by the ideas of the Hungarian philosopher Arthur Koestler, especially his concept of the '**holon**'. An earlier work, *Sanity Madness and the Family* (Laing & Esterson, 1964), was also influential. Based on research conducted with 11 families with a 'schizophrenic' member, the authors examined three interacting experiential levels: 'each person in the family; the relations between persons in the family; *the family itself as a system*' (1964: 23, emphasis added).

This is, as you will have gathered by now, a way of thinking that connects all things, from the most remote to the most proximate, and looks not just at what they are in themselves but how they are interconnected and how they interact with one another. It is a descriptive map of everything, not based on a theory of everything, but on close observation of our living and social worlds. The French mathematician Blaise Pascal foreshadowed the possibility:

> There is for example a relationship between man and all he knows ... since all things are both caused and causing, assisted and assisting ... providing mutual support in a chain linking together ... the most distant and different things, I consider it impossible to know the

parts without knowing the whole as to know the whole without knowing the individual parts. (1670: 64)

This could be a good manifesto for systemic thinking, which has enriched the analysis of all manner of different realities by showing how in mapping the organizational patterns we can direct human energies differently. Understanding the world more fully and using this knowledge beneficially has been a triumph of scientific empiricism. By detecting patterns and refashioning them it shares the aesthetic tradition of art; by doing so with the structures of power relationships and their negotiations it shares the tradition of political science. The *grand analysis* of the interconnection of the multiple systems that constitute our world offers those working at mending the effects of disrupted human relationships a new, clearer lens of unprecedented potential. Small wonder, though, that applied systemic thought can seem difficult to grasp since it appears such a chameleon-like term.

For the therapist seeking to harness the methods and techniques of family and systemic psychotherapy and its benefits, the learning is considerable. However, none would claim sole privilege to the fundamental ideas which underpin this holistic way of thinking about individuals, families and the many networks which embrace them in their social nexus. Many casework practitioners and professional mediators use systemic thinking with families matter-of-factly and would no more view themselves as family and systemic psychotherapists than psychoanalysts. The UK Association for Family Therapy has endorsed the title 'systemic practitioner' for those who have completed family and systemic training to intermediate level and want to use systemically informed practice more explicitly, though the term 'systemic counsellor' is preferred by some.

A critical time?

We are living in times of rapid social change which many see as having critical causes for concern. The description encompasses a large and growing list: the whole system of economic capitalism, family life, the quest for a tolerant, multicultural society, international relations, the future of the earth's climate, all human life stages, the increasing global population and its call on the natural resources of the earth. Everything seems out of balance. 'Crisis' is the new *Zeitgeist* replacing 'anxiety' to describe our age. We inundate ourselves with relentless narratives of 'dismal stories' through 24-hour news. There is a growing sense amongst all but a tiny elite that the expectations of a lifestyle of increasing affluence is no longer sustainable or realistic.

Perhaps all ages have had their sense of apocalyptic crisis? Certainly this was experienced strongly during the Cold War. The nature of the contemporary **unbalancing** is of a different order. A sense of political and economic insecurity is played out in the personal domain. Greece, once a country with the lowest suicide rate in Europe, now has one of the highest (based on 2011 figures). We seem to suffer from more collective dissatisfactions than ever, despite having increased life expectancy, greater access to affordable consumer goods, more opportunities for travel and rapid mass worldwide communication. This seems odd, though not to critics of consumer-led 'happiness' such as Oliver James (2007). So how do we reach some sort of perspective and identify which new ideas might assist us through 'crisis' talk, without minimizing the fact that there are many genuine social, political and existential concerns which need urgent attention? We cannot pretend to be able to change the systemic organization of the world alone, but can heed Gandhi's advice: 'You must be the change you wish to see in the world' (Ricard, 2007: 10)

In crisis, the psyche is highly charged and liable to make unguarded errors but, by the same token, it allows for new possibilities, a heightened creativity and directed energy to resolve issues. Likewise the energy of all living systems is activated more fully when faced with potential threats, when they receive 'feedback' that can disrupt the 'steady-state' functioning, and even threaten survival. In the case of human systems, the challenges of different truths and perspectives can cause a system to falter. With the collision of different analyses and solutions, no clear consensus emerges. In this respect, in political systems there frequently emerges an authoritarian force that imposes order through fear and violation of human rights. There are many past and current examples of both out-of-balance systems and good governance, without the need to cite examples. Knowledge of systems and their organization, therefore, does not necessarily imply an outcome of harmonious balance. To be effective and efficacious, systemic thought must be joined at the hip with ethical thought and practice, like Siamese twins.

The development of systemic thought

It is from the crisis of the Second World War, the social upheaval it generated and the technological solutions brought to bear to gain mastery and victory that our story of systemic thought and **attachment theory** begins. New sets of models were developed for mobilizing social and military efficiency in pursuit of a successful outcome to total war. This involved understanding and describing the complex web of inter-locking organizational patterns, communication information and regu-lation so as to function more effectively. Now known as *general systems theory,* or just *systemic theory* or *systemic thinking*, this descriptive model for understanding and energizing the interlocking processes of our organized world has had far-reaching consequences for human relation-ship development beyond wartime. In the family of ideas that accompa-nied it came *information and communication theory*, with the idea that the huge complexity of the evolutionary process, its development and main-tenance, comes through the transmission of information between multi-ple systemic linkages. This continuous, chattering flow of 'information', better known as 'feedback' between the different receptors, is essential for the viability and functioning of all organisms and organizations.

From the same family of systemic science came another member, *cybernetics*, from the ancient Greek word *cybernetes*, meaning 'steers-man', which examines the mechanisms of control and deviation correc-tion. The equivalent terms 'governor', 'governance' and 'government', from the Latin *gubernare* (to govern), describe their functions as system regulators. Cybernetics was developed first by Norbert Weiner as an engineering application to enable missile guidance. It really *is* rocket science, but its basics are not that difficult to grasp. The simplest cyber-netic analogy is driving. You use the accelerator to gain 'runaway' (posi-tive feedback) and the brake to retard it (negative feedback). Movement between the two operations maintains the **homeostasis**, or balanced regulation of the car's movement (and your safety), according to road, traffic and weather conditions. Your subjective mood state will of course be influential (neglecting speed limits to keep an urgent appointment?); however, the basic principle of corrective control remains your active responsibility.

The task of producing more effective computing during the Second World War led to the clearer formulation of information and communi-cation theories and their application in artificial intelligence. A seminal figure in this intellectual revolution was the British-born anthropologist Gregory Bateson (1919–85). Systemic thinking was defined by Bateson as seeing 'patterns that connect' (1980: 16), information as 'news of a difference' (1980: 37) leading to renewal or change in 'the difference that makes the difference' (1980: 78).These Batesonian aphorisms are best studied more fully in his seminal works *Steps towards an Ecology of Mind* (1972) and *Mind and Nature: a Necessary Unity* (1979). This revolution in science and technology has continued apace. The creation of the World Wide Web by Tim Berners-Lee in the 1980s had revolutionary effects on the free flow of information and ease of social networking globally.

'System' is derived from the ancient Greek word *systema*, composed from *syn* meaning 'together' and *histanai* meaning 'to set', thus meaning to stand together or to set alongside. We will see shortly how this fits with 'inclusive' reasoning and Bateson's 'double description'. In the application of systemic phenomenology to family psychotherapy that is precisely what happens: one perspective is put alongside another and they are looked at together to make a fuller evaluation.

Systema, or the 'organized whole' as a way of structural thinking in terms of parts and wholes, was developed by the Greek philosopher Aristotle in his *Politics* . One of the clearest and more recent developments of this structural analysis of systems is by the Hungarian-born philosopher Arthur Koestler (1980), through his concept of a *holon*. How things are organized or set alongside each other can be expressed 'holonistically' in terms of their 'partwholeness' and 'wholepartness'. On a hand, for example, a finger is both a 'whole' thing in its own right and at the same time a 'part' property of the hand (Hills 2002: 147). A Russian 'matryoshka' doll set, each one nesting inside another, yet complete in itself, is a holonistic structure.

Structure, function and process and systemic thought

So these elements, *cybernetics, information theory* and *general systems theory*, continue to have wide application. There are three other dimensions in which systemic thought has to be understood: the **structure** of the system, that is, all the interlocking parts of the system and their boundaries; the **function** of the system, that is, the aims and end goals of the system; and the **process** of the system, that is, the moving and interactive elements of the system that communicate with each other, providing informational and corrective feedback necessary for the system to preserve its integrity of structure and function.

This may be easiest to describe and observe in a simple non-conscious reflex system of the body, such as shivering. Here the structures are the receptor parts of the skin that respond to 'information' of temperature change. They then activate the muscle parts that induce the shivering so that this 'information' then passes to the conscious mind that either closes the window, turns up the heating or puts on a sweater. Here parts of the **structure** 'inform' one another, creating a chain of interactions. A comfortable, balanced temperature is restored through a chain reaction of different 'part-whole' (which can also be described as 'whole-part') receptors that feed back to manage the whole. This communication **process** then restores the comfortable state, and so is **regulatory**. The overall **function**, being mostly non-conscious, is self-referential. There is no higher functioning except that of all living systems responding to the invisible evolutionary imperative of self-sustainment.

The characteristics of a living system may be very different, for example, between human systems that largely rely on consciousness and reflected activity and ones that rely entirely on non-conscious intelligence. However, whatever the composition of the system, they all share three characteristics of process and structure:

- interactivity and flow in a series of chain reactions (informational flow);
- mechanisms of information that balance the functioning of the process between the threats of inertia and stagnation and the threats of chaos from 'overdrive' (cybernetic balance);
- the complex structural interlocking between parts and wholes to complete the entirety of the system - its holonistic structure.

We have seen how the 'mapping' of a system's organizational pattern helps highlight structure, function and process in shivering. Let us examine a more perverse example, leaving aside any ethical objections: the organization of a terrorist cell.

Within a terrorist cell, absolute secrecy about the membership and the boundary of the closed system is crucial to its viability. Whoever is a trusted part of 'the system' must be rigorously maintained to ensure the cell's survival. In order to demonstrate the 'terror' function of the group a target, time and place for an act of terrorism are selected and a trusted, committed member of the group assigned to carry it out. If this is done successfully then outrage is generated, terror is disseminated and retaliation is anticipated. The cell has fulfilled its function. The ethical intention which conceives this deliberate act of harm is a different matter to the process by which it is organized and implemented. The corrective action in the case of shivering is simple; in the second example it is the preparation and negotiation of obstacles in the situation that is crucial. It will be risky for members of the terrorist cell to communicate with one another if they encounter an unexpected difficulty. This process of correction and movement towards goal accomplishment is the cybernetic process of the terrorist system.

Some of these ideas can be used to different ends in working thera-peutically with family and workplace relationships. They have huge implications for organizational management. Hopefully, they may enable you to enhance your practice and develop a fuller experience of your personal and professional self, though they may at times puzzle you, since the ideas themselves ask unusual, counter-intuitive ques-tions. At times, they may infuriate with their seeming uncertainty and indeterminacy which the inclusive thinking of this approach requires. The reward for persevering, however, is considerable, by giving you a richer appreciation of the complexities of living in systems.

As you may be beginning to see, systemic ideas are a way of looking for meaning. They are an invitation to connect with the most seemingly discrepant elements in perceived existence; an invitation to appreciate the 'whole' as more than the sum of the parts and the equal importance of the parts in the creation of the whole. The Jains of India have a story of the 'Eight Blind Men and the Elephant' which helps to explain this idea more fully, for it provides us with another meaning of systemic: the multiple different experiential perspectives and narratives about the same phenomenon.

In this story, popularized by Rudyard Kipling, eight blind men come across an elephant. Each touches the nearest point to him, feeling its shape and texture, concluding that it is a certain object: a tooth, a pipe, a seat, etc. None of the men, of course, can see the whole animal (as the reader can imagine), and they may have no construct for 'elephant'. *We* can tell they are mistaken, for we have both object construct and the means of verifying the whole object through the reading of their attempts.

Systemic phenomenology and collaborative practice

There is much in our experience that is not as readily verifiable as an elephant, for example the nature of mental illness. Even if the diagnos-tic categories of mental illness were scientifically incontestable this would not necessarily lead to a social consensus about their nature and what should be done to alleviate them. It took time for a health consen-sus to emerge on smoking, but disputes as to the causes of global warm-ing (and therefore their resolution) continue. Mental illness remains a complex mystery, since the imaginative part of the mind draws together surreal, disparate, disturbing and chaotic inner experiences and images, usually contained in dreams or artistic creation. They are not enacted in lived experience except when the containing boundaries of the mind break down, whether because of severe substance misuse, the traumatic intrusion of war and civil violence into the immediate secure environment, or the intrusion into personal space of abusive relationships.

In **Jainist** philosophy this attempt to discover the 'whole' (literally the 'elephant in the room') from the different perspectives is called *anekanta* (meaning uncertainty, or non-exclusivity). The philosophical outlook it teaches is known as *anekantaveda* (the doctrine of non-one-sidedness, non-absolutism and non-exclusivity). This is of interest for systemic ways of thinking, since it is an ancient and culturally different articulation of what in the West we now characterize as 'holistic', since it considers the whole, and considers all creation holy. It is a pertinent reminder that what the West has 'discovered' through advances in scientific thought and technological development has actually 'uncovered' ancient 'pre-scientific' knowledge through an unexpected philosophical circularity. Fritjof Capra (1975) and others have written extensively about other such linkages between scientific paradigms and Oriental philosophy.

There are many situations where you may feel overwhelmed with different ideas about a person and their situation, for example, in a case conference. All seem to have some validity. You may equally have studied many forms of psychotherapy and counselling and puzzled over which modality seems to work best for you. You may have a medical, nursing psychiatric background and wonder how other professions cannot see the problems and issues in a situation as clearly as you can. This has been particularly true of the tragic record of child-protection failures, from Maria Colwell to Baby P, where not all members of the professional network were able to see 'the elephant' of harm and risk to the child and if they could, were unable to agree on a form of intervention.

Of course, these cases are well known because they ended in tragic failure. Risk is notoriously difficult to measure and predict with accuracy, for human nature is not robotic. There are no figures and statistics kept on the positive outcomes from collaborative, interdisciplinary work. All the same, how much time is spent in disputing different realities at case conferences and case reviews? How much energy is dissipated in trying to convince others of your perspective? How frustrating is it to have a line manager or member of staff who cannot see matters from your perspective? Such dialogues are essential and more often than not lead to a more accurate delineation of the 'elephant' of risk. When they end in tragedy, however, social criticism is severe and rapid. These multiple perspectives of the 'real', so clear in the Jain story, are the basis of systemic phenomenology, the whole organizational fit of different perceptions and experiences: core-disciplinary perspective, role responsibility, personal attitudes and belief, direct experience of the subjects, and so on. Whoever forms elements in a human system will always have different 'takes' on that situation. This is the essence of systemic phenomenology, and dialogue may reveal conflicts of difference as well as consonance, the ideal goal of the process.

For all the good intentions of training and protocols that emphasize the essential nature of multi-disciplinary working, it is remarkable how these can unravel in the face of critical and risky-case situations. The whole professional system becomes anxiety-activated. In the case of Henry Cockburn's decline into suicidal psychosis, the process is graphically described by himself and his parents in the book *Henry's Demons* (Cockburn & Cockburn, 2011).

However, within professional networks, it is not difficult to detect the operation of 'ghosts in the system': the invisible dynamics and subscripts of interprofessional rivalry, fear of wider societal blame, agency budgetary and manpower shortages, and legal rights considerations – all acting to distort the view of the 'elephant'. Ideals and principles sit awkwardly alongside situational circumstances and their experiential effects.

Systemic phenomenology seeks to cultivate a genuine respect and valuing of different positions and understandings expressed openly and respectfully. Besides 'double description', Bateson also used the term 'binocular vision' to describe how the merging of two different lens perspectives produces a clearer vision. There may be no single expert in this pluralistic approach (except squaring the paradox of being 'expertly non-expert'); the process of collaboration is the most effective way. A belief in 'non-exclusiveness' and pluralistic reality is difficult to hold to under the tension of having to move swiftly and decisively in difficult case situations. Many of the best teams, medical, psychiatric and social interventionist, however, are able to hold the tension between acting decisively and being collaboratively informed. Interdisciplinary systemic working requires practice, patience and respect in allowing each of the seven other 'blind perspectives' to emerge to advantage a better delineated elephant and more considered action to benefit the creature. The blind eight are, after all, a system.

Systems thinking and spirituality

The inclusion of all perspectives into the wider whole means that a strident demand for 'science-based evidence' must sit down patiently with the less visible, complex and softer processes of relationship building and experiential clarification. Jainism has a system of logic called *syadvada* (the reasoning of *both/and* truths) that rescues thinking from the dominant monopoly of Aristotelian logic (the *either/or* truths). The most common example of the latter (which also embodies the logic of prejudice and disqualification) is 'All Cretans are liars; this man is a Cretan; therefore this man is a liar.' This contains the rule of the 'excluded middle' – an assertion is either true or not; its contradiction asserts its propositional truth. We have witnessed the devastating use of this form of reasoning in the Nazi categorical, exclusive 'logic' of a 'master race'.

Syadvada reasoning has seven truth propositions that form the basis of 'non-absolute' reasoning. These proposition truths are that '*in some ways it is*', '*in some ways it is not*', '*in some ways it is and it is not*', and so on, concluding, '*in some ways it is, and it is not and in some ways it is indescribable*'. At first, this may seem odd to Western minds, but it asserts the importance of the paradoxical logic of reconciling contradictions: opposites may both be true, the '*both/and*' inclusively. Since Jainism is a spiritual system, all roads lead back to the sacred of the *indescribable,* even in their contrary opposites. The work of science has increased our knowledge of the world about us immeasurably. However, to appreciate the *indescribable* is an important dimension to understanding systemic thought. Spiritual philosophies universally maintain there is a sacred mystery at the heart of existence for which discourse and language is inadequate – 'God', 'Allah', 'Om', the 'Tao', the 'Word'. According to Wittgenstein, 'what we cannot speak about we must pass over in silence' (1981: 74). 'God's' mystery was revealed to Moses through the enigmatic 'I am that I am', rather like Oedipus's revelation of his true self. In the sacred work of Hinduism, *The Bhagavad Gita* (*c.*500 BC), Krishna says in his Dialogue on the Soul, 'I am the silence of hidden mysteries; and I am the knowledge of those who know.' Janet Sayer's excellent book *Divine Therapy* (2003) explores the connections between psychotherapy and spirituality in greater depth through an examination of the work of 12 influential philosophers and psychotherapists.

Few humanists who reject the existence of an intervening deity also reject the aesthetic wonderment at the fact of existence. Gregory Bateson wrote: 'Most of us have lost that sense of unity of biosphere and humanity which would bind us and reassure us all ... that whatever the ups and downs of detail within our limited experience, the larger whole is primarily beautiful' (1980: 27) This whole, the mystery at the centre of existence, never fully discloses itself (it is mystery after all) though reached through contemplative practice and aesthetic experience.

In *Henry's Demons*, Henry Cockburn (Cockburn & Cockburn, 2011) writes about communing in a similar pantheistic way with the energy of the natural world, though he believed it 'called' him into acts of near self-destruction. He was clearly attuned to the mystery of creation, but through the unmanageability of psychosis and the primary forces of destruction that coexist in our psyches. Respectful knowledge for the mystery which permeates human thought and experience is abundant in poetry and the sacred writings of the world's spiritual systems (Van de Weyer, 2003), though each has its own pathway to union with the metaphysical centre (or non-centre) of creation. Remarkable photographs from the Hubble telescope challenge us with the simple and basic existential questions. Holistic thought, like that of the Jains, is based on an appreciation of the unknowable and can only be approached by a different route than science or strict, Western evidence-based logic and reasoning.

As part of the holism of systemic thought, the 'personal self' is a forceful player acting on the different systems surrounding 'him' and the total situation in which he finds 'himself'. Particular situations shape and challenge the positioning and adaptation of the person. This is the ecology of being a person. We are both alone in the world, and in multiple relational worlds in which the self's multiple identities find expression. It is our experiencing self that is the starting and ending points of existence because these are the limits of our self-consciousness. The philosopher Ludwig Wittgenstein wrote in his journal: 'It is true. Man is the microcosm. I am my world' (1916: 84e).

The Chinese proverb says, the 'fish is in the ocean and the ocean in the fish', so the self exists in a host of systems: in partnership, family, workplace, local community and in human society, national and global. All these systems are also in the self, in an invisible chain linking and reacting one with the other. This is the experiential nature of a personal and systemic phenomenology. So the constituent elements of the personality, of the personal self (mind, body, feelings and action), are gathered in the invisible unity in what popular terminology calls the *soul* or *psyche*. It is worth remembering that 'psychiatry', 'psychotherapy' and 'psychology', as well as 'psychopathology', all derive from the Greek word *psyche*, meaning spirit, mind and soul. These different characteristics of our being may operate separately or can be brought together into some integrated activity, such as a collection of jazz or rock musicians in a jam session; and likewise in systemic-based therapy the three parts of the *psyche* is ever present.

Experiential thought maintains that, whether aware of it or not, each human actor is their own scientist, **hypothesizing**, testing, modifying and concluding (tentatively or with certainty) their truths in the open laboratory of their lives. There is no prescribed or predictable outcome. This is the personal freedom of our life choices. Not to choose is a choice. From such experimentation and openness to corrective feedback can emerge the desired end of well-being. R.D. Laing (1967) argued for the primacy of personal experience, known as 'personalism', over that of scientific positivism, as did the French existential author and philosopher Albert Camus:

> But you tell me of an invisible planetary system in which electrons gravitate around a nucleus. You explain this world to me with an image. I realise then that you have been reduced to poetry ... that science that was to teach me everything ends up in a hypothesis, that lucidity founders in metaphor that uncertainty is resolved in a work of art ... The soft lines of these hills and the hand of evening on this troubled heart teach me much more. I have returned to my beginning. I realise that if through science I can seize phenomena and enumerate them, I cannot for all that apprehend the world. (1942: 18)

In the light of the main principles of systemic thought, let us briefly return to how that might affect our thinking in understanding families and how we can apply this in greater detail to genogam work. The main points from systemic thought are: the structure, function and process of systems; the information process that activates difference to maintain the system or change it; the cybernetic function of balanced regulation or governance; the multi-perspective of phenomena 'put alongside each other' as the etymology of the word system suggests; while human systems are consciously directed and managed on the basis of the incoming data of experience.

Any human system is complex and difficult to attempt to look at organizationally, especially the family. The following template of its experience might be useful. The family's script perspective is bracketed alongside. This will be discussed fully in Chapter 8 and an explanation is available in the Glossary. However, this will alert you to the kind of experiential phenomena to which you will need to attend in order to follow and intervene in the flow of dialogue.

- power structure and family alliances (structural problem-solving script)
- cognition and thinking (all scripts)
- affect and mood (all scripts)
- behaviour/action (all scripts)

- issues of difference and cultural issues (assumptive identity script)
- existential, life-cycle transitions (assumptive script)
- communication (delivered script and subscript)

Power structure and alliances

You will have seen from your own genogram that the family is a political system with some basic hierarchy and disposition of authority. Some families derive authority from cultural tradition; for others it is developed pragmatically by experience. Authority is the homeostatic regulator between all the differing and competing demands, needs and disagreements. Where there is no clear experience of regulating authority, boundaries may become confused and behaviour embattled. However, families have their own operational understanding about where the power and authority are vested or where they desire them to be. Children or adolescents give the game away: 'Dad thinks he's in charge, and Mum lets him think that. But she is really. She's the one who makes up his mind for him.' The assumptive scripts about authority and its use can be discovered through the genogram by questioning the different generational beliefs. Much family dialogue is about the experience of authority and its effectiveness to achieve harmony and fairness.

> *Therapist* (to the father): Mick, in your family you gave us a sense your Dad was the boss.
>
> *Mick*: Yes, we'd never risk getting him annoyed. Me Mum knew how to work round him, though.
>
> *Therapist* (to Mick): Does it work like for you and Sharon? [his wife]
> *Mick*: Best ask her.
>
> *Therapist* (to Sharon): Is that how you think Mick sees your relationship? Has he based it on his parents?
>
> *Sharon*: No way. For one thing, he didn't like it like that. For another, I wouldn't have wanted it that way either, and I let him know it. It wasn't how my Mum and Dad were. We do this together as equals, is what we agreed.
>
> *Therapist* (looking to Mick): I see you nodding. Sounds like you agree with how Sharon sees it.

As Minuchin taught, the family is a smaller system of governance. As we shall see in Chapter 5, his model and method of structural family therapy (1981) is particularly good at identifying divergent power issues and finding ways, sometimes dramatic ones, to enable the family to negotiate these better and problem-solve through unbalancing, rebalancing and enacted dialogues.

Cognition and thinking: conception, perception

The cognitive, conscious life of a family system is as complex and multifaceted as the family itself. The cognitive attitudes may be overt and contested or in varying states of latency, depending on the danger and risk felt in voicing them. Each personal cognition is at the centre of the family's assumptive scripts:

> *Father to son*: If you don't knuckle down to accepting some kind of authority, son, no one in their right mind's going to give you a job, far less are you going to keep it.

Or:

> *Mother to daughter*: You shouldn't speak to your father as if he's a piece of dirt. Parents deserve some respect, you know.

Families are often unsettled places of dissenting exchanges where the feedback of different ideas and beliefs is seen as threatening the equilibrium of the family. This process contains a myriad of contextual issues, from the political (dissent and division over the merits of strike action) or cultural (desire to wear a burka in the face of parental anxiety that it may activate an Islamophobic reaction to the family in the surrounding white community). Notions about the negotiated feedback of life-stage changes, e.g adolescence or older age, may have been disconnected from the parents' or grandparents' remembered experience of how they negotiated these stages. There are many ways of asserting individuality and difference, and all involve taking on the basic conceptions and values around which the beliefs of the family are based.

Exercise 3.1: Ten points of family friction

As an exercise, devise a list of ten features likely to cause dissent and challenge the different beliefs in families you know. How would you work with these?

Cognitive beliefs involve conceptions. The 'elephant' of core assumptions (often unexamined) can lead to a perception that there is a threat to basic family values and stability. Circularly, perceptions can cause tensions, and lead to the conceptual beliefs that something is not as it should be. Shame, guilt and attributions to do with some violation of cultural norm, law or personal belief provide potent energy for conflict and dispute. The perception that a daughter may be pregnant, for example, still has powerful emotional resonance and social anxiety, whether the family's basic assumptions come from strong religious prohibitions or secular ideas about timing and the right circumstance for having a child. Likewise, the act of coming out as gay, lesbian, transvestite or transexual can set in motion complex reactions around dormant basic beliefs. Sometimes the outcome can surprise; perception may anticipate conception which has already been reappraised. In the containing space of a genogram and the secure alliance with the therapists, the open dialogue can produce effective listening and feedback to understanding. New information about attitudes and personal emotions to a family member can also produce change.

> *Mother to son*: You know you'll never get anywhere you want to without doing more homework.
> *Son*: So? It's my life, isn't it? Anyway, if you weren't going on at me all the time and trusted me more it might be different.
> *Mother*: Well, I'm only doing it because that's what your Dad would have wanted if he was still around. Anyway, you wouldn't do a single thing unless I had a go at you.
> *Son*: Well he ain't here, is he, and the way you keep on I don't want to be around, either.
> *Mother*: That's a terrible thing to say to your mother.
> *Son*: So who else am I supposed to complain to?

In this small extract there are all manners of assumptive scripts about family roles and relationships: motivating others, intrusion, ways of achieving in the world, filling gaps and losses and acceptable communication, and so on. Family dialogue is saturated with such richness, and it is as important to get hold of the content of the family's script as it is to follow the way in which emotional energy is expended in the interchanges.

Exercise 3.2: Family scripts

As a therapist, how might you reflect on your understanding of this situation to help the mother and son problem-solve? Write out one response you think might be reflected back to the couple.

Alternatively, the mother and son may become aware of where the fight is leading them and correct the direction, in which case they will have used their capacity to solve the problem in the service of preserving the unity of the relationship.

> *Son*: Look, Mum. I'm out of order here. It's not your fault. I know it's down to me. Can we call a truce?
>
> *Mother*: What you said was very hurtful. I'm only doing my best for you and your sister.
>
> *Son*: Yes, I know that. Sorry
>
> *Mother*: OK, let's try again. I'll hold my tongue and try not to nag and let you just get on with whatever you have to do.
>
> *Son*: Well, I do like you reminding me a bit 'cos I'm naturally not good at getting down to work. So perhaps you could just say something like 'how's the work going?'
>
> *Mother*: I know, I'll do more than that. I'll tell you to take a longer break until you feel really ready to work.
>
> *Son*: (bewildered) Well, OK, let's try that.

The mother has adjusted her attitude to one of inclusion, even been a little paradoxical.

Affect and mood

It is the informational data of our 'felt existence', our mood and feeling states and those of others, that give life its savour. When these are emotionally 'bad' states (experientially 'dis-easing'), they are not easily released and the sufferer feels enslaved by them and the 'caring other' disqualified. For many years family systemic approaches was impoverished by deliberately avoiding this essential dimension of our humanity. There are many affective states that arise in the self from external adversities which are experienced as persecutory. Perhaps the deepest of these is permanent loss. Such adversities are then fed back into the internalized state of 'badness' and alienation, which is then generalized to a pervasive, toxic experience from which the only release is felt to be death. The 'bad' states induced by adversities can be readily listed: despair, despondency, depression and hopelessness. In their most chronic and entrenched states they enter the classification work of psychiatry as pathologies, states of ontological 'dis-ease'. The knowledge (*logos*) of passion and pity (*pathos*) are its Greek derivatives. In an experiential approach to psychotherapy, we attune ourselves to listening, feeling and understanding the nature of the suffering rather than classifying it as a disease and looking to how different feedback from others in the system could make a difference.

We are saturated with accounts and experiences of sorrows and life troubles and we also have our own difficulties to contend with. Associative suffering, sharing the sorrows of others though listening, is itself distressing and requires resilience to bear for sustained periods. Constant exposure to distressed reality risks corroding our own sensibilities, the heart of our connective capabilities which need constant refreshment.

When conducting the genogram you will soon become aware of the predominant mood of the family, the family atmosphere: of tension, inhibited emotional expressiveness, depression or a jocularity and frivolity that somehow seem incongruent for a family seeking help. This is usually a property of the subscript and the therapist feels a way to helping it being expressed.

> *Therapist* (reflecting): I can see Tracey (partner/mother) that your father moving out of the family when you were 7 sensitised you to changes in the family's closeness. You all seemed very tense with each other when we first met, and even now when we've got to know each other better. Do you worry, we were wondering, with Jim (partner/father) serving in Afghanistan, that if the worst happened to him, you and the children would be left alone to get on with your lives in the same way as we've heard your mother had to when you Dad left?
>
> *Tracey*: I've never thought of it that way, but, I suppose so.
>
> *Therapist*: (to Jim) Did you realise Jim, that for Tracey, there may be more to you being on active duty than just worry about your safety.
>
> *Jim*: Well I did always wonder why she would never show many tears when I left, unlike some other army wives. I was glad in a way because I thought she was stronger than most, not putting up a fuss.

Behaviour/action

It can readily be seen from the systemic principle of considering different dimensions besides each other that they are not discrete entities but merge and interact with one another; change in one part can influence change in another. Action subjectively willed by me with all sorts of intentions, transparent or latent, is 'my behaviour' objectively characterized and experienced by you. It runs the risk of being 'thingified' or reified and split off from 'me' as if disconnected, usually because it seems both inexplicable and unacceptable. 'Behaviour' is not an entity in its own right, but is always expressive of the context in which it manifests itself, if one takes the time and trouble to search out the background. Seeking to understand its meaning in context, when it is disruptive or destructive to the self and others, is of course a difficult skill, not just for a therapy team but for every parent, grandparent and sibling. An adolescent who attacks his father and badly beats him may be understood differently in a context of having witnessed domestic violence towards his mother over many years, to an attack that arises from a father's refusal to give money to his son to pay off his drug dealer. Each requires a different kind of intervention.

The family genogram gives a fuller picture of the background expectancies and experiences from which the presented difficulty stands out like the observable part of an iceberg. The point, however, is not to present factors of extenuation or explanation (though both may arise naturally in the family's shared understanding), but to view them systemically, in the original Greek sense, that is to put separate pieces of information alongside each other. This is an equivalent of a team looking at different X-ray shots of a fracture. All are put alongside each other to get a clearer more accurate perspective.

The difference of difference: cultural issues

Experientially we cannot fully know the personal and social world of 'the other', especially when it appears significantly different to our own. Difference does indeed make a huge difference, and much human conflict stems from either the incapacity or unwillingness to seek a connecting bridge. When that difference is acute, it is easier to demonize it and put it into a category with attributes that justify fear, hatred and the desire to confine or, *in extremis,* to exterminate it. Such has been the sad history of the treatment of the mentally ill, minority cultures and ways of life in Western society (and perhaps in all societies) by those in powerful positions. This **'will to power'** permeates the collective nature of humankind but develops its pathways and energies in the experiences within the micro-system of the family.

There are two natural developmental stages of the 'will to power' (between the ages of 2 to 3 and again from about 12 to 15) which usually provoke crises and conflict in families. Both phases of 'insurrection' are important rites of passage in the movement to individuation. However, unmediated, this 'will to power' wreaks havoc and creates alienation in communal life, with the recent examples of extravagant self-rewarding bankers and the rioting groups in English cities.

British family therapist John Burnham (2011) devised an ingenious mnemonic to guide awareness through the main experiential domains of human differences and social relativities. You will almost certainly have personally experienced the tension of difference in one of these domains. This is contained in the acronym, the Social '**Grraacceess**'. These are: gender, religion, race, age, (dis)ability, culture, class, education, employment, sexuality and spirituality. Our own unique background and location in these areas are to an extent given by genetics and social circumstance. However, experientially speaking, we have the ability to seek to choose how these factors organize our identity, the process Jung termed 'individuation'. We learn from existence and human difference how best to position ourselves to 'stand out' from our situation and circumstances (from the Latin *ex-sistere*, meaning to 'stand out' or 'emerge'). Putting it more philosophically, 'to exist is to stand out from nothing' (Macquarrie, 1980: 62), or in this case from being different.

In an encounter between a white, male, Oxbridge-educated, British therapist and an Afro-Indian, all-female, migrant family, without work and with little English, there will be huge differences of conception, perception and unspoken expectancies about their ability to connect. How can these different realities be explored without prejudice? Equally, how can an East European therapist engage with a family who is convinced that the troubles in the UK are all down to the levels of immigration, especially from Eastern Europe, but who are desperate for help with their son, who shows signs of schizophrenia?

The easiest and most frequently used method is generally to say nothing and let the formal role of 'professional authority' do the work. Here the problem is that the unspoken tension of different domains and experiences *is* the work, and unless voiced and thought about conjointly it is liable to obstruct anything productive happening, however skilled and empathic the therapist. Chapter 8 has ideas as to how to cross the terrain of radically perceived differences. Meanwhile, it is vital to be able to orientate yourself to take the risk to do so, leaving behind the protective security of the 'expert' model. The first prerequisite is to be aware of your own default experiential perspective and identity through **self-reflexivity**. The Grraacceess give you a valuable map.

Exercise 3.3: Addressing your own personal challenges

Identify a set of Grraacceess factor differences that you know you would have difficulty connecting with experientially. Be brutally honest. Think about and write out a dialogue that would help you address it with the person.

Existential and life-cycle themes

One certain fact about human existence is that it is subject to change. Our lived experience can be seen in many ways as a homeostatic attempt to maintain stability and feelings of security amidst flux and movement: Hamlet's 'sea of troubles'. There are threats and worries about the adversities of ill health, unemployment and the loss of income, care or even a home. Wars, famines and disease, symbolized by the Four Horsemen of the Apocalypse, have always been sources of fear and dread, threatening the ability of human beings to flourish communally. These existential threats are a daily reality in many parts of the world, and the seeming comfort provided by affluence in the developed world should not disguise how easily it can change.

Families as systems also undergo the fears, panic and worries that change brings. They, like larger polities, have to work to adapt to the unexpected. These can be major losses that come with life-cycle changes: immobility in older age, illness in its many forms, migration to find work and income for the family – even the arrival of a child involves some losses and certainly worry about managing – and then the ultimate and inevitable death. Family life is punctuated by separation and loss throughout the life cycle. This is given dramatic voice in Arthur Miller's play *Death of a Salesman* (1949). In an exchange between the ageing and failing principal character, Willie Loman, and his wife Linda, Willy tells his wife with some bitterness and disappointment: 'Figure it out. Work a lifetime to pay off a house. You finally own it and there's nobody to live in it.' She replies with more stoicism: 'Well, dear, life is a casting off. It's always that way.'

It is the incursion of these existential events that shape family life and its patterns of attachment. In turn, patterns of attachment shape the way life and relationship events are understood and responded to. Life is indeed a casting off, but how we attune and orientate ourselves to such experiences shapes the pathway of the experience. (We shall look more closely in Chapter 5 at the ethical thought and systemic formulation.) For the purposes of the genogram, it is essential to map out the personal and different responses that comprise parts of the collective response. This can be accompanied by a question that invites a solution, for example in the exchange above, a therapeutic reflection could be: 'Willie, you seem to be taking it very hard that your sons have now left home and it is only you and Linda left in the house. Linda seems to be taking it better as if "that's life". What do you think is getting in the way of enjoying the freedom of owning your own home and having it to yourselves?' This leads us neatly to the final dimension of experience.

Communication

Relational intimacy is rarely an easy spontaneous activity, though it may be in the early days of excited passionate attraction and the arrival of a newborn. Enduring intimacy, an essential part of family relationships, can sometimes feel, well, like an endurance test. Communication is the informational conduit, the feedback process in all relationships; sometimes through dialogue, sometimes through a touch or a glance, meaning is conveyed. To have grown up in a family culture where emotion and different thought can be openly expressed without jeopardizing the security of the family or risking alienation is a significant experiential legacy. Much, perhaps all, therapy is both reparative and innovative in enabling fuller access to expressiveness. Like Cyrano de Bergerac's coaching of his protégé, it is not just about feeling the feelings but finding the language to convey them in ways which are not necessarily elegant, but which make for a better human connection.

However, much groundwork can be covered using a genogram when you get indications of obstructive styles of communication. Feedback to one another or from the therapists seems to find a *cul-de-sac*. This can sometimes be helped by a reflective question.

> *Therapist*: I can see the way you speak to each other seems to cause you to feel worse and drives you further apart.
> *Therapist* (to Linda): How would you like Willie speak to you?
> *Therapist* (to Willie): And you Willie, what is it about the way Linda talks to you that you dislike?

Communication culs-de-sac may be uncomfortable, but they give valuable data about the family's difficulty. Most of the time, in the dialogue, families provide their own openings and covert invitations to be curious.

However, when they do not, sometimes a family member sends out signals that the theme of the exploration is unsettling by reacting defensively, aggressively, anxiously withdrawing or challenging the therapist. You have touched on something in the family subscript and someone in the family warns you about proceeding or the rate of proceeding. Sometimes they will deny the simplest connection the therapist or team seek to make. It is important to note these cues of information and reflect aloud about it.

> *Therapist*: Jim, I'm thinking you're not too happy or even convinced we're heading anywhere useful with this. I have a feeling this goes on behalf of all of you. (*some nod*). Would it help to know what's in the back of my mind in asking? (*more nodding*)
> *Jim*: Well, David, it would. I was seriously wondering, where the hell is he going with this?
> *Therapist*: I was trying to link it with something Jean was saying about five minutes ago, that ... (*he reports Jean's earlier statement*)

The principle of systemic thought is to help open the 'informational flow' of cognition and affect and understand the meaning of behaviours by setting different perspectives and reactions alongside one another; always looking for different connections and the connection of differences. Above all, it is in freeing up and modelling open communication that invites the family to think a different homeostasis may be possible.

Summary

- Contemporary life seems punctuated by crises of different intersecting systems.
- The historical development of systems , cybernetic and information theory is explained, especially the contribution of Gregory Bateson.
- All living systems operate on the circulation of information and corrective regulation and have structure, function and process.
- Multiple systems and perspectives coexist to form our world.
- The allegory of eight blind men and the elephant describes the challenge of pluralistic perspectives.
- Jainist inclusive reasoning is explained as a way of non-reductive thinking.
- The holism of the experiential self, the *soul* or *psyche* is always embedded in the *indescribable* of creation.

- Applied to family systems, the genogram is an organic way to explore the different interconnecting domains of experience which form the script.
- These are power structures and alliances; cognition and thinking; affect and mood; behaviour and action; cultural issues; existential and life-cycle themes; and communication
- Each is examined and their implicit areas for exploration in systemic therapy.

4

THE FAMILY CRUCIBLE AND THE
ORIGINS OF FAMILY THERAPY

The 'family' as community: what and whom?

In the inaugural issue of *Family Process*, the first periodical devoted to the development of family therapy, the psychoanalyst Nathan Ackerman wrote:

> The family approach offers a new level of entry, a new quality of participant observation in the struggles of human adaptation. It holds the promise of shedding new light on the processes of illness and health and offers new ways of assessing and influencing these conditions. It may open up, perhaps for the first time, some effective paths for the prevention of illness and the promotion of health. (Ackerman, 1962: 31)

This clarion call was taken up by a number of other clinicians focusing on the family as the basic source of well-being. Carl Whitaker (Whitaker & Napier 1988) termed it 'the **family crucible**', the matrix of human identity. We are born as automatic members of it, our primary organization and community. When we speak of 'the family' we are not speaking of something that is uniform, simple or readily understood. Like the hunters of Lewis Carroll's epic poem *The Hunting of the Snark*, who discover that the snark they seek is actually a 'boojum', so 'the family' model in your mind will often turn out to have an altogether more exotic and complex form. Gill Gorell Barnes has written a very instructive and useful guide to the complexities of modern family structure, *Family Therapy in Changing Times* (2004), also in this Palgrave Macmillan series.

We cannot assume that the generic term 'the family' gives us any clues to the family or part-family we will encounter in work. Nor can we make universal assumptions from either our own family experience or social archetypes of 'the family'. There are as many forms of 'the family' as there are families; each family situation is configured in its own way. Initially, the systemic therapist should approach each family situation and ask them to help define who 'the family' is, as well as get them to explain their rules, beliefs and communicational style. You may have strong convictions about how a family should work or how it could work, how human happiness is found and promoted, or how harm, hurt and suffering may be avoided or remedied. These convictions may be valid truths based on personal experience. However, they are obstacles to discovering how the particular family members see one another as a living, organized system.

The family system is a community that functions like a club, with its own membership rules. It can be a highly exclusive club that demands a great deal of its members, sometimes very little; sometimes the qualifications for inclusion and exclusion are clear, sometimes they are ambiguous. When seeking to engage with it, it is essential to establish who 'the family' is seen to be and what it means to whom. Without this, and an emerging sense of its alliances and divisions, the work can soon get into difficulty. Sometimes, to extend the club analogy, it is not clear who comprises the membership or where they are, or the history of past members and who holds these stories. There are certain key moments of membership transition that may be experienced acutely: for example, when a child enters the 'looked-after' status of corporate parenting, or when an individual or sub-group suddenly finds itself excluded as beneficiaries of a deceased relative or on separation, divorce and reconstitution.

'Membership' is often defined by dominant figures in the family for a host of different reasons. Similarly, some members prefer to exclude themselves. The stories and perceptions about the membership usually emerge when using genograms, for they provide explicit clues to the more covert patterns. Much of the beneficial therapy work of a family-systemic approach comes from discovering how the family as a unique community perceives itself: its fears, its wishes, its frustrations, its conflicts, its strengths and its collaborative capacity to generate changes and solutions.

The cultural expectations, values and beliefs of a family are also shaped by the wider, overlapping beliefs of the institutional social structures, the political nation-state and religious affiliations, as well as social class, ethnicity and sexual orientation. In contemporary Western society, postmodern views of family relationships are portrayed through the media of film, television, radio, novels and magazines – narratives and images that are often used in the active manufacturing of celebrity. A strict Hindu family from rural northern India may find little in common with that of a contemporary British, white, working-class family from Manchester in lifestyle, beliefs, hierarchies or acceptable emotional responses. Were they to meet they would first have to set aside many presumptions of the other, though commonalities of experience would probably still emerge. The huge global and national inequalities of wealth, power, resources and access to opportunities should always be kept in mind. Family and child labour are still exploited in many parts of the world. Many families struggle to survive, and it is the desire for a better life for themselves and their families that fuels the economic migration deplored by the tabloid press and which separates families.

Families, then, are not randomly patterned, even so-called dysfunctional ones, but are micro-social systems enacting their beliefs, about, for example, care and organization; emotional expressiveness and concealment; speculative and spiritual beliefs about suffering and existence; coping with illness and existential threats to their survival; social behaviour, boundaries and compliance; achievement and success; making money and how it should be shared; and the valuing of family–communal relationships and connections with the wider national community; while adding new members through birth, marriage and social joining and losing members through death and departure.

Families are formed through combinations of sex, love, law (via marriage, fostering or adoption) and family planning (by individual choice or family negotiation). There is a variety of discrete family communities besides the nuclear/extended family: the lone parent-led family; stepfamilies formed through separation, loss and reconstitution; same gender-led families, foster and adopted families, and groups of friends that identify themselves as familial communities. (The US mass murderer Charles Manson's commune was known as 'The Family', though we cite this as a model of familial community, certainly not one of a model family!) The Argentinean-born American family therapist Salvador Minuchin (1974: 54) describes 'accordion families', where one of the parental figures, usually the father, moves in and out of the family for a variety of reasons whether working away, stationed overseas with the armed forces, in prison or just out of inclination. Such families' pattern of organization pivots around the movements of the periodically absent member. Indeed, as the *Observer* stated: 'One study five years ago looking at 5,000 households identified 73 different family types' (29 January 2012).

Changing attitudes to marriage and its decline as a normative institution in many Western countries means that the nature and structure of family communal life has changed hugely over the last 60 years or so. The fragmentation of traditional structures is not necessarily a sign of communal breakdown, however, but of individuals experimenting to find ways of living together more satisfactorily though more personalized arrangements, though these can bring as much complexity and distress as failed marriages. The 'family' is a group of characters in search of belonging; it is always an aspiring community.

CASE STUDY 4.1: LAURA AND ALEX

Laura was the babysitter for Alex and Rachael, who had two children, Charlie and Josie. Rachael had an affair with Paul and left Alex to live with him. Alex set up home with Laura, who already had a daughter, Angelina, by her first husband. Alex and Laura then had a child, Bethany.

Laura was referred to individual therapy for help with her depression and experience of childhood sexual abuse. The individual therapist referred her on to the family therapy service when it became apparent that there was a great deal of conflict in Alex and Laura's relationship. Social Services had been called to investigate sexualized behaviour between Josie (then aged 8) and Angelina (4) when Josie and her older brother Charlie came to stay.

Seven family therapy sessions were held with various combinations of the reconstituted family, including the four children and the three adults. The tensions eased considerably and the children were much more relaxed with one another. Alex and Laura talked about getting married, but Alex shortly afterwards left Laura for a mutual friend who had also acted as a childminder while both parents worked. Laura was initially very distraught but acted quickly to re-establish herself as a lone parent to Angelina and Bethany, finding a new home, and completed her ongoing work in individual therapy. Surviving family breakdown and relationship disappointment was her strength as well as her expectation that this was her life script. Alex was reported initially to be happier living with someone he believed understood him better. However, this relationship broke down and he and Laura got back together again. This time they decided to get married.

Through these crises Alex and Laura came to a better self-understanding which went hand in hand with greater appreciation of each other and their relationship.

The family: the basic community of care

Historically, the new family, often formed through family alliances and church-sanctioned marriage, and then procreation, was embedded in wider social networks of the family and the local community. Social historian Hugh Cunningham, author of *The Invention of Childhood* (2006), described the main threat to the communal life of the family until very recently as a high mortality rate. Death is (and was, even more so) a powerful social reorganizer. Through natural disasters and imperial conquests, death is written into the histories of every culture. In evolutionary terms, the reproductive ability and the community of care and belonging has made the traditionally organized family a potent source of endurance and stability through such catastrophic times as the mid-fourteenth century, when the Black Death spread through Western Europe. It has also proved resistant to ideological attempts to modify it, whether by Nazism, Soviet communism or the early Israeli kibbutzim experiments.

Almost all the myths and stories in the major world religions involve stories of family relationships and their dynamics. Adam and Eve in the Old Testament, the Holy Family of the New Testament, the dramatic narrative of Oedipus, the Kauravas and Pandavas in the *Mahabharata*, and the family of Prince Gotama, the Buddha. Narratives of family as community are deeply and archetypically embedded in the human consciousness and are transmitted from generation to generation, along with their relationship dramas and stock of stories, with the same constancy as genetic patterns of DNA. So, although the structures and forms of modern family life may vary, the passions and emotions that arise from family relationships are endowments of an ancient order and part of a world collective heritage. From the early Greek tragedies of Sophocles and Aeschylus, ancient folk tales and traditional folk song and music attest to the universal, enduring experiential fascination and instruction that stories of family life have.

During the eighteenth and nineteenth centuries family life in the UK underwent huge changes as part of the Industrial Revolution which saw a major shift from a predominantly rural-based agricultural economy to an urban industrial one. This process of internal migration is now a feature of many third-world societies around the globe. Migration has always been a feature of human behaviour in the quest for a better life. However, it was the dire working conditions of the white, working-class families in Manchester and their poverty and exploitation that prompted Friedrich Engels and Karl Marx to write their manifesto for change. *The Communist Manifesto* (1848) envisages a more humanitarian and just world order and has been hugely influential.

What is the family crucible?

We have seen that the family is a micro-community of care and mutual economic support. But what about the dynamic processes it contains? Traditionally, 'dynamic' refers to Freud's model of mental functioning, of forces in conflict within an individual's experience, but there is also its meaning of strength or power, derived from the original Greek *dynasthai*, in its more popular sense of empowerment. Both dispositions can be played out in family experience, as relational systems may be in conflict and veering towards destructiveness or empowering one another to live creatively.

The root word 'family' is shared with 'familiar', meaning 'the given' or 'the comfortable, taken-for-granted'. This is part of the sometimes fantasized comfort and strength of the family, that it is 'lived in' and not endlessly re-examined. The familiarity of domesticity can have the comfort and security of a well-worn coat, and domestic ease can act as an anaesthetic. However, the restlessness in unmet needs or submerged conflict requires the difficult challenge of reflection and the risk of articulating frustrations in relationships. The conflict this generates, or the anticipation of conflict, the exhausting and anxious uncertainty as to the outcome, mean that such a critique from the inside of the family is more difficult than with most other human institutions. Freud sensibly separated the alienated one from their family process for therapeutic work.

One of the pioneering and significant figures on the British family therapy scene has been the psychiatrist and group analyst, Robin Skynner. He was one of the co-founders of the Association for Family Therapy (AFT) and the Institute of Family Therapy (IFT) in the 1970s. His thinking, which integrated psychoanalysis, systemic theory and a holistic spiritual philosophy, was heavily influenced by the Greek Armenian mystic, G.I. Gurdjieff (1866–1949), and is best described in his book *One Flesh: Separate Persons* (1976). He worked for a number of years at the child and mental health service clinic at Woodbury Down in North London and characterized the important existential activities of the family thus:

> From our first cry at birth to the last words at death, the family surrounds us and finds a place for all ages, roles and relationships for both sexes. Our needs for physical, emotional and intellectual exchange and for nurturance, control, communication and genital sexuality can all exist side by side and find satisfaction in harmonious relationship to one another ... It exists to make itself unnecessary, to

release its members into the wider community as separate, autonomous beings, only to recreate their images of itself and anew. It has enormous creative potential, including that of life itself, and this is not surprising that, when it becomes disordered, it possesses *an equal potential for terrible destruction.* [1976: xi; emphasis added]

Like most definitions, this should not be taken as a final statement, but it is a helpful place to begin. First, we have a description of the enormous complexity of the family process. Skynner conveys a sense of optimism that all these different, potentially conflicting needs and desires can be brought into harmony and fulfilment for all its members. He is clear about the different identifiable threads, separate yet interacting, and implies, importantly, that we are enfolded by an experience that crosses gender and generational boundaries to create a shared feeling of belonging. The community of the family is a matrix, almost a 'socially constructed uterus', in which the person can feel held at every stage of their development and then is freed to re-create the pattern of family strength and accomplishment. Skynner's ideas echo Bowlby's in seeing the family as a secure base from which to venture into the personal dance between belonging and individuating.

The second part of his statement proposes a model of thinking in which the whole family rather than just the individual has to negotiate between opposites; between the forces of creativity, renewal and regeneration in which the arrival of a new child and a passing life are celebrated. However, Skynner points to the toxic capacity within family life and the possibility that the emergence of the full person can be constricted and inhibited at many levels. The destructive potential is immense, and thus, like any ecosystem, its sustainability must be safeguarded by those who govern it. When this does not happen, systems beyond the family become involved.

The emotional legacy from the turbulent and fragmented patterns of family life, which arise and find expression in the family crucible, are the centre of many universal stories of suffering, and certainly of great art, notably drama. From the ancient Greek tragedies through Shakespeare to modern dramas such as Ibsen's *A Doll's House* (1879), Arthur Miller's *Death of a Salesman* (1949), Tennessee Williams's *A Streetcar Named Desire* (1947), Harold Pinter's *The Homecoming* (1964) and Mike Leigh's improvised dramas such as *Secrets and Lies* (1996), the drama hinges on the disturbed passions, confusions, secrets, threats, power imbalances and violence and self-harming implicit in the artistic re-creations of the destructive dynamics of family life. From *Oedipus the King* (c.429 BC) to popular TV and radio dramas (the UK's family radio serial *The Archers* is the longest running drama in world history), family scripts prove a powerful attraction. Their conflicts of loathing, violence and insecurity cohabit closely with feelings of tenderness, love and loyalty and have a compelling capacity to switch. This is the nature of the crucible: the full dynamic properties of drama are unrivalled in the family process. When the wheel of its dynamics is spinning, the outcome is not always clear and could equally be tragic, farcical or result in a concord of deepened bonds of attachment.

The existential dimension of human experience

This book stresses the existential dimensions to thought and experience and their potential value to understanding family relationships and therapeutic work. Such deeper thoughts about living, its values and direction can come into the mind unbidden while we are apparently preoccupied with ordinary daily routines. We are a meaning-activated species. The theologian Paul Tillich (1952) identified a number of 'ultimate concerns' which follow from our mortality and the fear, anxiety and insecurity which sit alongside this certainty. The existential psychotherapist Irvin Yalom (1980, 2002), most recently in *Staring at the Sun: Overcoming the Terror of Death* (2009), took the following from Tillich: 'Four ultimate concerns, to my view, are highly salient to psychotherapy: death, isolation, meaning in life and freedom' 2002: (xvii). These ultimate concerns of life are powerful and natural dynamic drivers in the family process and therefore a key to understanding and aiding the family dialogue. In *Death, Family Scripts and Systemic Existentialism* (Hills, 2002), I attempted to show how an appreciation of this 'darkness' in the human condition is essential to understanding and attuning oneself to the heat and distress in the family crucible. In contrast, there are many importance experiences of 'lightness' that give life its joy and delight. It is experiential awareness of both polarities of existence that provides the basis for our well-being (see Chapter 6).

There are many stratagems, decisions and reactions that sometimes make no sense to the onlooker nor the actors in the family drama, without an empathetic connection to our shared 'ultimate concerns'. They form part of the promptings from an unseen script, the family subscript. Those who wish to work therapeutically with families begin to develop an acceptance of highly expressed (or repressed) passions, fears and threats while also preserving a cool, clear mind that allows them to connect while mimimizing associative, secondary suffering. As John Byng-Hall, a leading British family therapist, put it: 'Emotion provides the thread and colour in the tapestry of family life. The full range of every experience is felt most profoundly within family relationships: bliss, contentment, sexual ecstasy, loyalty, remorse loneliness, frustration boredom, fear, murderous rage and so on. Feeling provide the impetus for staying together and for leaving. They energize relationships' (1982: 111).

How to manage and redirect the destructive tendency of some passions into more harmonious and creative channels is a difficult task, and some ideas will be offered in later chapters. Sustained displays of high emotion might be compelling in the theatre or cinema, but they are only a part of enabling change in family psychotherapy. Psychotherapy seeks expressive understanding but it also seeks to convert reaction to reflection, and family group **catharsis** should always be led in that direction. Literature and the 65-year history of family psychotherapy offer some important methods, techniques and understanding to help in getting to grips with the powerful, destructive minotaur that sometimes stalks the secret labyrinth of family life.

CASE STUDY 4.2: CINDY

Cindy (20) wanted to meet me to check out that she could trust my working with her mother and three siblings. She was worried that my working with the whole family could unravel her work of 12 years as the family mediator and peacemaker. Her father, a highly successful and well-respected academic, had periodically terrorized the family, particularly her mother. Though he had finally left the home she did not feel elated or even easier; on the contrary, she felt more fearful and tearful than ever. She said she was the only one in the family whom her father listened to and he had confided in her from the age of 11 about his suicidal feelings and rages. Cindy said she knew how to read his moods and how to manipulate them so that he would not strike out (sometimes physically, but mostly verbally) and humiliate her mother, two sisters and brother. She felt strangely insulated because of her adroitness in managing him, though she was tired, tearful and felt burdened with the weight of responsibility for the family and for her mother's psychological health. Since living and working away from home, her father's standing within his professional field had increased and so she was less concerned for him since he now 'took it out less on the family'. She found it hard to concentrate on her literature studies, though her main interest was in Anglo-Saxon literature, notably the saga of *Beowulf*. For the first time in our meeting she laughed when I gently said I imagined her family experience

→

in facing such unpredictable fears and threats must have given her an excellent grounding in connecting with the disturbing narratives of such ancient myths and folk tales.

In the end I worked separately and briefly with all the children and their mother over two years. Knowing the whole family narrative, initially from joint work with the couple, helped the connection I was able to make with the siblings. They were more comfortable not coming together as a family, a decision I respected and did not attempt to speculate about.

Freud fully understood the envious, rivalrous elements making up the destructive energies in family dynamics. He would not have chosen to use the story of *Oedipus* to characterize this dynamic, and was clear that the road to therapeutic help for troubled minds did not require the direct presence of the family, who could be dealt with by proxy through 'the transference'. Analytically-informed psychotherapists interposed themselves between the internalized flow of the family dynamic in the patient's mind and their search for freer, more secure sense of their own separated identity. Eugene O'Neill's modern tragedy of his own family life, *Long Day's Journey into Night* (1941; O'Neill 1976), lays bare all the frustrated emotions of love and care and the impossibility of deflecting a self-destructive family member – in this case, his morphine-addicted mother – whilst simultaneously being part-contributors to her condition. Empathy, care and watchfulness prove insufficient to prevent her path into the darkness of the title; indeed, they have paradoxical effects. Truly to understand the power of the family crucible, this play, with its interpersonal moments of lightness and humour, teaches more than most textbooks on the subject, including this one! In writing this drama O'Neill finally achieved understanding, acceptance and forgiveness. The Tyrone family at the centre of the drama does not.

The origins of family group therapy

The origins of family group psychotherapy are usually traced to 1948. The child psychiatrist and psychoanalyst, John Bowlby, described how:

In the London Child Guidance Clinic where I worked before the war and also at the Tavistock Clinic we habitually saw as much of parents as we saw of children. No one, as far as I know, had ever seen more than one of them, one member of the family at a time ... I'd been seeing a boy of 13 or 14 [who] was a highly intelligent boy at a grammar school but he was not making much progress and was up against everyone. Initially we didn't see fathers. Well, anyway, when I went down to the waiting room I found father and mother and the 13-year-old boy there. On the spur of the moment, actually, I simply said to them, 'Well, come up'. It was a very fruitful session because I'd seen the mother once or twice ... and I asked 'What sort of childhood did you have?' She poured out a very sad story about all kinds of unhappy events.

I felt this was enormously important. First of all, it was useful for me, but much more so, it was useful both for the boy and for the husband, neither of whom knew a lot [about her story] and I would say the boy knew nothing whatever about his father's background either. Anyway, that was an eye-opener to me. From then onwards I had no doubt that family sessions were extremely important, but I couldn't persuade many other people to think so too. (1987: 3)

Bowlby published the work in a paper entitled 'The Study and Reduction of Group Tensions in the Family' (1949). The paper fell into obscurity, undeservedly so, for it is a little gem of an account of practice seven decades ago, containing the blueprint of much that was later developed through family and systemic psychotherapy. Like most discoveries and innovations, it was the product of a spontaneous, discontinuous leap of faith and connection. Speaking in 1986, Bowlby implied he was immediately intuitively aware that he had touched on something significant, although he was unsure of how it might be used therapeutically to change the treatment of mental illness of individuals in families. In a sense he felt alone with his discovery and was more immediately concerned to develop attachment theory. This paper was overshadowed by his later seminal work commissioned by the World Health Authority, published as *Child Care and the Growth of Love* (1953). This was followed by the trilogy *Attachment, Separation* and *Loss* (1969, 1973 and 1980), also seminal works, which provided an empirical basis to psychoanalytic thought, mental health and child care.

A selection of extracts will give a flavour of just how progressive and visionary the paper proved to be. It stresses the focus on relationships as the 'patient': 'With the child, the problem usually lies in the relationship between him or her and the members of the family.' Of the desire in family groups to find mutual satisfactions and collaborative well-being instead of the destructive, adverse elements of experience:

One of the striking things which we meet with in child guidance work is the tremendously strong drive in almost all parents and children to live together in greater harmony. We find that, though caught up in mutual jealousies and hostilities, none of them enjoys the situation and all are desperately seeking happier relations. Our task is this one of promoting conditions in which the constructive forces latent in social groups come into play. I liken it to the job of a surgeon: not to mend bones but to try to create the conditions which permit bones to mend themselves. In group therapy and in treating the tensions of groups the aim should be to bring about the conditions which permit the group to heal itself. (1949: 292)

He recognized the importance of listening, and forming a view of each individual perspective within the system and how this was contributing to the collective dynamic of tension and conflict. These observations were then fed back into the family system as reflections and a tentative connection made with early attachment experience, the parents' experiences and their effect as a 'script' influencing the tenor of their family relationships. The views and wisdom from the wider network of neighbours also emerges:

During this time I had spoken little but during the second hour I began making interpretations. I made it clear to them that I thought each one was contributing to the problem and described the techniques of hostility each used. I also traced out the history of the tensions starting, as I knew it had, in the boy's early years and gave illustrations of the incidents which had occurred. I pointed out that the mother's treatment of the boy especially her insistence on immediate obedience and her persistent nagging, had a very adverse effect on Henry's behaviour, but I also stated that I felt sure that her mistaken treatment of Henry was the result of her own childhood which I had little doubt had been unhappy. Father remarked that the neighbours had for long criticized them both for nagging the boy too much. We discussed father's educational ambitions for Henry and the bitterness his son's failure had induced in him. (1949: 294)

Having served to clear the air of the conflicting passions and desires, the way seemed clear to begin to think of better solutions and collaboration.

In this final half hour all three found themselves co-operating in an honest endeavour to find new techniques for living together, each realizing that there was a common need to do so and that their ways they had set about it in the past had defeated their object. This proved the turning point in the case. (1949: 294)

Bowlby was wary of his own anxiety at containing the potential violence of the passions released by a whole family exchange. He offers a sideways critique of individual therapy, as a safer, more easily contained and defended option for the therapist against associative suffering and the release of destructive forces:

When I first came to consider this technique, I felt not a little apprehensive of the scenes in which I might get involved. How much safer to keep the warring parties apart, to divide and conquer! But the recognition of the basic fact that people really do want to live happily together and that this drive is working for us gives confidence. (1949: 296)

He speculates about the 'not in front of the children' dilemma of open dialogue, and reassures himself that this is unlikely to reveal new information to the child and is more likely to have a freeing effect because of the containment of the different setting:

Even so, one cannot help asking oneself whether it is a good thing for all these problems to be discussed in front of the child. But, once again the answer is reassuring, in a fragmentary and recriminatory way they have already been discussed many times before. There is nothing new in the material discussed but the atmosphere in which it is discussed is different and, one hopes better ... I have come in fact no longer to be alarmed by the hideous scenes which may ensue in the use of this technique, the violent accusations, the cruel sarcasm, the vitriolic threats ... if they occur in one's consulting rooms, there is a chance that the parent may be helped towards a different view and the child can observe that the therapist is, at least, allying him or herself with his accuser. By focusing our work on the tensions between the child patient and the members of his family group we are adding to the child guidance techniques already in use (psychotherapy along psychoanalytic lines, therapeutic interviews with parents, remedial teaching and so on) and developing techniques which permit the direct study and therapy of the tension within the group. (1949: 296)

Bowlby concluded, in a key articulation of systemic thought, that the maintenance of different value beliefs in any open, respectful participative consultation is essential. This difference can create chain reactions of influence within whole sets of relationship systems to create a different context-changing a destructive (vicious) cycle of experience into a constructive one (virtuous):

> Dictatorial and punishing management is likely to increase the dictatorial and punishing attitude of the workers towards their children: equally, democratic and participatory behaviour by management will encourage such parental attitudes in their employees ... Techniques of changing key social relationships can thus have far reaching repercussions either for good or evil, in the same way that man's agricultural methods can greatly improve soil fertility or finally destroy it. We see furthermore that to attain the end of a secure, contented and co-operative community in which parents can give love and security to their children enabling them to grow up to be stable and contented people, able to sustain and further a just and friendly society, no one point in the circle is more vital than another. The vicious circle may be broken at any point; the virtuous circle may be promoted at any point. (1949: 297)

What he had set in motion and contained like fission in a nuclear reactor (but in the nuclear family) were the toxic chain reactions of freely expressed thoughts, feelings, wishes and intentions of family members. This helped free families to find a different and better experience of one another and made accessible the well-being of the one through the well-being of all, and vice versa. If the method and technique worked for the 'child-patient' then, theoretically at least, this could be adapted to any age group of patients and any symptom or condition. The skill required, Bowlby maintained, was in creating a safe context to examine and interpret the tensions springing from unresolved personal conflicts, and the pattern of relationships maintained through the live interactions. If this was accomplished successfully the emotional and mental health benefits to the whole family were immense, for it liberated their own resources to understand better and resolve their own difficulties. Here was the potential of a 'brave new world', but it was going to take a long journey for it to be realized.

Meanwhile, the story crossed the Atlantic. John Bell, a British-born American clinical psychologist, visited the Tavistock Clinic in London in 1951 and met the medical director, Dr John Sutherland:

> In conversation one evening before dinner, Dr Sutherland mentioned casually that Dr John Bowlby of the clinic staff was experimenting in

cases of problem children and adolescents with having whole families together for therapy. Before I could ask for details, the topic of conversation shifted and I took away a misapprehension of what Dr Bowlby was doing. I assumed he was using contact with the whole family as his sole way of meeting the problem child ... I discovered only much later through reading articles by Dr Bowlby and a personal meeting with him that the family approach he had used included only occasional conferences with the whole family. These conferences were adjuncts within the typical mode of dealing with children and parents where one therapist sees the child and another the adult. (Bell, 1961: 2)

On the sea voyage home to the USA in 1951, Bell 'began to think through the technical implications of meeting the whole family as a group'. Soon he was to try out the method he called 'family group therapy' on one family, extending it soon afterwards to 20 others. In 1955, on a sabbatical, he worked with the 'McAndrew' family at the Edinburgh Infirmary, and found the method had wider application than the middle-class white American families with whom he had trialled it. His work was subsequently published in a monograph, the first to detail how 'family group therapy' might be conducted, while in the USA his work stimulated much research into family process and the founding of the journal of that name in 1961.

These were the early psychoanalytically-based pioneers of family therapy, along with Nathan Ackerman (1958), Murray Bowen (1978) and Ivan Böszörményi-Nagy (Böszörményi-Nagy & Spark, 1973). The family therapy community, since discovering it was clandestine and a movement (Haley, 1962), has produced an embarrassment of riches across the whole spectrum of psychotherapy modalities. The fertile creativity of Milton Erickson (Haley, 1973) and the Mental Research Institute in Palo Alto, California, have been generous sources. The latter, under the influence of Gregory Bateson and visiting guests including R.D. Laing and Gianfranco Cecchin, produced seminal works such as *The Pragmatics of Human Communication* and *Change: Principles of Problem Formation and Problem Resolution* (Watzlawick, Beavin & Jackson, 1967; Watzlawick, Weakland & Fisch, 1974).

Many of these thinkers were irreverent, humorous writers able to provide powerful critiques of the psychoanalytic method, and they have had an enduring influence. Jay Haley's was another fertile mind. He wrote with great clarity, freshness and irony about his therapeutic relational work, though he would never have described it as systemic. From his earliest forays into the strategy of therapy (1963) with the mantra 'a symptom is a tactic in a relationship', he influenced many. His articles 'Why a Mental Health Clinic Should Avoid Family Therapy' (1975) and 'How to Have an Awful Marriage' (www.jay-haley-on-therapy. com/How_to_Have_an_Awful_Marriage.pdf) are masterpieces of originality and irreverence. His collaborations with Salvador Minuchin in the 1970s and with his partner, Cloe Madanes, were highly influential in developing the strategic therapy model of working.

From these bases followed brief therapy, known also as solution-focused brief therapy. Pioneered by Steve de Shazer (1982) and Insoo Kim Berg (1994) and Brian Cade and Bill O' Hanlon (1993), it focuses on what patients want to achieve through therapy rather than the problem that brought them to it. In the UK Cade brought his own brand of ingenuity and irreverent wit to the skill of therapeutic work. Michael White's *Narrative Means to Therapeutic Ends* (White and Epston, 1990) is a similar, social constructionist solutions-based derivative. Attempts have been made recently to synthesize different approaches within the family systemic repertoire and wider methods in the psychotherapy canon, notably Paul Gibney's *The Pragmatics of Therapeutic Practice* (2003) and Carmal Flaskas and David Pocock's *Systems and Psychoanalysis: Contemporary Integrations in Family Therapy* (2009).

The development of strategic, brief, solution-focused and narrative therapy have all presented highly original ways of thinking about how problems develop and how they can be alleviated – ideas that can be incorporated into a family and systemic frame. However, in most of these cases the method has tended to move away from its origins in whole-system work and be applied in one-to-one therapy. The feminist and postmodern critiques have raised important questions about the unexamined gendered and cultural assumptions in the work of many so-called 'master' therapists, who supplant the 'authoritative objectivity' of the scientific model with the 'expert' therapist. (Whitaker's Symbolic-Experiential Therapy, well demonstrated in *The Family Crucible* (Whitaker & Napier, 1988), and the humanistic approach of Virginia Satir (1983) are both examples of highly charismatic and original therapists though their methods are not easily recreated). However, though these critiques raise attentive questions for the self-reflexivity of the therapist, they do not constitute by themselves a sufficient methodology for conducting whole family dialogues. Family therapy has always itself been a huge crucible for the melding very different elements into new robust material. However, for the purposes of this book, the Structural and the Systemic-Phenomenological models remain the clearest guides to learning and creating an effective 'whole family' dialogue.

We will now look at some key aspects of family process, which may not lead to distress but may need assistance to negotiate in better ways.

Summary

- The 'family' is a community which changes over history and has many different cultural forms and membership rules.
- According to Robin Skynner, the family has many different operational functions and psychosocial goals, and can be creative and destructive.
- Experientially-based therapy takes account of the ultimate concerns of the human condition as well as the personal.
- Dramas such as those by Sophocles and Eugene O'Neill lay bare the complex contradictions of family dynamics.
- The first origins of working with whole-family systems go back to John Bowlby's post-war work and 1949 publication, which are described.
- Bowlby was the first to identify the importance of feedback processes in family experience and the quest for harmony.
- Pioneers and their models are briefly described.
- Emphasis is given to the centrality of structural therapy and that of Milan Associates in whole-family work.

5

KEY INTERACTIONS IN THE FAMILY CRUCIBLE

Early attachment: the 'call and response' of the family matrix

There are a number of key relationship interactions and movements within the family crucible that are sometimes sources of tension and conflict unless communication and negotiation are possible. Such movements, like dance movements, are not liable to correction and modification without full discussion. These are the early-attachment movements which start to define the structure of the family matrix, the alliances, triangles and distance-regulators that become embedded in the structure of family relationships, to beneficial or distressing effect. They form an essential part of family scripts, in particular the non-conscious elements of the subscripts.

A new baby is 'ejected' from the enclosed, dark, liquefied world of the womb, in which the neurological, sensate and cognitive systems start rehearsing their repertoire, to the open, live matrix of care and relationships of the outside world. A complex interrelational 'dance' begins between the primary carer (usually the mother) and the dependent infant. The process of this attachment dance is the subject of a thousand textbooks on child development research and almost as many of child psychotherapy.

On its arrival, the child is swaddled and fed, usually at first by the mother, and then by a whole network of familial and friendship relationships, to provide an interactional universe. In between the early stages of sleeping, feeding and expelling waste the child engages with and returns the gaze of the mother and father. A 'feedback loop' between the caregivers and the baby is established and other parts of her experiential repertoire are engaged. Through various emergent sights, sounds, tastes and touches a more complex interactional field is set up around the child.

The child's life is usually cherished and is a source of deep pleasure to the human community into which she has been born. However, the baby's needs must be balanced by the needs of the adult caregivers. The 'dance' is a complicated, vital, relational process, with attuned adult responses that settle and comfort the child, the 'call and response' interchange of mutual delight through language and movement between the baby and primary carer(s). The effect of that process is the formation of a secure self-experience and identity for the child, as has been well documented and supported increasingly by neuroscience research (Gerhardt, 2004) and well understood by common sense.

The elements of this 'call and response' dialogue can be summarized simply in a sevenfold way:

1. the communication of information
2. the perception of that communication
3. the interpretation of the situation
4. the emotional response to the situation
5. the action response into the situation
6. the response to any others observing the situation
7. the response to the response of others observing the situation.

This is the arena in which the complex drama of attachment is enacted. The circular drama will have a number of perspectives, depending on the role of the observer. The archetypal situation may begin with a monologue, i.e. a baby's cry. This communicates information of distress, which, as clear in research, has a carefully pitched frequency, that is, a universal, cross-cultural phenomenon, a triumph of evolution. To this opening monologue, also observing the associated reddening, facial tensing and possibly tears, the mother may make an active response, sometimes in language: 'There, there, my darling'; she may also respond physically by lifting and comforting the child by stroking or hugging it. The monologue is therefore transformed into a duologue, the mother and child forming a system of two people (a dyadic system). If the father has also heard the cry and arrives ahead of the mother he may respond to the child in a similar way. If he arrives later he may try to support the mother, baby and their relationship. These roles are not gender-specific and are interchangeable, depending upon the partners' beliefs about role flexibility. The dyad then changes to become a three-person system, a triad. We have the interactional coalescence of three actors, three voices (in a trialogue) and three different kinds of awareness seeking the immediate goal of comforting and alleviating the baby's distress.

At the same time – for these processes are simultaneous and interactive – the adult(s) will be interpreting the baby's cries, trying to understand their meaning and constructing a response. If, for instance, the baby has been fed and the mother constructs that the baby is tired and needs sleep, she may believe that lifting the child is the wrong response and may delay responding in order to let the baby settle. However, she may also experience anxiety at the baby's distress and want to alleviate this immediately, as well as she can. It may be a case that the baby's crying has a deeper resonance for her. She may feel tired, harassed, distracted or preoccupied with something else, or she may herself never have been effectively comforted when distressed and the baby's cry will be experienced as persecutory and the care for her otherwise cherished child seen as a relentless punishment.

Therefore, from an internal dialogue between perception, interpretation and emotional resonance, she will respond. Not responding in this situation is of course also possible. The duologue between mother and baby may continue for a while and the child's agitated state increase. Some theories hypothesize that a child may experience such a state of anxious distress that she begins to 'construct' the mother as a persecutory actor and the world as a place of unrelieved suffering and indifference. The mother (or father, since this not gender-specific) may find the child's cries hectoring and respond with withdrawal or anger, believing in an unreflected way that the child deserves such a response. From such small beginnings can emerge deeper and divided ontological feelings in the child's self-experience. The French philosopher Simone Weil (1982) wrote of the amplification of this oppression and ontological damage:

> In those who have suffered too many blows, in slaves for example, that place in the heart from which the infliction of evil evokes a cry of surprise may seem to be dead. But it is never quite dead; it is simply unable to cry out any more. It has sunk into a state of dumb and ceaseless lamentation. (1982: 72)

This perfectly encapsulates the experience that childhood neglect and abuse leave imprinted on the innate experiential openness of the child's psyche. The parental caregiver will invariably have been subjected to some equivalent experiences in their own childhood.

However, after a while, even if not feeling an immediate, spontaneous warmth towards the child, the parent may construct an idea that it would be more sensible to try to mollify the baby so as to secure their own peace of mind. Stage five then follows and the baby is maybe picked up, winded, interacted with, comforted, rocked and offered feeding in an attempt to restore its sense of equilibrium. We can call this process between parent and child a dialogue, using the term generically, as a complete interactional exchange of the two of them working towards a state of harmonized resolution. In terms of script conceptualization, it is an assumptive script; the caregiver makes a series of interpretations about the source of the baby's distress and how best to respond to it and restore the baby's ease.

If the other parent enters this drama as well, he will process the communicated information through his own cognitive and emotional repertoire of understanding. If he sees the mother responding in ways he experiences as good and effective, he will align himself with her efforts and actions. They may identify and agree their construction of the situation and the baby's needs and remedies aloud, or non-verbally, as an unspoken action of solidarity. If, however, he has a different perception of the child's needs, his needs or his partner's approach, he may align with the child against the mother and attempt to take charge of the situation. This is a shifting field of alliance. Although I have punctuated it from the starting point of the mother, 'the dance' is equally applicable if the father is the first actor on the scene. It is also applicable if the couples are in a same-sex partnership. These roles are as much socially and emotionally constructed as biologically influenced. They form a three-part, perceptual, constructional and communicational field, with differing degrees of emotional resilience, moving towards some kind of interpersonally enacted outcome. This simple drama may have a variety of outcomes or, as in Samuel Beckett's *Waiting for Godot* (1956), none of significance, just 'more of the same' in a continuous, circular loop.

This is the 'call and response' of dramatic tension in the family crucible played out in the privacy of the home. For systemic well-being, of course, a harmonious, concordant outcome is sought. There are other exceptional passion-based responses that under certain conditions could lead to an outcome of harm or the threat of harm to all three characters in the drama. The interactional elements at work in this situation can be plotted, but not predicted. As in all competitive games or political movements for change, systems can move to unregulated destructiveness without the participants perceiving the attendant risks of the interactions and so influencing a different homeostasis. Sometimes a systemic group process has a collective life of its own and is self-activating, 'virtuously', like the Mexican Wave at a sporting event; 'viciously', like a lynching or a rioting group.

A family's experience of family therapy

It is time to listen to an account of family therapy from one of its recipients. Hayley Andrews wrote this description of her experience of family therapy and of life in her family crucible:

CASE STUDY 5.1: HAYLEY ANDREWS

I have been suffering with anorexia nervosa for a number of years now and have had a number of different therapies to try to help me overcome it. Some therapies I would consider forced upon me but some I have been more open to; some I found helpful and some not so. Recently my parents and I reached the 'graduation' stage of family therapy, which means we no longer attend the group sessions as we have been deemed functional enough to cope without them. The therapy sessions were more of a help to my family and I than I expected them to be. Before we started, in all honesty, I had begun to lose faith in my family, my recovery and myself. However, as a family we undertook yet another challenge.

In the therapy I had prior to the family therapy sessions, everything concentrated on me, my illness and what I did wrong, which furthered my sense of self-blame. I didn't expect family therapy to break the mould and be any different. I was, therefore, very wary and sceptical of family therapy as a whole. I envisaged sitting in the corner of a room with my parents and a therapist looking in at me and pointing fingers. I thought I would be told off, told how I was wrong, how I have a negative effect on the family relations. Therefore, from the outset I bestowed that role upon myself. I spoke very little, answering questions with various tones of grunt; I stared at the floor and counted the minutes until I could leave.

Due to the nature of therapy, the initial sessions tend to be an assessment of sorts, running through your history and reasons why you are there in the first place. So the first few sessions were indeed centred on me, which made it easy for me to conclude that my preconceptions were indeed correct and that I was in for a rocky ride. However, in later sessions I was proved wrong because our therapist soon showed me that he understood more about me and how I feel than I had given him credit for.

I think the first thing he opened my eyes to was that although it is the common belief that eating disorders are suffered solely by the diagnosed individual, this isn't actually the case. Although it is the 'central person' who bears the physical symptom, in cases where the person lives in the family environment the family are 'ill' and suffering too. It was put to me that the whole family had problems that each member dealt with in a different way, my way being anorexia. So I did begin to feel less attacked and less guilty. We all started to take responsibility for our own actions and the consequences of those actions.

The sessions were by no means easy. Each week it felt like a different person was in the firing line, the person whose actions were brought into question. One week it may have been Dad, the next Mum, and the next me. The thing is that as a family there is fault on all our parts, all of us do things that perhaps have a negative impact. That isn't to say that any of us mean to hurt each other. In fact I think our main problem is that we love each other so much that we cannot bear to hurt each other.

We will suffer in silence if it means saving someone else's feelings, therefore dancing around each other and treading on eggshells. It didn't take long to realize that this isn't healthy for anyone but it took longer to actually find the courage to change it! The therapy opened up our family dialogue and made communication easier, by giving us a forum to discuss exactly how we feel about each other, what each of us does and what effect that has.

Far from the grunting creature in the corner hiding under my hair, I have now opened up and expressed how I feel about things. The bullies at school had discouraged me from maintaining the good open relationship with my family that I might have had, but the therapy has finally rekindled it somewhat. Aside from keeping my parents at a distance, I also held things inside for fear of how they would have been taken, but have now developed a certain ability to express myself and I think the same is true of my parents too. We learned to take criticism and not take it to heart. We learned how to accept that we do hurt each other, whether we mean to or not. But we also learned that we love each other dearly and would never hurt each other intentionally.

Family life is never easy, nobody claims this to be the case, but our family life has been made so much better with our increased and ever-increasing ability to communicate without making assumptions and taking things personally. Of course, our increased faith in our love for one another has helped no end too. I am so glad that we all persevered with the therapy sessions even when we found it challenging. I'm glad it challenged us and pushed us to our limits because otherwise we wouldn't have learned the valuable lessons we learned from it and we would still be treading those eggshells rather than living the comfortable, more-functioning and happier life together that we do now.

Hayley's description shows how the emotional climate in her family was regulated by the smoothing-out of conflict and how she, conscious of these tensions and her own from being bullied at school, in part found a 'solution' in anorexia. It was also clear, like Bowlby's first family intervention case, that conflict, stress, anxiety and the experience of adversity conceal the care and competencies in the whole system. Personal experiences of responsibility become defused and paralysed by guilt, recrimination or indifference.

We have seen how early patterns of attachment and the self-experience of each adult carer helps form the direction of the family process in the care of a baby. These patterns are deeply embedded, often beyond our active awareness. We have also tried to show how the process emerging in the parental-couple system is dependent on how they communicate their different perceptions of a situation and work towards a shared view that fosters mutual well-being.

There is now a great deal of research and clinical evidence of an invariant connection between early secure attachment and family interactional patterns conducive to well-being, and early chaotic, disorganized attachment and interactional patterns that activate and maintain distress, troubled mental health and abuse. The development of these experiential scripts and subscripts is well known and not surprising, given the circularity of relational patterns. In examining a family's micro-transaction it is possible to observe elements of the wider whole; Salvador Minuchin describes this process as 'isomorphic' (from the Greek, meaning 'equal form'). How to intervene to change it is, however, the major question, and Minuchin developed a specific approach he called 'structural family therapy'.

Structural analysis and alliances

Salvador Minuchin's classic works *Families and Family Therapy* (1974) and *Family Therapy Techniques* (Minuchin & Fishman, 1981) are landmark contributions to the literature of family therapy. Along with the Milan Associates, Salvador Minuchin has provided one of the clearest and most comprehensive guides to working therapeutically and experientially with whole families. The trainee therapist or counsellor would best experience these texts directly, as they will repay personal perusal more than any summary (a DVD of Minuchin's techniques and life can also be obtained through the Association for Family Therapy at www.aft.org.uk).

With his background in political radicalism, psychiatry and psychoanalysis, Minuchin fashioned a model of family intervention work through connecting many different intellectual sources. It is likely, with his Latin American education and a keen interest in drama, that he was aware of Augusto Boal's *Theatre of the Oppressed* (1998). There seem to be many parallels between their work, especially Minuchin's work with families from the slums of Philadelphia. Many of Minuchin's techniques (e.g. enactment, unbalancing, focusing and an active style of intervention) resemble those of a film director. His is a very personal and charismatic approach and led to much criticism, particularly from feminist family therapists, that he was insensitive to issues of difference and power, often using his own gender and cultural assumptions, like a benevolent patriarch.

Minuchin did, however, understand political power as the vehicle of both oppression and liberation. These ideas emerge in his understanding of the family as a basic political system, an arrangement of power balances and structures that may or may not work for the well-being of everyone. Structural family therapy provides a synthesis of the political, the ecological and the psychological, weaving together a feeling for the passions, aspirations and everyday struggles of the lives of the socially and economically marginalized and alienated. It seeks to assist them to use their resources to challenge these experiences and find self-empowerment.

Structural family therapy, influenced by Koestler's ideas of the 'holon', sees families as a system that, like all 'whole' systems', can be subdivided into its component 'part-wholes'. So leadership, the authority for care, love and control, is vested in the parental or executive subsystem. This archetypical and essential role function may, in fact, be undertaken by a grandparent or, in the case of a 'looked-after' child, be distributed between the local authority (as 'corporate parents'), the child's kinship network or their professional and surrogate network, including foster carers (Hills, 2005). Bowlby stressed that, as part of the attachment bond, a child needs a direct experience, socially, psychologically and ontologically, that someone 'owns' them in the vastness of the social and actual world. It is essential that there is at least one caretaker who takes unconditional responsibility for their love, the direction of their social, ethical and emotional development as part of that 'ownership' and who does so, as far as possible, with generosity, commitment, dependability and discernment.

Children themselves form a different subsystem, which Minuchin named the 'sibling subsystem'. This is, at times, a private, playful relational world away from the intruding reality and potential disapproval of the 'parental subsystem'. It can generate fiercely loyal attachments and solidarity, protectively dispatching threats to playground bullies, challenging inaccurate and unjust misunderstandings from the 'executive subsystem', sharing opportunities, social networks, clothes, music and possessions, and can be generous in its altruistic support of the 'other(s)' and the relational bond itself. It can also be potently destructive in its competitiveness, even murderous, in the passions aroused. There are many such examples, though Cain and Abel are the forefathers (forebrothers, perhaps?) of all destructive and rivalrous sibling subsystems.

In a well-regulated family culture, Minuchin contends, there is an openness and respect for the differences between generations and their experience, views and emotions, and so on. Family dialogue is openly democratic and produces shared decisions and solutions. The parental subsystem acts generally with a confident authority, consults and is collaborative and modifies its approach and expectations in accordance with the changing developmental needs of the sibling subsystem. Conflict is contained because all parts of the system share information about their needs, perspectives and emotional responses to one another. There is an emphasis on 'age-appropriateness and fittingness' which permeates the frequent renegotiation of family relationships, requirements and expectations as the whole family passes through the human life cycle. Such a model of optimal relationship functioning was partly based upon the major family research studies in the 1960s and 1970s at the Timberlawn Institute in Texas (Lewis, 1976).

Though such descriptions can sound like a Hollywood stereotype of a 'happy family life', they were not, nor did Minuchin intend them to be so. The family crucible is a place of conflict, where boundaries and hierarchies are worked out (or not) in the heat of impassioned experience. Minuchin's work implies that, irrespective of culture, open negotiations and boundaries that facilitate relationships and reduce conflict are important goals for the common good. The structural family therapist operates almost like a sports or life coach to assist families to find the cybernetic point of harmony between differences and taking charge of regulating themselves in due course.

In terms of analysing the process, a systemic therapist would be looking for patterns of alignment and alliance and their flexibility e.g. mother to child, mother to father, father to mother and father to child. The more inclusive these alliances are and the more flexible, usually the freer, clearer and more likely the family processes are to enhance well-being. Structural family therapy mostly focuses on effective boundary-making and confident use of authority that empowers, in family situations where the 'will to power' is individualized, random and uncontained. However, besides creating a better sense of coherence, unity and family community, there is much more going on experientially to change the family's sense of their relationships. Minuchin's

95

experiential style is worth examining for the nuancing of a skilled, empathic communicator, operating at levels more profound than the claims made for his model.

The triangulation drama and a warning from the Greeks

The notion of **triangulation** arises in both the early formulations of family therapy and in transactional analysis where it is known as the Karpman or drama triangle (Karpman, 1968). Certain constellations of family interaction can be seen as a pattern of family interdependent roles; there are those of *destroyer* or *persecutor*, the *victim* of any scape-goating attack and the *'family healer'*, *rescuer* or *conciliator*.

In this dynamic activated by/or activating situations of high emotional arousal and conflict the roles can become highly inter-changeable, switching between *persecutor*, *victim* and *rescuer*. The process can be seen in a simple three-way scenario. Supposing you see a fight between two people late at night on the street in which one seems to be seriously hurting the other. You intervene to try to break it up and in the process, the attacker inadvertently hurts himself. Immediately, the 'victim' protests to you, the 'rescuer', that he resents your interference, for now you have hurt his friend. So, in this triangular exchange the 'perpetrator' becomes 'victim'; the 'victim' becomes the 'perpetrator' of a verbal attack on you and the allied 'rescuer' of his friend, while you as 'rescuer' become simultaneously 'perpetrator' and 'victim'. One just can't win! Alan Carr (1997) has written how these triangulation dynam-ics are part of the counter-reaction in family therapy and can lead to burnout if they are not understood.

The wise Greeks also understood that an overweening and dominant self, confident to the point of arrogance (*hubris*) would inevitably attract correctional role functionaries. The resulting nemesis and catastrophic destruction of the person's dominance (or the person) then may lead to reconstruction and healing. This is certainly a theme of Freud's elevated tragic hero Oedipus, triangulated as he is between two different families, two different sets of parents and between the humans and the Gods in Sophocles' drama of that name (1998).

This pattern is also triangular: the rise in triumphant power; the cata-strophic, destructive fall from grace and then the restoration and a contrary force, either from fate (attributed to the intervention of the gods) or renewal. The pattern is archetypical and sometimes embedded in relationships, society itself or, indeed, civilizations. Those who attrib-ute catastrophe or its threat to 'divine will' fail to see the underlying unchecked human activity that the Greeks were communicating. It is the individual 'will to power', as Alfred Adler pointed out (1956), that could create mayhem if not accompanied by an ethos of social collaboration. In the competitive 'bear pit' of social life, it can generate experiences of oppression/victimhood in those unable to exercise their own 'will to power' (inferiority feelings). In balance, this energy is allied to fulfilling some of the creative potential of individuation, on becoming a mature, adult person. However, there is something in the dynamic energy of triangular roles that cannot easily be checked and, usually, Greek drama ends tragically for all concerned, so 'healer' beware.

When, for instance, a police officer asks to see a motorist's driving licence, it depends on the way the police officer presents himself and how the subject feels about authority as to how the request is received. In all relationships of unequal power and/or authority there is always a see-saw of persecutory feeling attached. In the case of dominant and terror-activating systems (such as the Mafia or al-Qaeda) the persecutory force is real and its affects amplified in the imagination of the victim. In trauma and terror-activated family systems, such as Frederick and Rosemary West's family, the dominating figure is actively persecutory in controlling the system. A closed system, no 'healer' role was available to it until a member disclosed. Inevitably, the persecutory 'hearing voices' that plague mental health sufferers can be traced to an actual influential dominant figure in their earlier life, distorting the patient's ability to process reality experientially.

CASE STUDY 5.2: BERNARD

Bernard is a 70-year-old father of seven children, two from his previous marriage. He has been receiving help from the Older Adult Mental Health services for about two years for depression that had psychotic and suicidal features, and bizarre thoughts in which he believes he will hurt children, though he knows this to be unreal for he is a devoted father and grandfather. He attends for family systemic work with his wife Liz, who is 20 years younger than him. Bernard has been hospitalized because of his depression for over a year. He is reluctant to be discharged and Liz is equally reluctant to have him at home. He is artistic and musical but hates everything he has ever produced, except for one painting.

A story emerges of the struggles in this couple's marriage to bring up five children after the small business they both ran went into bankruptcy. They both stated it was the relationship with their children and their partnership strength as survivors that kept them together although,

→

essentially, intimacy and communication between them had ceased a long time ago.

Using a genogram, it became clear that Bernard, brought up during the war, had nothing but bitterness and hatred for his mother. She had black hair, and he'd 'always hated women with black hair', adding, before the team were about to point it out, 'until I met my wife'. He was hospitalized for diphtheria in 1944, refused visits from his mother and destroyed all his toys. He was dying. A clergyman was called to baptize him and his father was brought back from Normandy, where he was fighting, to be with him at the end. 'I remembered the dream I had when they thought I was dying. I was in a tunnel and there was a horse and cart just clip-clopping its way through. I decided it wasn't going to come for me. Silly, isn't it?' Bernard recalled the small indications of his recovery in hospital by the way they would build up the pillows as his breathing got stronger.

At the next session, his presentation was different. He gave a more balanced picture of his mother: 'She wasn't very warm, it's true, but she had six of us, no money, surviving the Blitz, Dad away in the army, how else could she hold everything together?'

Bernard's level of self-persecution seemed based around the death anxiety of a serious illness (for the 1940s) and the reality of death. His mother became the receptacle and scapegoat for all his fears and hatreds. Hospital was a place of safety, as were doctors and medicine. We hypothesized that he re-enacted the basic drama 64 years later, with the whole mental health service acting as containing rescuers. He felt secure with the relationship and attention of the senior doctor and the levels of medicine prescribed. The intervention of a different doctor lowering those levels had triggered another crisis, keeping him on the ward. Though Liz and his children, who came for the family session, were very caring, it was clear there was a covert agreement for him not to return home. He was transferred to a half-way hostel. There was a sense he felt inadequate to the demands of his five young adult children and persecuted by his depression, as did Liz. Though they appeared to want a homecoming, there was no energy coming from anywhere in the system to balance the persecutory power of the depression. The team believed Bernard was repeating an ancient life script of insecure attachment, but this time in older age. This connection did not help reconcile family relationships, however.

A common experience is the triangulation of a child between two disputing parents. As overt witness of the emotional see-saw and atmosphere of threat between his caregivers in such a conflict-activated system, a child can react by withdrawal, attempts at peacemaking through excessively good behaviour and pleading. He may produce signs of psychological distress and disruptive behaviour which calls a diversionary truce to the conflict and may bring the parents together out of concern for their child. The difficulty, though individually presented, is contextual and systemic.

These situationally developed roles create very distinctive feedback loops. They are the basic meat of drama. Jean-Paul Sartre's play *Huis Clos* (1944; translated as *No Exit* or *Vicious Circle*) takes its tension exactly from a rich triangular interplay of different shifts of alliances, and the persecutory, conciliatory and victimized stances of each of the three complex characters. 'Hell is other people' is its oft-quoted line, and it is a play that should be studied by every family systemic therapist wishing to understand triangulation more fully.

Distance regulation and the attachment dance

The idea, illustrated in the child example above, was a variant of one of the early formulations of systemic theory: the victim unreflectingly sacrifices themselves to rescue a relationship on which they are dependent and for which they have catastrophic fears. The child's behaviour acts as a distance regulator between the parents. This is a variation of a triangulated role dynamic, though in this case the triangled 'patient' acts like a homeostatic device to try to keep a dangerous system from destructiveness. They are filled with the atmosphere of power conflict and menace which they internalize, at the cost of their own mental health and well-being. This idea is formulated extensively by John Byng-Hall (1995).

CASE STUDY 5.3: NATALIE

Natalie has severe depression and an eating disorder. Her mother Jean, a former senior mental health nurse, has just recovered from cancer. She and her father David, a lecturer in law and ethics, have been married for 30 years. David leaves Jean suddenly and without warning for someone else. Natalie, the youngest of three, has for a long while believed her highly achieving brothers put her emotionally in their shade and have bullied her at home in the past. Suddenly she has to absorb her mother's fluctuating mood states between tearfulness, violent rage at her father and constant depression. She is alone at home with her mother, her brothers having moved out a long time before.

She also has to absorb the change in her father from a rather introspective quiet man to an extrovert, driving a sports car and visiting some of the local nightclubs she frequents. He has a new girlfriend. Natalie feels in between her mother – confiding angrily in her and denigrating her father, whom she still loves – and her father, filling her with the angst of his 'mid-life' crisis and the guilt of suddenly abandoning his marriage. Her eating disorder has intensified significantly. However, this has prompted the triad to respond to the invitation to attend family therapy. The parents have confronted one another with their different perspectives on the marriage and Natalie can give voice to her position in the triangle. The parents have pursued mediation and reached an agreement about their financial futures. Jean has attended individual work with a colleague in the psychological services. After six sessions she has improved markedly to the point where she can see David's decision to end the marriage has freed her into a life of richer possibilities which she now pursues.

A person is in the family and of the family and its crucible. He or she draws on their family experiential repertoire, their script, to help shape and fashion their identity, character, beliefs and responses to the wider social world and are open to being influenced in return. This is the business of living and being fully human. Attachment formation and its various dance options are fundamental to optimizing this experience. From the direct sensory experience of care, touch, playfulness and warmth in the interactional exchanges, and encouragement of the child's intellectual grasp of the surrounding world, the child develops as a person, cherished and protected, viewing the world as a place of coherence, justice, of belonging and worth. What may also follow, as William Wordsworth described, is a feeling of sublime, spiritual connection with all that is, an intimation of immortality that is life-long. Such experiential riches may be rarely accomplished, but they are attainable.

John Bowlby, who with his collaborators Mary Main and Mary Ainsworth, formulated the first working principles of family psychotherapy, viewed his main legacy as attachment theory. This process is at the level of linguistic attribution:

There are parents who disconfirm a child's observation. The parent is self-righteous, doesn't accept any criticism and can sometimes systematically disconfirm a child's observations ... the child is rebuffed and rejected. The child grows up to be anxiously-avoidant and self-sufficient' (Bowlby, 1987: 6); and of ingested learning from experiential proximity, 'Subsequently the model of himself that the child builds reflects also the images his parents have of him, images that are communicated not only by how each treats him, but by what each says to him ... once built ... are so taken for granted that they come to operate at an unconscious level.. (Bowlby, 1988: 130)

Bowlby frequently used the following example from the Blitz to explain why the tactile, sensory experience of the child and the proximity to a secure attachment figure was so fundamental in the development of good self-experience and that external threats do not necessarily trigger the potential existential terrors of death or anxiety. During a war, he said, a child during an air raid in a bomb shelter, without their familiar attachment figure present, is more likely to be physically safe but psychologically distressed than a child in the open air sheltering underneath her mother (or attached parental figure, whether father or grandmother or aunt, etc.). Thought much less safe from harm, the major subjective experience will be one of safety and security, belying the apprehension.

The attachment framework of interactive possibilities described by Bowlby, Ainsworth and Main are fourfold: securely attached, anxious-avoidant, anxious-resistant, chaotic-disorganized. This repertoire of possibilities shows remarkable convergence with studies of family functioning, of which the best known are the early researches at the Timberlawn Institute (Lewis, 1976). There is also congruence with Minuchin's structural model of family alliances to promote optimal functioning. This is scarcely surprising. Though the family relational dance may have many subtle variations, it has a central human goal: the parental relationship provides comfort, encouragement, consolation for loss and boundaries for respectful behaviour – what Bowlby (1987) called 'amicable control' – mentoring for meaningful accomplishment and sufficient mastery of the deviations and somatizations of existential anxieties.

Finally, stories of two young adults, each with experiences of disrupted, chaotic attachments in childhood: I met the first when I was a probation officer and the latter when a psychotherapist. The outcomes of their lives have been very different, but perhaps their experiences have not.

CASE STUDY 5.4: PAUL AND WILLIAM

Paul's story

Paul (19) was released on licence from Rochester Borstal and I was his supervisor. I got to know him as well as his landlady, who formed something of an attachment to him. He had been brought up in the care system from the age of 5 and lost contact with his family years before. Paul had great difficulties resisting opportunities to steal. When I challenged him over a pointless theft that jeopardized the conditions of his licence, he broke down in tears of helpless remorse, leaving me feeling bad about my action. Later, after I had left the Probation Service, I learned that he and a friend had stolen a car, lost control, and hit a tree. Both were killed instantly. I attended his funeral with his landlady. Members of his family were present, including the father whom he had not met for at least 14 years after he abandoned Paul's mother. Concerned and curious, he was asking everyone how old Paul was. Someone directed him to the brass plate on the coffin. Satisfied with this knowledge, he started telling the rest of the family. I mused privately about the irony that Paul had finally encountered his family's closer attention in death than he had had in life, by which time it was too late to be of much help. Paul's ultimate act of destructive, rebellious rage against his existence deprived them all.

William's story

William, a looked-after child, came through the care system with his sister and was eventually placed at ISP in Kent, one of the first independent childcare agencies in the country. William's family attachment patterns were chaotic and disorganized. His mother separated from his violent father when William was 4 years old. Her new partner continued the pattern of mistreatment both William and his older sister had experienced from their father. His mother could not cope with them both and they were placed in care.

Innumerable placements broke down and William was finally moved to a foster family for over three years. I worked as his individual therapist for much of this time until this placement also broke down and William moved on. Eventually he was placed in a children's home in his home county in the east of England. At a conference involving looked-after children and the hierarchy of his local social services department, he launched a blistering attack on the director, who was present, for the department's

→

failure to provide for him consistently over the years. He was 15 years old at the time and wanted a passport and agreement from the department that he could live with his mother who, by that time, had relocated to the USA. Moved by his request, this was all set in motion and William went to live with his mother in New York. It proved disastrous. Both discovered there was no basis for a relationship. William got involved in drugs and turned to crime to support his habit. A final conflict with his mother finished abruptly when she told him, with passion, that she wished he had never been born. This echoed a sentiment in his own mind at his worse moments of personal distress. He made a hasty exit from the USA in part to avoid arrest for a series of drug-related charges. Out of the blue, 16 years later, he traced me and wanted us to meet to discuss his life. He was in a secure relationship and due to become a father, an experience which filled him with apprehension and excitement. He had been imprisoned for drug offences in the UK but persisted with his education in prison and secured a place on release at Goldsmiths College, London.

'I think everyone has worries. Most of the time I think there is love there. Obviously you don't just turn up at a placement and they love you. It's like a respect thing. Talking is a big thing. You talk to people and tell them how you feel instead of bottling it up, hoping it will go away. As I found out, it doesn't always go away. I don't think you should ever be ashamed of your past because there is nothing to be ashamed of in who you are. You might not have the best upbringing but when we get to bring up our own child, then we're gonna be a hundred per cent times better fathers and mothers than what other people are! You're gonna be much more willing to make sure it works for your family! When your family breaks down, and you have a family of your own it's something to look forward to. Your original family is something from the past.

When it comes to foster parents, I've been in a lot of foster families. They tried to show love but as they weren't my parents, I didn't feel they had any connection to me. They were just people who 'looked after' me. So, I used to push them away because they had no ruling over me. Sometimes you can push too many people away and end up with nobody.

There are other circumstances. I was in a foster family where my foster mother got very ill, which was nothing to do with me. I was with that lady – her name was Wendy – for about two years. She was such a lovely lady and when she got ill it felt like she was getting rid of us; she didn't love us anymore. You shouldn't think like that because you know it's not always the case but you tend to blame yourself and shouldn't because it's not always your fault, even if, like me, it's your behaviour, you rebel.

I used to test. I used to test throughout my life. I'd keep testing and testing and testing and seeing if they would push me away. I tested them further by stealing money off them. If they didn't get rid of me, I'd think 'Well, the next thing I do they must get rid of me.' Finally they'd have enough and did get rid of you. Then I'd think, 'Well, I told you so.' It's a silly thing you do. I always felt like second best, especially when you live in foster families with their own children. You never feel like you've quite made the mark. You always feel that you are separate. I don't think that's always the case.'

There is a Buddhist saying to the effect that whilst pain is universal we do have some choice over how we suffer. Both Paul and William made different life choices, though it was doubtful Paul at that time constructed it as a choice. He was probably living in the moment of the frisson of stealing a car and being driven at speed. It may have been the only thrill in a life that from his perspective looked bleak and without prospects. William conveyed more of a sense of the future, albeit with some foreboding, from a better understanding the past. In the next chapter we shall look at what ethics has to teach us about the good life, and how not only may we make the right choices that avoid suffering but that we may even find what the Chorus in Oedipus reflects to the audience, that elusive experience of happiness, which 'like a bird in flight flutters and is gone' (Sophocles, 1998).

Summary

- The first key transactional dance, as a family system first configures, and its seven steps of call and response are described.
- A family's experience of family therapy is described.
- The structure and process of authority, co-operation and subsystem in the development of family life, and Minuchin's structural family therapy are described.
- Triangulation – where role-switching between the archetypes of persecutor, victim and rescuer occurs under stress – is explained.
- A similar process observed in the role of distant regulator is examined.
- The four early-attachment patterns in the family and their formation towards the script are described.
- Two case stories of disorganized attachments, with very different outcomes, are presented.

6

THE SEARCH FOR WELL-BEING: THE ETHICAL DIMENSION OF SYSTEMIC THOUGHT

The individual or the common good?

The post-war British Minister of Health, Aneurin Bevan, who was instrumental in the creation of the British National Health Service, and whose guiding principle was entry for all according to need not to means, wrote: 'Not even the apparently enlightened principle of the "greatest good for the greatest number" can excuse indifference to individual suffering. There is no test for progress other than its impact on the individual' (1952: 167). This politician who introduced the most collectivist organisation in British history (it remains the third largest employer in the world) saw no contradiction between the good of the many and the good of the individual. In Bevan's view, the 'common good' of social well-being was best safeguarded through the universal provision of good health care and was an unconditional given of a civilised society.

Individual suffering in its many forms is a powerful driver in the search for treatment and healing. Medicine, psychology, different therapies, faith and meditational systems and philosophical systems all offer pathways of relief to the sufferer; so many, in fact, that it is sometimes impossible to know where to begin. Each has its basic assumptions and models: some are science-based, whose evidence is objectively tested; some are from the age-old traditions and practice of intuitive evidence; some are from combinations of different approaches. There is no final and given way. Current political and psychotherapeutic discourse is full of ideas about the importance of well-being and happiness; like fresh air, few would dispute their value. However, there are many contenders as to what well-being and happiness are, and how they are to be discovered. The veteran existential psychotherapist Victor Frankl (2004: 16) stated the happiness paradox thus: 'Happiness ensues; it cannot be pursued.'

A systemic family therapist is, of course, involved in this search and in the demand for evidence of the value of their chosen approach. Having an inclusive and pluralistic ethos, systemic thinking is able to embrace elements of many different therapies within the framework of understanding family organization, the relationships and scripts. Indeed, the inclusion of such elements, and the effective collaboration with practitioners of a different therapeutic discipline, only increase the therapeutic efficacy through the value of 'double description'.

Working with the smaller political organization of the family, the therapist is faced with the same definitional dilemma as Bevan: what is the balance between the good of the group as a whole and the good of the individual? The patient often feels estranged from the 'common good' of their family through their difficulty. Indeed, they may feel their family has no ordered or coherent sense of the common good and that they are alone with their difficulty. Individuation may mean getting out at all costs; there may appear to be no safeguards. Individual therapists, whether systemically informed or not, are aware of the centrifugal force of the invisible family system with its definitional power to influence the identity and well-being of the person seeking to escape. Rarely are 'flight' or 'fight' desirable options, but the patient sees no alternatives.

For the systemic-based therapist, assessing, understanding and facilitating aspects of the family group seem the most productive ways to problem-solve and help alleviate personal distress. It makes the assumption that the seeds of well-being are in the family relationships but that they are untended, even upended. In this chapter we shall look briefly at the qualities of well-being from the history of human ethical thought, and ways we might facilitate them in family work.

Systemic thinking in itself does not contain any ethical implications. The mass manufacturing, distribution and marketing of commodities use systemic analysis to maximize their effectiveness; increasing their profitability and 'brand visibility' and manoeuvring to best advantage through the complexities of the marketing systems in which the enterprises have to operate. The capability of totalitarian regimes to perpetrate mass genocide in recent history is a stark example of how the application of organizational thinking can be implemented for dehumanized political and ethical ends.

However, the potential of systemic thought to help make a more just, better self-regulated, sustainable, harmonious world, with fairer distribution of resources and acknowledgement of human rights, would seem to be immense. Could we find a way to a similar sustainability of intimate relationships, an ecological revolution in family life? This may seem a utopian fantasy, but there is always part of the human psyche that will be reaching out for a better world. Systemic and ethical thought belong hand in hand if there is to be any hope of building a more connected world, even if this is to start small, with the basic human living community.

Human beings: 'political and familial animals'?

Around 320 BC the Greek philosopher Aristotle described man as a 'political animal' (1995: 59). He meant 'man' as a collective noun, though women had little status in Ancient Greek society, and although he was certainly no feminist nor an egalitarian, we could give him the benefit of the doubt. He asserted that a person exists to best advantage in an organized society, and that Politics, as a philosophical discipline, provides the thinking as to how it could be organized. We have seen how, like Russian 'Matryoshka' dolls, the organization of any society can be broken down into its systemic 'sub-communities' of which the family is the foundation. Aristotle could equally well have described a human being as a 'familial animal', a member of a micro-political system within the macro one. He added a supplement to his work on political philosophy, the *Nicomachean Ethics*, in which he described the kinds of virtues that are needed in an effective political community. This is a key work of ethical philosophy. In it, he sought to define the characteristic of happiness and how it might be pursued. In more recent times, Bertrand Russell, the rationalist philosopher, made similar attempts (1930).

All cultures have rules and moral codes about how people ought to behave: some of these are decreed and sanctioned by religious beliefs and enforced through an all-knowing, all-judging deity; some by social custom and practice; others by criminal and civil codes and systems of law which vary between societies and which may be in conflict (e.g. between the tradition of English common law and European law). Developments, through the Enlightenment (and such radical thinkers as the author of *The Rights of Man*, Tom Paine) and the effects of two global wars, led to the Declaration of Universal Human Rights in 1948 by the United Nations. This enshrines a code of basic human decency to which all people are entitled, although it remains a utopian aspiration rather than a collective global achievement.

However, with all this welter of different national laws, moral codes and religious and secular customs and practices, as well as their systems of enforcement and sanctions, the questions Aristotle examines remain fundamental humanistic ones. All of us ask, usually at a time of crisis or conflict, but without such analytic clarity as Aristotle: 'What should I do in this particular situation and in life generally?' 'What is the "good life?"' 'If it is happiness and well-being, what is that?' 'Even if I know what it is, how do I find it?' 'Do I find it just for me or for others as well?' 'If so, what then is the "good society" or the "good community?"' 'What happens if what I believe to be good, right and ethical, and a human right, puts me into conflict with law, statute, religious and secular codes and family definitions of right?'

Ethics, then, as a formal study, is the rational analysis of behaviour, seeking to find personal principles and meaning behind and beyond the stated requirements of operating codes. The novel *Alone in Berlin* (Fallada, 1947) brought out immediately after the war is a beautifully written fictionalized account of a German couple who for two years conducted a secret poster and postcard campaign against the Hitler regime. Having lost their only child on the Russian front, they 'felt out' their ethical position and acted on it, in the face of one of the most viciously repressive regimes in human history, until the inevitable happened. No doubt, many such quiet unseen acts of ethical defiance are exercised daily out of a desire for for freedom and human rights in the face of repressive authoritarian regimes.

Philosophical and spiritual views of the good

There have been many attempts to describe the characteristics of well-being and happiness in ethical thought. The good, for Aristotle, was a state of happiness he termed *eudaimonia*. The philosopher A.C. Grayling explains:

> By this he meant an active kind of well-being and well-doing, a much richer notion than is now generally meant by 'happiness'. More precisely **eudaimonia** means a flourishing state of the soul ... The appeal to man's rationality is an important feature of Aristotle's view. Man is part of the natural world in that, like the plants he ingests nutriments and reproduces himself and like animals he moves about, perceives and has desires. But in addition and alone among all

things, man is rational and this is his defining mark or essence. To be human is to reason – more particularly to employ practical wisdom (phronesis) in thinking how to live ... 'in accordance with virtue'. By 'virtue' Aristotle means what reason will choose as the 'middle path' or 'mean' between opposing vices. (2003: 27–8)

A more systemic way of restating this 'golden mean' might be that well-being is to be found by constantly locating experience between the extremes of desires, impulses and moods. This might be seen as 'being sensible', a practical, experiential ability to use the basic cybernetic process to navigate the path of well-being. It is a common experience, seeking to be moderate after periods of excess, that Aristotle's view is immediately recognizable.

In his seminal guide to practical wisdom, *The Conquest of Happiness*, the British philosopher Bertrand Russell is unequivocal about his own pathway to the 'golden mean':

The golden mean is an uninteresting doctrine and I can remember when I was young rejecting it with scorn and indignation since in those days it was heroic extremes I admired ... The golden mean is a case in point: it may be an uninteresting doctrine but in a very great many matters it is a true one ... One respect in which it is necessary to preserve the golden mean is as regards the balance between effort and resignation. (1930: 178)

Aristotle's contemporary, Plato, dramatically reconstructed Socrates' dialogues presenting the main ethical virtues as justice, courage, temperance and beauty. The 'Good' was seen as the perfect form in the hierarchy of virtues but, though pursued, was, in truth, unattainable. The Platonic view, rather like Carl Jung's archetypical psychology of the collective unconscious, was that once experienced metaphysically they could be converted to 'lived experiences'. Just how this was supposed to happen was never made clear, except through Plato's allegory of the prisoner in a cave. The prisoner realizes that the images on the cave wall are shadows created by the firelight. He escapes into sunlight and at once discovers that his prior experience was a false one; he knows a deeper and more essential evaluation of the good at first hand. Attempting to remedy their false consciousness, he is shunned by the other prisoners; his insight and experiential knowledge are disqualified and discounted. This revelatory experience was at the heart of the Socratic paradox: that it is only the unawareness of false consciousness that prevents human attainment of well-being and the good. 'No one errs willingly' and 'virtue is knowledge' were the Socratic aphorisms. 'The whole and only point of the Socratic inquiry is to engender self-knowledge in the form of a knowledge of one's own ignorance. So that virtue is an aim rather than an achievement' (Macintyre, 1967: 22–3). In a common theme with the classical ethical systems of West and East, Plato's views are a synthesis between the humanistic and the mystical, though of a particular Greek form: 'One is the thought that an unjust person will be denied the friendship of the gods and other people if he is not capable of sharing. The second is the even more significant thought that to live well is to have an ordered soul, one which is in harmony with itself' (Grayling, 2003: 24).

The Jewish ethical system, the foundation of the Christian system, is based on the rules of the Torah, but with an emphasis on personal, situational questioning:

> If I am not for myself who will be for me?
> And when I am for myself what am 'I'?
> If not now, when?

the Jewish philosopher Hillel inquired of himself, in a very modern existential fashion. Jesus of Nazareth issued a variation on this thought in the ethical assertion of the primacy of developing the tripartite personal experience based on love and faith to the interpretation and application of Jewish ethics 'Love God and your neighbour as yourself.' This could be seen as a metaphysical parallel to the enlightenment of Plato's prisoner in the cave, and subsequent philosophical attempts were made to produce a synthesis between Platonic and Christian mystical explorations. Some have understood the various paradoxical and enigmatic fragments of ethical advice, especially the aphorisms of the Sermon on the Mount, as Zen koans (parables) to clarify and deepen awareness of one's own autonomous ethical and existential position. Jesus' ethical direction to delay a rush to condemnatory judgement ('judge not that you be not judged') seems more evident in its breach than its honouring, as a very cursory glance at Christian history reveals. As we saw in Chapter 5, Jean-Paul Sartre's *Huis Clos* produced the famous line 'hell is other people'. He later clarified 'hell' not as judgement in the afterlife but excessive reliance on the judgements of others for self-identity in this life. Judgements are powerful identity organizers in human groups for good and ill, and thus the basic material of all therapy.

Religious or spiritual-based ethics are best understood as existential guides to living at this time, in this world. The idea of an afterlife judgement is superfluous to the production of ethical behaviour and, at its worst, is used as a specious justification for basic ethical transgressions of human rights and well-being. At the centre of Jesus' teaching was a theme, universal to all ethical teaching, that of the 'Golden Rule'. This 'Golden Rule' of ethical reciprocity unites non-religious humanists and at least 21 spiritual systems of belief. The Hindu idea of karma is based entirely on it, and expresses the chain reaction, often invisible and long delayed, of our actions and activities. The Chinese sage Confucius (551–479 BC) is thought to be the first to have articulated it. When asked by his disciples what they could practice all day, he replied: 'Perhaps the saying about *shu* ("consideration"). Never do to others what you would not like them to do to you" (Armstrong, 2010: 10).

This principle can equally be expressed positively ('do unto others as you would wish to be done to'), or negatively, and is an ethic so plain, true and simple that a 4-year-old child can grasp it. Its logic, however, often dissolves under the stresses and demands of the adult world. As Groucho Marx famously remarked in the film *Duck Soup:*' 'Find me a 4-year-old and get him to explain it to me.'.

It also invites a different and particular quality of mindful activity which has been referred to many times in this text as the essential ingredient in an experiential approach to helping others, the imaginative ability to move outside the confines of our own experience and into the perceptual state of another. This has a number of labels: empathy is one, attunement another. It involves more than just connecting with the suffering of another, but this is most relevant in this context. For the writer Karen Armstrong, as for Dostoevsky, for whom it was 'the chief law of existence', the word is compassion: 'Compassion means to endure [something] with another person to put ourselves in somebody else's shoes, to feel her pain as though it were our own and to enter generously into her point of view' (Armstrong, 2010: 16).

In many ways this is the consummate, often under-developed ability of the human species, the solidarity that comes from the communal experience of suffering. There is an element of the tragic about our human species and our condition; adrift on a planet in a vast cosmos, without any certainties except death and having to let go of all the activities and relationships which enriched our living. 'A person who is dying calls forth a special kind of feeling. Our attitude to him is at once softened and lifted to a higher plane. We then can feel compassion for people whom we did not love. But every man is dying, I too am dying and must never forget about death' (Berdyaev, 1976: 301).

It is not surprising that, linked to compassion, the German existential philosopher Martin Heidegger (1927: 237) should identify the core human ethic as *sorge,* or care. This is a central virtue and quality to cultivate in all human services work, especially therapy.

The two major thinkers about ethics in Western philosophy have been John Stuart Mill, whose core principle of utilitarianism was 'the greatest happiness of the greatest number' (and whose mentor Jeremy Bentham sought to identify a number of virtues that constitute happiness), and the German Enlightenment philosopher, Immanuel Kant. Kant thought the test of behaviour was to determine whether it could be rendered a universal law without contradiction and exception. Close to the idea of the 'Golden Rule', this introduced a legalistic criteria into assessing and judging behaviour. Human rights legislation may be traced back to Kantian thought, as well as Tom Paine.

The best definition of the Enlightenment of the Western rationalist intellectual tradition came from Immanuel Kant, in September 1784, in response to the question posed by a Berlin magazine:

Enlightenment is man's emergence from his self-incurred immaturity. Immaturity is the inability to use one's own understanding without direction from another. This immaturity is self-incurred if its cause is not lack of understanding but lack of resolve and courage to use it without another's guidance. Dare to know! That is the motto of Enlightenment. 'Dare to know!' (Kant, 1784)

That bold if stern challenge has echoes of the central secret to well-being articulated by the Oracle at Delphi, to 'know thyself', and Socrates' 'virtue is knowledge'.

A very different kind of enlightenment and use of mind, practised and advocated by the Buddha, has been imported into Western psychology and psychotherapy under the heading of 'mindfulness'. This kind of knowing is experiential, unique only to the one who has discovered it through meditation and an emptying of the mind of its attachments and processes to reach a total state of unknowingness. Buddhism is a highly disciplined practice and search for well-being, wisdom and ethical action, as may be seen from the following selection from the 423 Buddhist aphorisms in the *Dhammapada* (*c*.300 BC), the Buddhist pathway guide:

Look upon the man who tells you your faults as if he told you of a hidden treasure, the wise man who shows you the dangers of life. Follow that man: he who follows him will see good and not evil.

He who for happiness hurts another who also wants happiness shall not hereafter find happiness.

If you can be in silent quietness like a broken gong that is silent, you have reached the peace of Nirvana and your anger is peace.

Being open to the experiential knowing of enlightenment is an essential pathway to well-being, but how many of us in the swirl of our lives manage this level of joyful peace of mindfulness? The other is the principle of the golden mean, or the 'middle way' advocated by Buddhism. There are many other spiritual systems which also develop the capacity for self-harmonization, synchronised harmony with others and with existence itself. One of the keys to well-being springs from an appreciation of the fullness and rapture which existence delivers to us if we are open to it: beauty and the good spring from many sources around us, in nature, literature, the arts and companionable, loving relationships as well as spiritual illumination. These come from sources deep within us and have their bases in experiential, meditative learning, not specifically from academic learning. They need to be cultivated through studied attention, a contemplative awareness from practised silence, just as therapeutic skills are cultivated.

Well-being and health: the political dimension

Systemic thinking invariably joins ethical thought with political thought since resource allocation and social initiatives that promote well-being are almost always dependent on governmental direction. This may not affect your therapeutic practice directly, but it certainly will affect the economic and social stresses that impinge on each family's experience from access to education, effective health care, employment opportunities and social and housing benefit. You may work with affluent families who bring different kinds of relational conflict unconnected with such wider systemic pressures. However, even such families may fall into straightened circumstances that challenge their already debilitated emotional resources. Aristotle was correct to assert the importance of the political environment of mankind.

Countries that are small and with a strong religious, ethical and spiritual belief may also be conducive to the 'good society'. Anecdotally, the Buddhist Himalayan Kingdom of Bhutan, with its 'Gross National Happiness' instead of 'Gross Domestic Product', may indeed be a Shangri-La; certainly the idea serves to unify that society. Though 'families' and 'social classes' may be descriptive categories, their experiential worlds in any given society may be so different as to seem totally disconnected. It is scarcely surprising, therefore, that most societies remain a potential battlefield of simmering tension between groups with hugely different access to social networks of opportunity, economic and political capital. Often what passes as a sectarian, racial or religious conflict has its roots in a marginalized group which exercises little political influence and thus is prey to economic disadvantage and discrimination.

An immediate example is Northern Ireland, where archaic sectarian beliefs have provided a thinly concealed pretext for structural discrimination by one part of the community against another. This was accompanied by random acts of violence, private vendettas and the breakdown of the 'rule of law'. Our adult mental health systemic team was recently working with a Protestant family, fringe members of which, on the husband's side, were members of a Protestant paramilitary group. The core family had sought refuge in England because of a violent 'honour feud' between the husband's family and his wife's over the alleged sexual abuse by one of the wife's brothers of one of her husband's nieces. According to the anxious accounts of those present, some family members had had their homes set on fire and open threats of murder and intimidation made over a 20-year period. The husband disowned his own family and their behaviour; his depressed wife felt rootless away from Northern Ireland, but relieved as well. Her adult children couldn't understand her desire to return to the communal conflict they had just escaped. As a team we were amazed by the different levels of context and how closely one interacted with the other to create profound inescapable personal and familial distress.

The system of world order is palpably and inexcusably unjust. The wealth creators generally hoard and resist reasonable attempts to distribute assets more fairly and universally argue for their personal entitlement and just desserts. Many see the need for a different global ethos to emerge that cultivates a greater fairness in resource allocation and long-term sustainability. Future scenarios do not give rise to optimism; whilst pessimistic ones, increased religious fundamentalism and terrorism, destruction of whole global eco-systems, and serious intercommunal violence all have their Jeremiahs.

The social location into which you are born largely determines all manner of outcomes, particularly health: the life expectancy of a man living in a poor suburb of Glasgow and one in the richest metropolitan authority in the south of England, Kensington and Chelsea, has a discrepancy of at least 20 years. More examples can be found in *The Spirit Level* (Wilkinson & Pickett, 2009) where the association between poor physical and mental health and inequality is carefully and tellingly made. Similarly, serious wealth and health discrepancies in the

USA are forensically analysed in *23 Things They Don't Tell You about Capitalism* (Ha-Joon Chang, 2010). These are huge political challenges if there is ever to be a real aspiration to promoting greater social harmony, inclusion, universal rights and access to opportunities. Tom Paine expressed this ideal in 1791: 'Every child born into the world must be considered as deriving its existence from God. The world is as new to him as it was to the first man that existed and his natural right in it is of the same kind', with its echoes of Plato's 'All men [and women]are by nature equal, made all of the same earth by the same creator.'

There are glimpses in the diverse protest movements that have emerged in recent years in different parts of the globe that there is a wind of change springing up, though as yet without a coherent manifesto. Perhaps systemic analysis provides the means for unravelling some of the complexities of our inherited world to make way for a different ethos?

An alternative experiential model

It is now time to introduce a different kind of framework for thinking about mental health and well-being, not one based on disease characteristics, such as the US Diagnostic and Statistical Mental Disorders (DSM-IV, 2000), but on experiential characteristics. In earlier chapters we looked at the importance of attachment theory in helping to describe key experiential characteristics. From this we can create a different template drawn from the ethical properties of those experiential values that lead to well-being, designated 'virtues'; and their opposites, the experiential values that erode well-being, activate distress and debilitation, designated 'adversities'. These terms are less pejorative than most and help to get away from the language of sickness and pathology to one of existential choice and possibility. At the root of all experience, however, is that of the 'good' experience and the 'bad'; these described experiences are not immutable, for what may have been felt by individual and group at one time as a 'good' may become re-evaluated on reflection with time, and vice versa.

The symbolic-interactionalist psychiatrist, Harry S. Sullivan, describes more clearly the threefold elements of this process of the development of the person built up interpersonally:

Satisfactory, tender and secure interpersonal experiences are organised into the self-personification which Sullivan called the 'good-me'. Interpersonal experiences associated with disapproval, forbidding gestures and general tension in the other are organised into the personification of 'bad-me'. The 'not-me' personification arises from interpersonal experiences of severe anxiety. (Barton Evans, 1996: 211–12)

However, he does not speak of the re-evaluative capacity of the person, the core possibility of therapeutic change. Psychotherapy is in part a redemptive relational art that seeks to disentangle the accumulation and circularity of bad experience (literally, the 'vicious circle') and make well-being more accessible through clarification, understanding and, on occasions, forgiveness. In Sullivan's examples, the different response repertoires produce different self-experiences in their recipient. These can be in the form of emotional or mood states, active characteristics of mind, or willing. They will invariably create feedback loops and chain reactions unless something different happens, or is done, which makes a difference.

Exercise 6.1: Virtues and adversities

Take five minutes to generate your own list of virtues that enhance the experience of well-being and of adversities that are detrimental to it. It should not be difficult to find at least 20 qualities of each.

On your list may be such virtues as honesty, transparency, humour, kindness, consideration, generosity and determination. Empathy, care, love, nurturance and understanding are interpersonal virtues, while some qualities belong to group relations, such as collaboration, co-operation, discipline or solidarity. Others relate to spiritual virtues, values of transcendent faith or hope; while some may be cognitive, such as reflectiveness, discernment, solution-finding and rationality; and some even bodily fitness or suppleness.

Family systems may also be activated by the predominant virtues of care, concern and empathy. In situations like this we may refer to them as 'concern-activated systems', 'care-activated systems', 'empathy-activated systems' or 'resilience-activated systems'. Such family characteristics often emerge most distinctly from conditions of stress, pressure and tension, but this is not a given and conflictual characteristics may be displayed instead.

Equally, there are many adversities. Some are corrosive systemically to the body, whole person and family group: violence, sexual abuse, neglect, rejection, illness. The severity of the adversities may damage the life force and confidence of both person and group, creating a chain reaction over time that disguises its origins. Cognitive conditions such as disassociative states and many mental ill-health conditions arise from the active or delayed effects of adversities from group relations such as disparagement, humiliation, alienation, invalidation, bullying and a general sense of group exclusion. The effects depend on the intensity and length of these experiences and the resilience and strength of the person's already constructed reality.

These states of response can be replicated by whole families isolating themselves from larger community relationship. Bob Dylan's 'Ballad of Hollis Brown' is a stark and tragic narrative of such familial phenomenology. Similarly individuals and family sub-systems can detach themselves from the wider family system, saturated by a culture of adverse qualities. Family systems can be activated and driven at moments by predominating adversities: we may speak of 'trauma-activated systems', 'conflict-activated systems', 'stress-activated systems', ' 'addiction-activated systems', 'violence-activated systems' or 'illness-activated systems'. These describe the culture, atmosphere and major organizing characteristics of the family system. Such family patterns are not permanent, but may emerge when the system is under stress. Revelations by celebrities and adversity-activated families are the stuff of media stories.

This is not to supplant the medical and psychological models based on research-based outcomes with the process- and interpretative-led models with their more tentative and uncertain outcomes. There is place for both, though the different ideologies of change seem to deny the value of the other. However, all practitioners need some basic communicational skills in helping the experiential rebalancing of distressing and well-being experiences in ways that patients follow. The established methods, for example, of reframing and positively connoting to shift the interpretative process within the family through a working alliance and open dialogue can both be productive and evidentially effective.

So also is the therapeutic work of seeking to help a family system rebalance itself. This concurs with the ethical wisdom of the 'golden mean' or 'middle way'; that experiential positioning and the pursuit of well-being is always a choice, even if it is not seen to be so at the time by the person making it. The failure to achieve well-being, according to Socrates, comes from insufficient understanding, not necessarily weakness of will. The effect of accumulated experiential adversities erodes the ability to think, know and therefore to choose differently. Pursuit of well-being is an activity derived from the cybernetics of experience originating in family relationships. From daring to know these and their influence on the present volume, change is possible.

Erik Erickson (1902–94) wrote of eight developmental stages that pose the options between experiential virtues and adversities. In childhood, at stage 3 (ages 3–5) it is between 'initiative' and 'guilt', and the successful negotiated virtue is 'purpose'; at stage 8 (ages 55/65–death) it is between 'integrity' and 'despair', and the successful negotiated virtue is 'wisdom'. For Erich Fromm (1900–80), the eight virtues of well-being (he postulated these as needs) are 'relatedness', 'transcendence', 'rootedness', 'sense of identity', 'frame of orientation', 'excitation and stimulation', 'unity' and 'effectiveness'.

It takes a great deal of skill, practice and belief to help a family identify and rebalance its value systems between the poles of the continuum between virtues and adversities. They may be helped to see that virtues, once enacted, generate their own momentum towards well-being, whilst the adversities do the opposite. Such is the experiential feedback of virtuous and vicious circles and part of the therapeutic redefinition co-scripted with the family. It is more than just 'accentuating the positives', but helping to move experience further into the domain of well-being, using the parts of family system that wants to go there as natural allies.

Virtues and adversities: the Timberlawn research

In a US landmark study in the early 1970s in Dallas, at the Timberlawn Psychiatric Hospital (Lewis et al., 1976), an attempt was made to research the different characteristics of family process and functioning, the elements (virtues) leading to well-being and those (adversities) leading to impaired mental health. It was based on the major theoretical models in family therapy at the time, particularly that of Murray Bowen, and examined eight dimensions of family life: 'power structure', 'differentiation' (that is, the level of individuality the family group would permit), 'communication' (the quality and nature of interchanges), 'relationship' (their main characteristics), 'reality sense', 'affect', 'attitude to change and loss' and 'types of disorder' (emergent, personal mental health difficulties within the system).

By describing these characteristics, the research pointed to the level of mental health functioning of individual family members. As with John Bowlby's first paper (1949), family group culture, the systemic, organizational characteristics of the family, has a crucial influence on the well-being of each individual within it. This is not a surprising revelation. Though the sample was small (153 families), the work has been highly influential, notably in the work of Robin Skynner (Skynner &

Cleese, 1983), and can be seen in many of the assumptions of structural family therapy.

As with Bowlby's models of attachment and Laing and Esterson's (1964) family studies, the description of the different processes provided an enormous navigational aid to the family practitioner in identifying and seeking to help the family change 'bad' experience to 'better' or 'good enough' experience. These observations have been confirmed by many studies since, including most recently the British research tool SCORE. It should not be read as another typology but as a rather useful guide to unravelling the strands of a family's experience.

The extremity of family process that showed severe signs of mental health distress co-related with Bowlby and Main's chaotic, disorganized attachment patterns. Here appeared a huge clustering of adversities detrimental to well-being. The *Power Structure* showed signs of chaotic patterns of parent–child coalitions, triangulating and excluding the other parent (usually the father). For *Differentiation*, the adversities showed up as patterns of blurred boundaries, shifting roles, blaming, scapegoating and invasiveness. *Communication* was sometimes vague, evasive and contradictory, with mystification and imperviousness. *Relationship* patterns tended to be distrustful, with an expectation of hurt and harm through betrayal and desertion; swings between extremes. *Reality Sense* was often dealt with by denial and inconsistency. *Affect* had patterns of cynicism, hostility, hopelessness and despair. *Attitude to Change and Loss* were encountered with an inability to cope and a repetitive quality to the patterns.

The opposite process extremes showed patterns of many virtues and little mental health distress. *Power Structure* showed patterns of clear hierarchy, with mutual respect and strong, equally powered parental coalitions, but children were consulted and decisions made through negotiation. *Differentiation* revealed well-defined, secure identities, allowing for high levels of closeness and intimacy, with high levels of personal responsibility. *Communication* was open, clear, direct, frank, lively and spontaneous; new ideas were encountered with receptivity and responsiveness. *Relationship* revealed trust, expectation of positive response to positive approach; warm, caring, mutual regard and responsibility; ambivalent feeling was accepted as normal. *Reality Sense* showed that perceptions of self and the family were congruent with each other and outside observation. *Affect* was characterized by warmth, enjoyment, humour, wit, tenderness and empathy. *Attitude to Change and Loss* was characterized by the embracing of change, growth while separation and death were accepted realistically.

Several caveats need to be made at this stage. First, the extremes have an almost archetypical quality to them which can make them seem unreal. On first reading, 'Surely no family can be so clearly "good" or "bad" as that?' is a common response. Secondly, the research also identified mid-range characteristics of family experience which are variants of the extremes. Thirdly, as with evaluating and locating attachment patterns or mental health diagnoses the descriptions and observations are never quite as clear-cut as the attributions that the research findings suggest. Fourthly, there was no clear idea of the structure or cultural background of the researched families, though by implication they were mostly nuclear families, and since the time of this original research family structures have undergone radical changes. These are important caveats and the same can rightly be made against some of the normative assumptions of structural family therapy.

However, this does not invalidate the value of the work in giving markers for well-being and distress in family systems' experience. It enables the family systemic therapist and team to listen fully and communicate a genuine understanding of the process of distress and the effects of adversities within the different elements of the family system, as well as legacies from earlier family scripts; to probe the level of commitment or faith in change; to highlight the virtues in the form of care, survival, humour, acceptance, resilience, tenderness and unused potential for better communication and dialogue, affect and reality testing through attempted solutions. How this is done is another matter. Therapeutic work is as much about the ownership of not changing as changing. In the last analysis, the freedom to choose lies always with the family, not the therapist. The therapist's skill is helping the family experience rebalancing towards the circularities of the virtues and away from the adversities, through dialogue. We shall now look at how to manage this

Summary

- The branch of philosophy concerned with well-being is called ethics.
- Aristotle's concepts of *eudaimonia* and 'the golden mean' are discussed.
- The social rules and customs of communities and the historical development of human rights are described.
- Spiritual definitions of the good, the 'golden rule' of ethics, compassion and care are explored.

- The systemic importance of politics in creating the 'good society' for all is examined.
- A template for well-being, the 'virtues', is described, together with that of detrimental characteristics (the 'adversities'), and an exercise to develop these for yourself is given.
- Erik Erikson , Erich Fromm's and John Bowlby's conceptualisations of the virtues are described.
- The Timberlawn Institute's research into family characteristics and their virtues and adversities is summarized.

7

THE PHENOMENOLOGICAL PERSPECTIVE AND METHOD

The experiential world of self, others and systems

We shall now look in closer detail at what constitutes an experiential approach, in particular its primary method and set of historically developed assumptions called phenomenology. Like any 'ology', the term can sound forbiddingly academic until we begin to connect it with our own experience of seeing the world.

Its origins lie in the history of philosophy and, more particularly, the work of Edmund Husserl. Phenomenology (from the Greek *phainomenon*, 'that which appears', and *logos*, 'study') is concerned with the analysis of the structure of consciousness and the appearance of things within it, such as judgements, conceptions, perceptions and emotions. It is an approach that concerns itself entirely with the subjective and the personal: the world is entirely how you and I perceive it to be. This does not mean that everything is relative to our perception, for there is a common, shared heritage of suffering and distress, the 'sea of troubles' which beset Hamlet. Each form of distress may be different, as may each interpretation. Alfred Adler wrote: 'It is not the child's experiences which dictate his actions; it is the conclusions which he draws from his experiences' (1956: 209). Since we exist socially in a world with others, we are constantly influencing one another through dialogue and perceptions of each other in potentially endless sequences of circular feedback. So, 'my experience of your experience of my experience shapes my experience in return, which then shapes yours', and so on. This all sounds remarkably convoluted, and it can be, as is brilliantly demonstrated in R.D. Laing's book *Knots*, which illustrates the circularity of the two-person phenomenological process which forms the basis of the method of **circular questioning**.

Besides distress, the other absolute given of life which prevents phenomenology becoming a relativistic theory is the fact of death. This departure from existence is as important as birth, and sets a common inescapable context in which our consciousness forms its constructions, perceptions, feelings and beliefs about the 'appearances' around us and our actions. Phenomenology was linked with existential philosophy to provide a potent way of thinking about felt existence. Through the philosophers Martin Heidegger and Jean-Paul Sartre, and psychiatrists like Karl Jaspers, Ludwig Binswanger and R.D. Laing, existential-phenomenological thought has had a huge impact on psychiatric practice.

Though phenomenology started out as a method of personal perspective (**personal phenomenology**), it also emphasizes the inescapable relational world shared with others that shapes meaning and interpretation (**interrelational phenomenology**). We can now add to the mix the systemic world of organization and patterns, mostly but not exclusively of human systems (systemic phenomenology). The relevance this has for therapy is apparent, for therapy is a particular context in which, through open dialogue, one or more persons' experience is offered to another for help to find a different understanding and meaning for a better life experience. This holds true whether the particular therapy is individual-, group- or family-based.

The effectiveness of all therapy is based on the therapist's experience being accessible to others, by it being accessible to him/her or the team. This openness and availability to others is a loop of mutual learning and influence from which the experiential self of the therapist is also changed and develops through participation.

The personal phenomenology of the self

In recent years much of the intellectual basis of family and systemic therapy has been drawn from social constructionist thought. This, however, is just one branch of the social phenomenological intellectual tradition; its other was symbolic interactionalism, whose major exponent was the Chicago sociologist, George Herbert Mead (1883–1938). Mead characterised selfhood thus:

The self is an object to itself ... This characteristic is represented in the word 'self' which is reflexive, and indicates that which can be both subject and object' ... For he enters his own experience as a self or individual, not directly or immediately, not by becoming a subject to himself, but only insofar as he becomes an object to himself just as other individuals are objects to him or are in his experience ... The importance of what we term 'communication' lies in the fact that it provides a form of behaviour in which the individual may become an object to himself. (Mead, 1934: 202–3).

Mead's theory is 'symbolically interactional' because he saw the interpretation and attribution of description to 'the other' (their character, intention and behaviour, their whole identity) as a product of social, communicational exchange. These articulated descriptions are the symbols by which the 'other' or 'others' may characterize the 'me' of the self. There are an infinite number of such symbolic descriptions, many denigratory (such as 'lazy', 'bitch', 'bastard', 'chav', 'white trash', 'pikey', 'dike', 'straight' and 'queer'), and used in specific contexts with the intention to disqualify, distress and voice contempt or even hatred. In many cases, one person 'may enhance his self-esteem by disparaging the other person, in the most serious cases becoming lord over life and death, his own life as well as that of the other person' (Adler, 1956: 236). Symbolic interaction is the very stuff of social life and its linguistic process of exchanging meaning. There are linguistic symbols for all seasons and settings.

Symbolic representations may denigrate and imprison in alienating linguistic categories, but they can also liberate in such descriptions as 'he's a really sweet, considerate person', 'she would do anything for anyone' and 'she's so hard-working as a mother'. There are remarkable parallels with Sigmund Freud's statement about language from the *Introductory Lectures*:

> Words were originally magic and to this day words have retained much of their ancient magical power. By words one person can make another blissfully happy or drive him to despair; by words the teacher conveys his knowledge to his pupils; by words, an orator carries his audience with him and determines their judgments and decision. Words provoke affects and are in general the means of mutual influence among men. Thus we shall not depreciate the use of words in psychotherapy and we shall be pleased if we can listen to the words that pass between the analyst and his patient ... But we cannot do that either. The talk of which psychoanalytic treatment consists brooks no listener; it cannot be demonstrated. (1912: 12)

In the USA a tradition of symbolic interactionists and social deviance theorists in sociology grew around Mead's work. The most notable was

Edwin Lemert (1912–96), who developed the idea of a two-level process in the formation of identity. First is the external linguistic attribution and its associations (the primary process); second is the internalized acceptance by the person of those attributions. This can be heard in Louis Armstrong's 1933 recording of *Black and Blue*. He sings with palpable feeling: 'I'm white ... inside ... but that don't help my case:

> That life ... can't hide ... what is in my face.
> How would it end ... ain't got a friend;
> My only sin ... is in my skin ...

Armstrong had more personal resilience and creative genius than to be deflected by such disparaging 'first-order' denigration (itself a word of symbolic significance, if you are black).

The American family-therapy pioneer Carl Whitaker (1984: 2) used to make the Zen-like utterance: ' "Me" is the only "You" I know', which encapsulates the whole basis of personal and relational phenomenology. Arthur Koestler conceptualizes the self as the wholeness of the person ('the individual'), which is simultaneously embedded in the partness of others ('the dividual'):

> No man is an island; he is a holon. Looking inward, he experiences himself as a unique self-contained independent whole; looking outward as a dependent past of his natural and social environment. His self-assertive tendency is the dynamic manifestation of his individuality; his integrative tendency expresses his dependence on some larger whole to which he belongs, his partness. When all is well, the two tendencies are more or less evenly balanced. In times of stress and *frustration, the equilibrium us upset, manifested in emotional disorders*. (1980: 467; emphasis added)

The basic unit through which we enter and experience the world is the subjectivity of our self. We both are the world and are not the world; we are part of the other and are not part of the other, to follow the paradoxes of Koestler and Jain reasoning. Similarly, we are and are not the descriptions and definitions others give to us. Irvin Yalom's substantial text *Existential Psychotherapy* (1980) has many examples of how living on the experiential edge of distress and despair can be a precursor to transformational experience. History, myth, legend, fairy stories, folk tales and case histories are full of the archetypical journey from despair to hope, confusion to enlightenment, emptiness to fulfilment.

The psychotherapist or counsellor is presented with a series of inter-woven if disconnected narratives about the disappointments, failures, anxieties, dreads and losses of patients. These stories are also part of the family script, the intersecting, systemic phenomenology. The self, itself a system, has been looked at in a number of works that see individual psychotherapy from a systemic perspective (notably Boscolo and Bertrando, 1996; Hedges, 2005). How can we understand the different elements of the self? Metaphysical thinking has largely gone out of favour in the West, except in Carl Jung's work. However, there is now an emerging awareness that the phenomenology of the self has a mysti-cal, unquantifiable dimension. The growing literature about 'mindful-ness' takes this as a central place of truth from which to discover good self-experience.

Towards the end of his life Carl Rogers articulated the power of intu-itive knowledge working in him:

> When I am at my best as a group facilitator or a therapist I discover another characteristic. I find that when I am closest to my inner intu-itive self, when I am somehow in touch with the unknown in me, when perhaps I am in a slightly altered state of consciousness in the relationship, then whatever I do seems to be full of healing. Then simply my presence is releasing and helpful. There is nothing I can do to force this experience but when I can relax and be close to the transcendent core of me then I may behave in strange and impulsive ways which I cannot explain rationally which have nothing to do with my thought processes. These strange behaviours turn out to be right in some odd way. At those moments it seems my inner spirit has reached out and touched the spirit of the other...profound growth and healing are present. (1986: 198)

Neuroscience has made huge advances in observing and understanding the neural processes of mind and body. However, from a phenomeno-logical position, we are less concerned with what goes on 'under the bonnet' than how the driver understands, experiences and modifies the direction of the vehicle. But let us see if we can map the different dimensions of the system of the self.

The dimensions of self-experience

The five conjoined and interacting dimensions that comprise the expe-rienced, phenomenological world of the person as a whole system are *mind, affect and mood, interaction, body* and *soul or spirit*. The 'mind' is the cognitive centre from which the assumptive scripts are developed; affect and mood form the delivered script and subscript; interaction, the feedback cycles of action; body the non-conscious centre of all sensate feedback; and soul/spirit the non-conscious element of our total psyche.

Dimension of mind

The opening lines of the collection of Buddhist aphorisms known as *The Dhammapada* (*c*.300 BC) read: 'What we are today comes from our thoughts of yesterday and our present thoughts build our life of tomorrow; our life is the creation of our mind.' This idea is present in modern psychology under different guises, 'Mindfulness' has a long philosophical tradition which need not detain us here, except to say that expanding our conscious awareness of self and the world is at the centre of all experiential learning. The aspiring therapist must seek to learn to be quiet, still and attentive, the better to hear the other and themselves with a fully open mind.

The mind is usually identified with the physical organ of the brain, and is sometimes described as a large blancmange situated inside the thin shell of the skull. The brain is a wondrously complex mechanism, containing millions of pieces of neural receptors that pass information which activates cells and maintains the self as a system in some kind of integrity and shape in the face of change. Its development has been a triumph of evolution and adaptational skills. All neural pathways ultimately lead to the brain, and it is through this exceptional receptor that the self largely configures itself. However, 'mind' exists in all parts of being, both the consciousness and in the large domain of the non-conscious. 'Mind' is itself a system, able to open a window onto the infinite through reflection. Whatever its restricted physiological characteristics, in the multiplicity of its functions and accomplishments the mind seems limitless. It can travel across the universe, focus closely or at a distance, rule the world, build empires, transform society and being, and have endless erotic and travel adventures. It can envisage almost anything; the only limitation is the willingness to do so. The novelist William Boyd wrote that rather than carry out research,

> I've been all over London with my eyes open, and talked to a few people. But I've discovered that imagination and intuition often bring you incredibly close to the reality, whether it's something middle class or the daily life of a prostitute on a sink estate. If you've looked closely and read a certain amount, then your *imagination is a*

more direct route to a truth than interviewing twenty working girls'. (interview with William Boyd, 2009; emphasis added)

Imagination can also be a source of destruction, and such extraordinary potential carries a health risk to those who are burdened by its power.

We know from neuroscience that different processes operate in the various areas of the brain, as Jungian analyst Robin Royston describes in *The Hidden Power of Dreams*:

As well as the cortices located from the front to the back of the brain, there is a difference between sides. Like a walnut in its shell the brain seen from above is divided in two: these cerebral hemispheres are joined at the bottom of the crevasse by a broad band of fibres, the corpus callosum. (Royston & Humphries, 2006: 47)

In mammals, including apes, both hemispheres function similarly. However, about 100,000 years ago, the human brain underwent a radical change and developed the capacity for art, and later, speech:

The two sides of the brain became specialised with the crowning glory – speech and language – located in the left brain. Mathematical ability, reading, writing and logic are also associated with the left brain. The right brain deals with more artistic abilities: visual and spatial, musical and the recognition of emotional values ... It is the right brain that fills in the blanks, reads between the lines. Socially, the left (logical) brain is relatively incompetent. Autism resembles pure left brain. The right brain makes sense of a situation, giving it context and emotional significance: it is skilled in reading others' intentions, the nuances of negotiation and intuition. (Royston & Humphries, 2006: 47–8)

Similarly, neuroscience indicates that where patterns of attachment are not secure, higher levels of cortisol are released in a child's brain, which causes distortion and inability to read situations more empathetically (Gerhardt, 2004). The interconnection between the different systems of relationship networks, the mind's homeostasis, training and development are irrefutable. Developing the mind's ability in both hemispheres is central to training in psychotherapeutic empathy and ability to analyse information and problem-solve.

The mind uses language in an infinite number of ways. All these capabilities are expressed through communication (derived from Latin and Old French root words meaning 'common sharing') and relationship. Relational intimacy is, according to Shakespeare, the 'marriage of two minds'. *Psyche* has its origins in *soul, spirit* and *mind*. Thus mind not only contains the darker influences of the amygdalae but the numinous and ecstatic influence of the spiritual, conveyed in artistic forms, religious ritual and worship, philosophical reflections and contemplative silence.

Dimension of affect and mood

Affective states, moods and feelings, are aspects of the self. Though they operate via different pathways in the body and seem separate systems, they are interactive, as the French mathematician Blaise Pascal acknowledged three centuries ago: 'We know the truth not only through our reason but also through our heart. It is through the latter that we know first principles and reason which has nothing to do with it, tries in vain to refute them' (1670: 28).

Our emotional world of feelings, passions and moods provides the texture and motivating energy for much of our thinking and responding. Emotions can feel like obstacles, inhibitors, destabilizers or enhancers. In the case of mood perturbance, experience can move distressingly from one extreme intensity to the other. Much that is labelled 'mental illness' is more accurately described as disruptive intrusions of feeling states that overwhelm the mind's capacity to mediate with calm thought. The dense clusters of powerful, contradictory emotions pulling thought in contrary directions (ambivalence), or as 'complexes' or 'gestalts' producing restricted stuck thought and action are the experiential material of the self.

CASE STUDY 7.1: JOANNE

Joanne is a 40-year-old married woman with five children. A highly successful teacher, her life had been punctuated by periods when persecutory voices tell her to kill herself. She had made several serious attempts at suicide which led to her hospitalization, and on one occasion she was chastened by a near-death experience. Diagnosed with borderline personality and bipolar disorders she rejected both diagnoses, and for periods tried to lose weight and refused medication (for her, the signifiers of her illness). To be designated with a psychiatric illness was a deep source of shame and weakness in her Catholic family. She acknowledged that she enjoyed the adrenalin rush of crises and being the centre of attention, and thought that these 'adolescent strategies' were connected with being the youngest of many children in her family. As many with her conditions

→

report, when she ceased taking her medication she experienced an extraordinary sense of ecstasy and mystical revelation, it is then that she is also at her most personally self-destructive.

In therapy, over a number of years, Joanne and her husband explored and reinterpreted the emotional complexes from their families of origins and their emotional fit as a couple. She hid her drugs from her husband to keep control, and accused him of violence towards her, summoning the police on one occasion (he was kept overnight in the cells). In a subsequent joint session, she said (with a smile on her face) that if she were him she would really want to beat her up, too. A long-compliant, mildly suffering part of this elaborate game, the husband was both perplexed and mildly amused. His indignation about the humiliation of the arrest (the first of its kind) was not altogether convincing.

Therapy felt like a triangular game without end. Eventually we decided to change the 'minimum sufficient system' from couple to family, and three of the children attended. Joanne erupted in violent rage at their 13-year-old daughter's defiance; the children, outside the family for the first time, voiced their anxiety and anger about their mother's destructive episodes when she would disappear and her violent outbursts. Working with others in the mental health team using a psycho-educational approach complementing the therapeutic work, Joanne's regulation of her moods, behaviour, empathy and understanding improved

Taking the systemic view of Joanne's family, she was a key player as 'victim' and 'persecutor' in a 'depression- and anxiety-activated system'. Her daughter's angry defiance could trigger her mother's depressive episodes and contribute to her impulsive suicide attempts (she nearly died on one occasion); there was no containing influence in this 'fear-activated system' except the therapist and mental health team. The chain reaction of these systemic transactional patterns had to be addressed as fully as any individual help to the person.

Of all passions, loss is the most potent, and in unexpected death, particularly of children or a young parent, the burden of the associated feelings and their mental accompaniments are often unbearable. Some of Freud's greatest insights came from his understanding of melancholia, the seemingly irredeemable loss that can precipitate an experiential crisis of meaning, ontological void and existential persecution. The loss can lead to profound destructive passions that are sometimes acted upon. In African-American blues, a genre of music born out of enslavement, there is a compelling personal immediacy of expression that gives voice to the universal experience of unconsoled life distress.

Dimension of action and interaction

The third domain of personal experience is that of social relationships and broader interaction with the world. We describe it as interactional, for every action or piece of behaviour provokes a reaction, whether sought, realized or expected. This is the Hindu/Buddhist concept of *karma* and a kind of Newtonian law of ethics: no action without reaction. We cannot always judge the consequences of our actions, and sometimes their effects are outside our lifetime. Such patterns of action/reaction are not just in the domain of personal experience. World history is full of them. Intentionality is not the same as the outcome of an action, as a patient's story illustrates:

CASE STUDY 7.2: PETER

Peter had wanted to end his life. His relationship with his partner had recently ended and his Ph.D. research was going badly. He could see no point in going on. He thought the best way to do this was via a kerosene stove which, once lit and the flame extinguished, produced toxic gas. He made himself comfortable with his choice whisky and some favourite music, texted his friends to bid farewell and settled down to ignite the stove.

Alas, for his self-destructive wish, he bungled the attempt and instead set his leg and part of his flat alight. Fortunately for his life-wish, friends alerted the emergency services, as did he, lest his flat burn down. He was taken to hospital, where he soon made a good recovery. The irony of his situation was not lost on him when it was pointed out in a therapy group. He managed to laugh at himself, along with the others.

However, intention is a vital stage in the development of an action, as is the emotional background that shapes it. In Peter's case, he had felt helplessly depressed for years, and saw himself as an academic failure, disappointed in love and an unwanted only child, an ontological error. He persisted in finding an alternative meaning to his life besides suicide, and is still searching.

Dimension of body and soul

Our physical self is the shell thorough which we 'body forth' into the world. In the words of the comic songwriter Allen Sherman's 'You Gotta Have Skin', 'it helps keep your insides in'. Using and directing the full range of our five sensory experiences of touch, smell, taste, sight and hearing, we monitor and seek to respond with the necessary sustaining feedback to our situation. These receptors are all information providers that lead to some kind of corrective response which may be completely non-conscious. We are 'hard-wired' for life and living and the ethical values that preserve this for ourselves and our 'cared-about' others. Without relational attachment at some stage of our development we have no meaningful existence. Our bodies are relational systems, as well as self-contained ones.

At times, sensory information from the body may be turned into descriptive narrative to inform another (e.g. a doctor, if there is a rise in body temperature or we feel out of balance with ourselves). We are, according to the phenomenologist Edmund Husserl, living scientific experiments, constantly monitoring evidential data. The body has very specific needs, desires and urges to sustain itself and maintain some level of immediate, organic satisfaction. These elements, essential but difficult aspects of our evolved nature, set up conflicts with other domains of self-experience and the wider relational world of others. However, in contrast to the immediacy of desire is the capacity for the transcendent, that which raises consciousness out of the here and now, in a manifestation of the complexity of being human.

Much of what we experience of the ecstatic and the mysterious is not reductive to scientific explanation, despite attempts to do so. Aspects of relationship intimacy, love, tenderness and generosity touch depths in us, often intuitively. These moments are not always open to analysis and yet feel vital parts of what it is to be human.

Using the phenomenological method in dialogue

The pioneering integrator of psychoanalysis and family systems, Nathan Ackerman, wrote in the first issue of *Family Process* : 'The moment we shift to the second conceptual model, a two or more person interaction, we have a true social experience: an interaction between two or more minds, as compared with patient and analyst recreating the symbiosis of one mind in the infant-parent union' (1962:41). The different 'true social experience' of a two-or-more mind interaction creates a very different open dialogue than that of analytic therapy. Earlier chapters of the book should have given a foretaste of this.

'Dialogue' is derived from ancient Greek words *dia* (meaning 'across' and 'through') and *logos* (meaning 'knowledge'), an exchange of meaning and knowledge through relationship. It holds rather more intent of exchanging ideas than 'conversation', and it is sometimes used inter-changeably with *dialectic*, a term again derived from ancient Greek, though this has a more specific meaning of the discourse in formal argument in which different positions are articulated and used to reach a better clarification. The term has been imported into therapy to define certain approaches, such as dialectical behavioural therapy.

The two principal aspects of phenomenological approach are ulti-mately derived from the history of philosophy from Plato's mentor, Socrates. He was, by Plato's account, the master of the dialectical process. He would invite an opponent to formulate a proposition or a definition. Through a series of questions he would deconstruct the truths of the proposition and invariably showed the limitations of the other's thinking, often to their professed incredulous appreciation. The strategies he used in his dialogues are those of the *epoche* and *maieutic*.

'I suspend judgement': the *epoche*

Husserl advocated that in order to disclose the full appearance of a phenomenon you had to 'put in brackets' any assumptions or emotional disposition you might hold about the nature of the other's experience, which is known as the *epoche*. Such a positioned stance would provide optimal conditions for seeing the emergent organization of that experience, with its processes, tendencies, patterns and value structures. Freud and Husserl were both pupils of the philosopher Franz Brentano (1838–1917) and took his teaching into different directions: Freud, into the practice of 'free association' and psychoanalysis; Husserl, influenced by the 'vitalism' of William James's 'stream of consciousness' from his 1890 publication, *The Principles of Psychology*. For both, the different and entwined levels of described experience could best be obtained by minimal intrusion, except to prompt clarification and greater depth to the accounts given by their subjects.

It is clear from the recent work of Sarah Bakewell (2010) that the sixteenth-century French essayist and free-thinker Montaigne had developed a similar method. He cultivated a position of ironic scepti-cism to all received truth in the search for better ones, in the spirit of Socrates' *'que sais-je?'* (what do I know?) and the Greek philosopher, Pyrrho:

> Pyrrhonians accordingly deal with all the problems life can throw at them by means of a single word which acts as shorthand for this manoeuvre: in Greek *epokhe*. It means 'I suspend judgment'. Or in a

different rendition given in French by Montaigne, je soutiens: 'I hold back'. This phrase conquers all enemies: it undoes them, so that they disintegrate into atoms before your eyes ... The Pyrrhonians did this not to unsettle themselves profoundly and throw themselves into a paranoid vortex of doubt but to obtain a condition of relaxation about everything. It was their path to ataraxia and thus to joy and flourishing. (2010: 124–5)

This setting-aside of all prior knowledge – 'all I know is that I know nothing' – is central to *epoche*, an idea popularized in recent therapy literature as the 'not-knowing position'. Such a stance involved suspending any hypotheses and judgements and reaching into the constructed narrative of another's experience and their truth and manner of presenting it. Husserl believed this was the most authentic, objective way to look at the experience of others. We construct the 'aboutness' of the world around us through our directed awareness towards perceived objects. Invariably we are drawn to what we know ('perception' follows 'conception') of 'objects', persons, places and things. Unexamined, this becomes our 'objective' knowledge, an absolute, hard-and-fast, taken-for-granted reality. What passes off as knowledge and opinion is thinly disguised habit or prejudice (literally 'prejudgement'), usually based on unreliable information. Dogmatic, fundamentalist thought and self-righteous moralizing are frequently the outcome. For example, in this circular observation of a bystander: 'Drinking to excess is crazy and weak-willed; only losers do it. Look at that guy across the road, drunk out of his head again. Such a spineless waste of space.'

Exercise 7.1: Setting aside our prejudices

Draw up a similar piece of self-justifying, circularly constructed argument about, e.g., the poor, bankers, or any kind of fundamentalist group or set of ideas that come to mind.

Setting aside assumptions helps the curious enquirer to see what lies behind first impressions or appearances (the *phainomenon*), to a different level of understanding. Phenomenologists have some communality with mystics, with their emphasis on the process of discovery through waiting for meaning to emerge (as George Fox, the founder of Quakerism, put it in a spiritual context: 'stand still in that which shows and discovers'). Tolstoy's character Pierre in *War and Peace* points to the relationship between condemning judgement and contextual knowledge; he contends that the more we know of the background situation and motivational pressures on a person, the less likely we are to judge severely.

It is intuitively waiting and feeling for the unformed to articulate itself. This hermeneutic process is the basis of developing appreciative, interpretative skills in the arts or the vexatious multiple meanings of scriptural texts. R.D. Laing based his family explorations in both clinical work and research on the use of *epoche*: 'We must first of all put this manoeuvre in brackets in the situation as we see it. Whether or not there was anything the matter with an elected scapegoat to begin with, there soon will be if this process continues. It is one of the most ancient, well documented, pervasive social processes known' (Laing, 2002: 4).

There is a contextual difference between the use of *epoche* for research and for therapy. The family comes for help in one case; the researcher for help in the other. Though the methodology may be the same, there is a different level of engagement and intention in trying to connect experientially with the distress. Both are looking for patterns: the researcher for information for wider and more general application, while the therapist searches for information to help the family develop resources for change.

Applying your understanding of *epoche* effectively is to be willing to embrace the full implication of its method and requires your open, attentive mind and free self-awareness. This is a highly demanding task which may carry some risk to you, and we again emphasize the importance of mentoring support. To listen attentively, suspending assumptions involves a capacity to embrace the instinctual forces of human nature through their presence and manifestation in yourself, as well as rational, discursive thought, and the intuitive and spiritual forces in human nature which are also embodied in you. As Rogers puts it: 'It includes communicating your sensings of his/her world as you look with fresh and unfrightened eyes at elements of which the individual is fearful. It means frequently checking with him as to the accuracy of your sensings and being guided by the responses you receive. You are a confident companion to the person in his inner world' (1980: 142)

The *maieutic* method: the experiential midwife

Socrates described the *maieutic* method as acting like a 'midwife' to facilitate the birth of the 'fullness of ideas'. Gradually, as Socrates developed his enquiry, so unrealized knowledge emerged through the dialogue. In the *Meno* (380 BC), Socrates demonstrates that Meno's slave boy, an uneducated child of 8, had an intrinsic ability to solve mathematical problems guided by Socrates' skill at 'bringing forth' his knowledge. The conclusion drawn is that the mind's capacity for thinking and knowing is hugely underdeveloped, and that consciousness has more depth and extensiveness than its possessor allows, or is credited with having.

Though Socrates used this method in a philosophical dialogue to disclose basic assumptions, the ancient Greeks used the 'drawing-out' of the *maieutic* function dramatically. From the interactional process in any given situation (and family dramas were generally the most potent), the secretly held memory gradually emerges. The concealment through shame and guilt is broken down by a *catharsis* which reaches beyond the taboos of tradition to the ontological inner truth of the 'soul'. With Oedipus' deconstruction of his origins and the trans-gressed social taboos, the drama moves to his 'blinding catharsis' in which he finally sees the truth of his background, but at the cost of his sight.

This process is apparent in modern drama from the discovery by Big Daddy in *Cat on a Hot Tin Roof* of the 'system of mendacity' surround-ing him and his terminal illness (Williams, 1955). This then liberates him to reveal his 'truth' to the family uncompromisingly. In the ritual requiem in the last act of *Who's Afraid of Virginia Woolf* (Albee, 1962), the fantasy baby 'Sonny Jim' is finally 'killed' in a brutally moving act of parallel emotional midwifery. The couple is left abandoned yet free with the possibility of designing another script. In each case, the explo-ration of truth is an experiential dialectic, though different from the deconstruction of a philosophical truth. These acts are powerfully unsettling and momentarily perilous and their participants are trans-formed in their own ways through the 'purging' of false conception and repressed passion. *Maieutic* method embraces a belief that there is a universal and archetypical knowledge stored in the human conscience, preserved in the wisdom of past generations and able to be actively 'drawn out' in a crisis of false knowledge, as in the popular idea of the 'wake-up call'.

In family therapy, it is important to use the *maieutic* method with sensitivity and some tenderness to help the family discover their unre-vealed experiential truths. This is not always through a catharsis, though latent feelings contained in the unsatisfactory relationships – the subscript – frequently emerge. The intention is to help them access their basic assumptions in order to replace them with ones that better serve their well-being.

Dialogue: the systemic phenomenology of multiple voices

Using the open curiosity of suspended judgement and bringing forth latent beliefs, feelings and intentions lie at the heart of the phenomenological method in drama research and therapy. However, what of the implications for the multiple voices contained and constrained in families? Can we have a systemic phenomenology? How can the strategising of *epoche* be made to work in the tightly knit social group of the family, with its many perspectives and strong desire to safeguard its privacy?

Achieving the open curiosity of *epoche* comes less easily when there is a two or more person system in the therapy system. We can easily be pulled into partiality and lose the free-floating attention to move from one experience to another. This can be exhilarating as well as terrifying. If you have truly attuned yourself to be comfortable with such free-floating attention you will find yourself moved between different truths, each of which convinces you of its validity, rather like a jury listening to the different pieces of evidence. However, your discerning abilities will not be asleep even if suspended for the moment, for you will be prompted to clarify and check out any inconsistencies or disjunctures.

The team is valuable in constantly challenging one's own default position which is essential to the effective maintenance of *epoche*. When the therapy system gets stuck in the family's fixed constructions and creative flow is lost, change via dialogue, compromise or negotiation seems impossible. It is as though a group of jazz musicians suddenly finds itself unable to improvise. Sometimes the family atmosphere feels tense with an undercurrent of violence; their constructions will not permit anything but a 'game without end' or 'game to the finish' and certain traits the participants demonstrate tend to escalate (e.g. pride, obduracy and the will to power). Compromise and agreement are constructed as capitulation or defeat in the relational 'war'.

Such a state of oppositional symmetry, with its exchange of negative attribution and invalidation of the other's experience, creates an experiential *invalid*. Laing and Esterson's (1964) book abounds with vignettes of such experiential disqualifications, while family process abounds in personalized invalidations. All social groups and organizations operate such powerful dynamics of experiential disqualification, indeed, this is their most toxic and potent power (as indeed is the converse to heal and validate). It is challenging to work in a climate where the adversities seem to dominate the virtues. However, the creativity and ingenuity of many family and systemic therapists and the widely available literature, cataloguing different ways through a mired process, usually help to find a fresh resource.

The early formulations of the Milan Associates essentially developed a family systemic-phenomenological approach; the *epoche* was termed 'neutrality' (Milan Associates, 1980), and later 'curiosity' (Cecchin, 1987). There was also an awareness of the circularity of information, and the free-floating attention from one family member's perception and experience to another's. Attention sometimes lingers on a particular experience and then moves on freely, like jazz musicians in a jam session. The movement can be between different family members, different team members and between different parts of both system. Charles O'Leary recently describes this process as 'multi-directional partiality' (2011).

Attempting to integrate the work of the non-psychotherapist Gregory Bateson with psychoanalysis and psychiatry, the Milan Associates developed 'circular questioning' (Fleuridas et al., 1986; Brown, 1997) or 'interventive interviewing' (Tomm, 1987a; 1987b; 1988) and produced a highly effective way of *maieutic* inquiry. In the process they decodified Laing and Esterson's (1964) family processes, the relational muddles in Laing's *Knots* (1970) and provided a reliable therapeutic way of disentangling communicational confusion (Hills, 2004). In the next chapter we will look more closely at how dialogue may be deconstructed using the circularity of systemic phenomenology.

Summary

- Phenomenology and symbolic interactionalism are explained.
- The self is a system that constitutes the world, through our subjectivity is proposed.
- The five dimensions of self-experience are described.
- A case of a whole anxiety-activated family system is described.
- The historical origins of phenomenology and its use in Roger's and Laing's work are summarized.
- The two pillars of phenomenological method, the *epoche* and *maieutic* processes, are discussed.
- Adapting the method to a whole family system in the creation of a systemic phenomenology is explored.
- The connection with circular questioning developed by the Milan Associates is described.

8

DIALOGUE ANALYSIS: SCRIPTS AND SUBSCRIPTS

Deconstructing dialogue

The nineteenth-century American transcendental philosopher Henry Thoreau said of the authentic communication of truth that 'it takes two people to speak the truth; one to speak it, the other to hear it' (1849). All therapy, like all human exchange, is a dialogue. In fact, all thinking is a dialogue with oneself, with imagined or long distant or barely remembered 'internalized others' 'joining' the conversation. Our thinking is built on long processes of retaining in the mind presences, influential ideas and beliefs whose exact origins we cannot remember, but which become the thoughts and beliefs over which we stake ownership. Ideas and beliefs are always derived from minds that have conceived and constructed them, even if those people have long since died. Thinking is a relationally derived process.

Words are the straw and clay from which language, the bricks of thinking, are put together in the grandest or modest architecture of systemic ideas. Each language is unique to its cultural roots, to its own family vernacular, the *terroir* from which it grows and cross-fertilizes with other social class linguistic codes, whilst remaining particular to its local origins. Language can dress ideas up in a million guises to make the reality and intention the thought is seeking to communicate more or less palatable, exhilarating, alarming, or just bothersome. The different choice of words can have very different effects, therefore intention is crucial in their selection.

The statement 'these are all misleading statements' elicits a very different response in the reader to 'these are all very thoughtful statements'. Intentions and effects go together. It is not just the language that communicates but the tone and inflections in its delivery. So the expression, 'Well, I'm utterly appalled', said with anger, clenched teeth and squinting eyes, has a very different experiential feel to the same phrase delivered with a self-mocking, ironic tone, exaggerated look and twinkling eyes. Understanding the nuances of language and the specific cultural associations of gestures, intonation in delivery is something that must be attended to carefully, especially in therapy. If in doubt, check out the meaning with their user. Language can be used by the therapist to intensify or dampen down, to inspire or to soothe. Words, language and thought can also exist in the sometimes artless form of a spontaneous and unreflected response, 'a raid on the inarticulate ... in the general mess of imprecision of feeling', as the poet T.S. Eliot put it (1958: 31), or sometimes in the artful utility of human expertise, whether that of the lawyer, the salesperson, the propagandist, the advertiser, the poet, the parent or the healer. Much of the work of the therapist is to seek greater precision of feeling and help to give voice to what has hitherto lain unspoken.

Facilitating dialogue in family and systems therapy is central to the whole enterprise, as we have stressed. Because it operates in the three simultaneous dimensions of person, relationship and system it is complex and demanding. Individual therapy has an important collaborative place in helping to strengthen, clarify and validate the personal perspective of a family member, which the power of family group process may have habitually undermined. Generally it is important that this is done in close conjunction with family or relationship work to avoid splitting and the formation of exclusive alliances, which undermine the open feedback process of family process work. The implicit aim of this kind of therapeutic approach is to give confidence and empower all family members through safe experimentation with openly expressed communication.

The model does not seek the creation of long-term attachment or to disentangle the so-called transference distortions. From the beginning the therapists and team attempt to identify the potential relational basis of the unarticulated emotional energies. The genogram and direct observations in the session of interactional tensions are the material for this. All the work is attempted via conjoint dialogue with the family.

We saw in the last chapter how to apply the principles of the systemic phenomenological method to help create the right mindful and emotional conditions for developing the family's descriptions through dialogue. We must now look more closely at how to draw out the less understood meanings and hidden elements of experience, as well as how to analyse live dialogue, therefore being able as an active therapeutic participant to join the 'call and response' of co-scripting. Sometimes this also involves just sitting back and observing the family working out their own connections that lead on to a different experience with one another. **Script analysis** is an essential part of training for family and systems therapy, involving recording and examining dialogue so that this process becomes second nature in the consciousness, accompanied by facility and depth of interactive response.

We have already introduced the idea of 'script' in Chapter 1 in showing how you might use these ideas to explore your own genogram. Taking the example of writing a play, a completed script must contain four elements: the circumstantial script, the assumptive scripts, the delivered script and the undelivered subscript. Families, of course, are both actors and playwrights of the immediate; they improvise with each other according to the particular situation in ways that are difficult for the outsider to appreciate. However, the **circumstantial script** is the 'storyboard' background of events, their history; the whole situational context from which the participants derive their thinking and responses. Working with families, the genogram sets the scene for the family story, past and present. The **assumptive scripts** are the total set of attitudinal beliefs and emotional attitudes each person has to one another and their roles and relationships beyond therapy in the world outside. In drama this is usually called their character. There are many examples of this in the Individual Psychology of Alfred Adler, with its echoes of John Byng-Hall's script theory:

> Unhappy experiences in childhood may be given quite opposite meaning. One man with unhappy experiences behind him will not dwell on them except as they show him something that can be remedied for the future. He will feel 'We must work to remove such unfortunate situations and see our children are in better places.' Another will say 'Life is unfair. Other people always have the best of it. If the world treated me like that, why shouldn't I treat the world any better … I had to suffer just as much when I was a child and I came through it. Why shouldn't they?' A third man will feel 'Everything should be forgiven me because of my unhappy childhood.' In the actions of all three men their interpretations will be evident. They will never change their actions unless they change their interpretations. (1958: 209)

A dramatist and family-orientated therapist look at the family system as a whole, how it configures itself and how it believes it is doing so. The **delivered script** includes the actual words exchanged between family members and, of course, the therapist. This is the vehicle of communication from which the assumptive script emerges, sometimes by inference, sometimes explicitly. It is the means by which information is shared through language, emotional tone and body language. In seeking ways of deepening the descriptions, the therapists seek clarifications of the family's assumptions.

The **subscript** is the undelivered and unexpressed, the inarticulacies which have not found a voice. This can be for a number of reasons: concerns for safety (their expression believed to potentially damage already fragile relationships and persons in the family) and apprehension (they may not have been clearly formulated), or may be non-conscious (containing deeply felt wishes, longings, sorrows and anxieties). Open speculative empathy as to the unexpressed nature of the subscript is at the heart of the therapeutic art, in sensing frustration and distress, as well as wishes and desires, and help bring them into life *maieutically*. This involves risk-taking by the therapist and is usually done tentatively at first by checking out and, if well received, can be delivered again with greater conviction. If denied, it may be reintroduced in a different form at a later time if the therapist feels certain of its importance as a situational truth.

Practising the circularity of phenomenological enquiry

Having taken the family through their genogram, you will have begun to ask questions which arise naturally from the exchanges. However, you will have prepared some areas of enquiry at the outset. This process is the basic circularity of phenomenological enquiry. It has pattern and structure and is not a random narrative exchange that, however absorbing and fascinating, can become more maze than labyrinth. Constructing questions, like Ariadne's thread, will help you, steer a way through the labyrinthine nature of the family's experience.

Exercise 8.1: Practising different questions

Let's take a simple example of a four-part family scenario. The problem is less important than the focus, which is on the interface between the family's delivered script and your own. Sophie (14) has been drinking while underage and has not been coming home on some nights. She's from a traditional nuclear family of father David

→

(44), mother Jane (42) and brother Jack (16). Remember the 'spect-actor' duality. Each person in the family is both agent (actor) and observer (spectator) of the others. Phenomenological knowledge need not be gained directly from the subject themselves but circularly from others through this means. Remember, too, that questions can be statements, trialled prescriptions to different connections, choices and solutions.

Questions can centre on **comparative (more than/less than) descriptions** which seek an evaluation by referencing one person's experience against another's in the family. The quest for evaluation is even-handed from each family subject:

> *Example* (to mother): 'Who do you think is most worried about Sophie's behaviour? Who least worried?'

'Other-observer' questions about emotional responses which seek an evaluation of how the responder thinks another in the family feels. This both tests and makes mindful in the family the experience of empathy:

> *Example* (to brother): 'How do you think Sophie feels when your Dad has a go at her?'

'Other' questions about cognitive responses which seek evaluation and information about the thought process of a different family subject:

> *Example* (to mother): 'Jane, what do you think is in your husband's mind when he has a go at Sophie?'

Checking-out, feedback questions use the gathered informational responses to elicit the perspective of the temporary focus subject of the enquiry theme:

> *Example* (to father):' David, you've heard what Jack and Jane think about what you're trying to communicate to Sophie by having a go at her, and how they think she feels. What do you think?'

Relationship questions seek commentary, not on content issues, but on relational process issues, easily overlooked by the subjects them-selves in the anxiety to get difficulties 'fixed' and family tensions reduced:
$\rightarrow$

Example (to Sophie): 'Since you've been experiencing these difficulties, have you noticed any change in relationships in the family? How would you describe them, then?'

Solution-invited questions seek to acknowledge in the face of other acknowledged connecting tensions some positive potential energy that could start to make a difference. These also suggest and encourage the family to trust to more of their own thinking.

Example (to Jack): 'We've heard from Sophie that Mum and Dad have often fallen out about things but that it's got worse since she's been having difficulties. What would you like to see them doing differently that might improve the situation, or don't you think it can improve?'

Explanatory-hunch questions an invitation to members of the family (or the family collectively) to use their own theorizing and intuition (and implicitly trust their own expertise not the oracular expert's):

Example (to David): 'What's your personal hunch about why Sophie has been experiencing difficulties right now?'

Whole-family wish questions invite a bit of 'magical thinking' and release the imaginative resources of vision and hope. There should not necessarily be an expectation that this will make a difference, but it is a further invitation to the family to dream, not just distress:

Example (to all): 'We've heard there's a lot of concern for one another in the family, but things tend to go round and round. How would each of you like things to be?'

Solution-invited, reality-testing and comparative questions carry on in the magical thinking of imaginative resourcefulness but grounding it in the quest to identify a small fragment of achievable action for change:

Example (to all): What small thing would each of you have to do differently to achieve this? Could you do it? Who is least/most likely to try this?

→

There are many variants of these questions, most of which should build on the feedback from the family. It is useful to be clear in your own mind how you want to structure a question and who you want to direct it to. Since all will be listening, the replies elicit comments from others. This is the value of the *epoche* mindset of the therapist and the *maieutic* effect the freely moving inquiry has on the consciousness of the family.

Exercise 8.2: Developing your questioning techniques

Imagine a family of three attending a session. Tom (23) is a young adult struggling with strong feelings of depression; Trevor (56) is his father and Becky (25), Tom's sister, has come to support her brother's search for help. All you know is that their mother Siân (55) died a year ago after a brief illness. You may have an idea that this could be a strong influential factor in Tom's depression, however, you should not allow this to organize your thinking, and the priority is to create an open dialogue at all the phenomenological levels of the family experience. Develop a list of at least 20 questions that help lead them into describing that experience and its many different personal and collective levels. Again, be clear and specific to whom you are addressing each question, and try to keep specifically to encouraging their descriptive, narrative abilities. You can add refining interventions that seek difference and change later as you build up the collective narrative. Here are some suggestions to check with afterwards.

> *Therapist to Tom* (personally directed inquiry): 'Tom, describe for us if you can what this depression feels like and when it seems to be at its worst.'
>
> *To Becky* (personally directed observer question): 'How do you experience Tom's depression? Is there anything different you see in watching it from close up?'
>
> *To Trevor* (personally directed observer question): 'And what about you, Trevor, how would you describe Tom's depression? Has anything he and Becky have just said come as a surprise to you?'
>
> *To all* (system-directed question): 'How do you think things are for you as a family at the moment? Does the way Tom is experiencing his life have any echoes for the whole family?'

To all (system-directed question, looking for virtuous exceptions to distressed adversity): 'How much do you do things together that help to lift Tom and your spirits?'

To all (system-directed speculation, followed by a question): 'I do know that you all lost Siân, your mother (looks at Tom and Becky), and your wife (looks at Trevor) recently. This must have been as sad as it was overwhelming and almost unbearable.'

To Trevor (personally directed comparative question): "Who do you think was most affected by that, Trevor?'

To Tom and Becky (personally directed response question): 'Your Dad thinks you both were, Tom and Becky, equally. What does each of you think about that?'

To Tom (relationship question): 'Do you think losing your mum has brought some of you closer together, or does the grief just seem unbearable at moments? Who do you think it has made closer?'

To Becky (confirmation and clarification questions): 'Do you think Tom's right about that? Anything different you want to add? What about you, Trevor?'

To Trevor (personally directed system enquiry): 'Can you tell me a little about how you keep the memory of your wife alive in each other's minds in the face of such hurt and pain? Who do you think is the best at doing that?'

To Becky (responds to follow Trevor's reply): 'So you, Becky, Dad thinks does this best. He says you are the best comforter, though he does try?'

To Tom (personally directed question) 'Becky says she thinks you're pretty good at keeping the memory of you Mum alive but (reflection) I wonder if you find it hardest of all to take comfort from anyone in the family about Mum's loss? Do you find it possible to find this outside the family, with friends, perhaps?'

Looked at in the starkness of print, this may read rather like a research questionnaire. It is important to bring it alive in the way you listen and attend to the family members with interest, empathy and warmth in such a context of loss and depression, and draw out, evenhandedly, with 'sustained voluntary attention', as William James called it (1890, I:9), the different layers of personal and interrelational meanings and the organizing emotional state in the whole system. In this phenomenological search you are also looking for traces of the virtues of well-being and re-presenting them to the family. The point at this stage is to develop the material present in the emerging dialogue, not to impose interpretations on them, except by tentatively suggesting experiential connections.

As a conductor of the dialogue, the analogy of the helmsman, the mythical boatman of the Styx who gave his named role to cybernetics, is a good one. The helmsman is one who manoeuvres between the cross-currents of differences in attitude, mood, character, activity and belief but steers the travellers to a better destination than the one of myth.

An extract of family dialogue

Let us look this time at a brief extract of family dialogue from a family session. Much family dialogue follows a well-worn pathway, whose twists, turns and predictable outcomes are familiar to the family. There is comfort in the familiarity of its patterns, rules and homeostatic balances keeping it in check from becoming dangerous or stale, some compensation for the frustration of not being able to change it. Hatred and hostility can be powerful drivers where families feel stuck in co-dependency with one another. All families have such psychic mechanisms, or 'checks and balances', though the tiny minority that do not can be exceeding dangerous in releasing unmediated destructiveness.

Sometimes the delivered script is explicit, barbed, provocative and reactive, seeking release of frustrations and issuing warnings to others in the system. Sometimes this is a repetitive script, full of habitual redundancies known to the family but not to the therapists. In some cases it is subjugated, inexpressive, giving no clue as to what is thought or felt. Whether explosive, or tacit and controlled, there is always a **subscript**, the existence of an emotionally defensive substratum that may not be articulated because of anxiety about worse consequences or aspirational disappointment. The paradox of high-expressive emotional families is that the defensive substratum is present, though they present as if it were not; that aggression is the best form of defence.

R.D. Laing, writing in 1969, could see the clear parallels between drama and family discourse: 'We can just glimpse in this family a drama perpetuated over three generations ...The play's the thing. The actors come and go. As they die, others are born. The new born enters the part vacated by the newly dead' (2002: 4). He was also acutely conscious, with David Cooper, author of *The Death of the Family* (1974), just how destructive to individuation, personal safety and mental health such family dramas could be. Like Cooper, he was not able to formulate an adequate treatment method for such family processes, however.

Below is family dialogue recorded from a session at Mount Zeehan, in Canterbury, formerly a NHS-pioneering treatment centre for alcohol dependency. It took place between Cherie (21), a recovering heroin addict and her father Carl (44), a recovering alcoholic. Both had received sustained periods of individual therapy, which had made a difference. Her sisters Marie (19) and Jane (14) and mother Teri (41) also attended. The genogram had helped the therapists' team form a strong alliance with the family and revealed elements of the basic experiential script. Their exchanges had an honest, raw vitality tempered with care. The talk flowed spontaneously, with very little need for intervention by the therapists. Cherie leads this dialogue, so it is her assumptive script which dominates, but the muted responses to it suggests it contained widely shared assumptions.

CASE STUDY 8.1: CHERIE AND CARL

Cherie: 'Your drinking, though. It was horrible.'

Carl: 'Yeah, I know.'

Cherie: 'You don't like me when I've been on gear for the whole two and a half years [reminding her father of his experience of her 'addictive' experience]. Yeah, for a couple of months we'd all be all right, then "bang" the whole house would be smashed up. (To father) Do you know what I mean? Staying at Uncle Brian's at birthdays and Christmases and that. It has an effect on other people [reminding her father about to the background of the circumstantial script and her and other's experience of his addiction].'

Carl: (appealing to wife) 'It's only been once or twice, hasn't it?'

Cherie: 'No, Dad, it hasn't been once or twice. It's been a lot of times.' [emphasis on the facts of the situation]

Teri: (emboldened) 'It has been a lot of times.' [supporting the circumstantial script]

Cherie: (with rising indignation) 'For three Christmases we were all meant to be together. It's never happened because you used to get pissed up all the time, Dad. (Marie and Jane look at her with silent endorsement) Look, we've had two Christmases as a family out of how many Christmases when you've not been drunk?' (silence in the group) [powerful statement of an assumptive script, a spoken heartfelt truth]

Cherie: (warming to the task) 'Even when we was at primary and secondary school Mum used to come in and say, "Cherie and Marie

→

have got appointments at the dentist." It was 'cos you had an argument and couldn't be with us. Like we've been down Uncle Bri's and stuck in the attic. You know what I mean? (looking to mother for endorsing support). Like Jane, why is she the way she is? 'Cos it affected her. It's affected me. It ain't just this. It's being with Darren [Jane's former boyfriend] as well.'

Carl: (calmly and pointedly) 'So all my drinking has actually made you a heroin addict, then?' [movement from defensive position to attacking one]

Cherie: 'No, I'm not saying that. I'm just saying it's had an effect on me, all them times we've had to do that. It's had an effect on me, like scars. The only way for me to deal with that is by going to counselling and sort me head out. [able to have help to articulate her subscript] Then I've had all the answers for what I always wondered when we were kids and when I asked you questions and that. When I go to counselling I start to answer my own questions and that's when I get back on track. (Carl nods knowingly as if connecting with something in her experience). I ain't blaming you, Dad, for all of that. I ain't blaming you that I'm a heroin addict. It affects other people. Do you know what I mean?'

Carl: 'Yeah, I do, mate.'

Cherie:'It affects all people differently.'

Teri: (to Carl, meekly and compliantly) 'I don't want you to sit there blaming yourself.'

Carl: 'Er?'

Teri: 'We're not all blaming you. It's all down to circumstance. It's not anybody's fault.'

Cherie: 'It's just my opinion (motioning to sisters). They might have a different opinion. It's like you and your Mum. You think you blame your Mum for some stuff in the past, don't you?'

Carl: 'I blame her for letting it happen, but I forgive her.'

Cherie: 'Exactly, I blame Mum for going back to you.' [relational pattern in the assumptive script]

Teri: 'She says if I had left you she wouldn't be in that situation.'

Within the dialogue there are a number of different communications, operating across one another and producing various emotional reactions. There are no 'raids on the inarticulate' here, for Cherie wants to berate her father for the disruption his drinking caused to her and to the whole family. Looking across to her sisters, she clearly believes she is acting as an advocate for them too. Their silent assent encourages her further. Her mother's failure to separate from Carl also comes in for voiced dissention,

→

but nothing on the scale of that towards her father. Carefully, she avoids directly blaming him for her own struggles to come off heroin but she articulates a 'soft' connection with the unregulated distress and conflict in the family and her own journey through dependency. There are implications of a three-generational failure to properly nurture, a basic script of familial conflict, neglect and inattention that has been repeated in addictive behaviour, but also reparation sought through understanding, honest exchanges, acceptance of personal responsibility and corrective behaviour.

Her father, though slightly disconcerted by the attack on his drinking, does not deflect or excuse. He invites her to blame him for her struggle against addiction, which she resists. Teri offers what can only be described as a rather sentimental and inauthentic attempt to reassure Carl it is circumstance not choice. She sounds to have replicated a pattern between Carl and his mother. In structural terms, the family at time of crisis has no effective executive function; the father had vacated it through alcohol misuse and the mother through indecision and conflict of loyalties. Cherie, the executive role spokesperson in childhood and adolescence, comes into that role formidably in this exchange. Partly as result of this session, Carl and Teri decided to work with the team as a couple, with a good outcome regarding their more open, respectful communication. Listening to the exchanges, it was difficult not to feel the powerful subscript drawing everyone into the encounter. This was about the sorrow and disappointment at the closer times that could have been and a sense of being cheated of a childhood. Though Cherie articulates this, both Carl and Teri share the guilt rather than anger at the lost possibilities that come from the emotional unavailability that addictions bring with them. Cherie's own transformed awareness of this seems to act as a spur for her to want the whole family to share in the acknowledged understanding of this truth.

The family-script process and the experience it engenders in therapy with the interplay of assumptions, beliefs and feelings has been well described by Harold Pinter's acceptance speech for the Nobel Prize for Literature (2005):

But the real truth is that there is never such thing as one truth to be found in dramatic art. There are many. These truths challenge each other, recoil from each other, reflect each other, ignore each other, tease each other, are blind to each other. Sometimes you feel you have the truth of a moment in your hand, and then it slips away through your fingers and is lost. (2005: video transcript)

However, the difference is that the curiosity of the therapeutic enquiry draws out the dialogue and enables selective attention to elements of the exchanges that can lead to more productive thinking.

Some guiding principles of script analysis and commentary

It takes time and practice to feel able to give accurate, empathic and immediate therapeutic feedback in the midst of a family dialogue. This may be difficult enough in the growing climate of rapid case through-put and 'box-ticking intervention'. It is also difficult in a one-to-one dialogue, so working to co-script the dialogue of a family who are, if nothing else, experts in their own script exchanges, is even more challenging. It can feel like plunging into a fast-flowing stream, which without proper anchorage can easily create an apprehension of being swept away. However, there are certain guiding principles which should be held in mind.

First, the value of co-working gives time to orientate yourself to the attitudinal beliefs, perceptions, emotions and behaviours of the particular family. You can take an observational break whilst your partner takes over. It is important to work at the pace you can process. Expect to get it wrong at times and in places, but always be openly encouraging for the family to correct you, so you have 'got it' accurately.

Secondly, be sure you have understood the personal attitudes of belief, perception, emotion and behaviour (the personal assumptive script), the differences between the personal assumptive scripts and how they seem to fit together (the systemic assumptive script). This will be done tentatively at first until you have engaged the family more fully.

Thirdly, try out your understanding with the family. This is a familiar process in individual counselling and has many names such as 'reflecting back', 'précised feedback', or 'position summary'. It is essential to do this regularly, in part as a safe default position for you and the family, so you do not feel disorientated in the informational flow and powerful counter-reactions coming your way. As with individual work, it is a sign to the family that you are actively listening and seeking to gain some purchase on their experience. It thus encourages them that you are trying to get alongside them and grapple with their difficult reality; that you have credibility and sincerity in the search for solutions and ways through. If you are open to your own 'que sais-je/ what do I know?' the family will help you get the position right and clearer, so there'd no need to feel your efforts have to be exact or perfect. The quest for perfection in such communicational interchanges is a disabling distraction. Try to extend your understanding to the whole family each time you reflect back. Having a reflecting team makes this task easier, for the obvious reason that the labour is divided and difference an active ingredient.

It is good training to do this frequently, and in particular when the family presents their situation you should experience all the characteristics of their impasse, and indeed join them in it. Recapitulation is always an important element in problem-solving, whether it is in mathematics, knitting or following an unknown route from a map. You can reflect back to the family something like this:

I'm/we're getting a very clear sense, Jones family, of how you're all finding the current situation impossible. You Tom [son] seem unable to manage your drug use at the moment; you, Tina [Mum] are driven to distraction by worry about him and have some health worries of your own; whilst you Jim [Dad] just get angry with him and his seeming inability to see the effects on the wider family; you also feel at a loss to know how to support Tina with her worries. Is that how it seems? So 'Mission Difficult', but not quite 'Mission Impossible'?

This may then release some different energy lurking unrealized in the system once the narrative of near-impossibility has been heard.

Fourthly, besides following the content of the script exchanges you will also be visually following the movements between people and the physical space they occupy in relationship to each other. It was an early requirement of practising structural therapy in the 1970s and 1980s that you had to move the seating arrangements in the session, with some reflection about why you were doing so. This is no longer considered necessary, but it was an important training in observation, seeing who sat next to whom and the postures they struck in conjunction with the content flow of dialogue. It is informational 'grist to the mill' and you might want to use it in reflecting back: 'I noticed you seem to turn away from Dad, Tom, whenever he starts to speak and you're sitting as far from him as you can. Are you trying to tell him something that's more difficult to say? Can we guess what it might be?'

The same applies to being attentively aware of the tone of voice, lapsed vocalizations and vocal emphases. This provides a different kind of information, called 'analogic communication' in the classic text *Pragmatics of Human Communication* (Watzlawick, Beavin Bavalas & Jackson, 1967) and will give clues and cues to the subscript.

Fifthly, as you feel yourself growing in confidence and proficiency in working with the innumerable differences of family situations and assumptive scripts you will begin to trust yourself to provide a commentary that addresses their unspoken subscript: their disappointments, longing for peace or closeness, aggressive feeling of injustice, and so on. You will feel more able to use your direct experience in the reflection back and commentary, as in: 'Jim I can feel your quiet rage in the room, so I wonder how Tom and Tina experience it at home at moments?', or 'Tom, I can feel your sense of helplessness over this drug use and, I will say it, the kick you get from using drugs. It feels as if a part of you doesn't want to give it up, because if you gave up the highs from it you feel there's not much else in your life for you? Tell me if I'm way off beam over that.' Similarly, 'Tina, it is really difficult sitting with you and not feeling a sense of your great sadness and despair over things and not finding much consolation from those you love that helps you feel better.' These counter-reactions are the very basic material of human connection in therapy, joining both the particular conditions of persons in the family, their systemic collectivity and the condition of being human. At all times it is important to be accurate, inclusive and balanced between the competing perspectives without allying to any except through such empathic reflections that come from your counter-reactions. However, once the secure alliance is in place you may choose to intensify or unbalance the homeostasis in the family for a specific therapeutic purpose before returning to the default position of attentive curiosity. Sometimes midwives require the expectant mother to push harder.

Exercise 8.3: Reflecting on scripts

Find a DVD or CD of a film or play that you really enjoy. Select five minutes of interactive dialogue. It need not be a heated or passionate interaction, though it should be an exchange of personal difference. Summarize each character's attitudinal, behavioural and emotional stance on a piece of paper and a sense of how they experience the different positions of the other(s). Then imagine they are seated in front of you listening to what you have just observed. Reflect back your understanding of their different positions and, if you feel you can, on the basis of enough reliable knowledge from the drama, reflect back elements of the situation (the circumstantial script) and how you think that might be affecting their positions and interplay. Reflect back on your experience of witnessing their drama (your counter-reactions) and any sense of apprehension or optimism about the

→

outcome of those exchanges. It is largely the function that a chorus in ancient Greek drama fulfilled, though you are practising it essentially as a therapeutic tool.

Take some time out to do the same with a couple or part of a family you are working with, and get their consent to record a session (you will also need managerial consent for this from your agency before you start). Be very specific about the uses to which you intend to put it. Examine about 5–10 minutes of dialogue in a similar way to that suggested above. Think of ways you can use what you have practised alone in the next session and try it out. It may help to preface this with 'Studying the recording you kindly agreed to me making last time, I have come up with a number of ideas I'd like to share with you …'.

This will be part of your training on a family and systemic therapy course, but there is always a need to practise your skill and become more proficient. It is essential to have a systemically trained supervisor to help you develop a greater range of script analysis. You should try to practise this at least once a fortnight, whatever the pressure of other work. It is important to instil this discipline into your routine so you begin to feel less swamped by the demands of the work. If you can't find a supervisor, a like-minded peer to act as a 'learning buddy' and who is training in systemic practice is a useful alternative.

Case study 8.2: Malcolm and Joan

We will now look at some work carried out in an older adult mental health service. There is no transcript here, but a summary at the end of the very different assumptive scripts and their difficult coexistence. The case summary is in the form of a Laingian-type 'knot' as part of a training presentation. You are urged to study Laing's *Knots* (1970) to get a feel for the experiential realism of relationship entanglements, which seem endless and, sometimes, lacking in warmth or intimacy.

This work is based on a therapeutic dialogue over four sessions with a couple and our team. There was plenty of dialogue but no 'synthesis' between their two different positions, at least not at the beginning of the work. Both were in their sixties, married for over 40 years, with grandchildren. Malcolm was originally referred for an assessment, having shown signs of some cognitive impairment. He and Joan were referred for an assessment for couple work as there were also relational and health difficulties. Malcolm was tested independently midway between our four sessions and there was evidence of early-onset Alzheimer's. The subsequent couple session revealed him to be in surprisingly good spirits after receiving this news. The team worked with Malcolm and Joan, using a phenomenological approach to encourage them to describe their relationship.

Malcolm had been brought up in a rural, working-class family that worked the land. The youngest of three brothers, his mother died when he was 5 and his main carers were his father and elder brother. He would get very tearful recalling his early life. He worked in a local factory, and was a fitness fanatic (his wife's description), working out regularly throughout his life and cycling compulsively. As would be expected he was well-built and muscular, in contrast with his frailer looking wife. He had been successfully treated for alcohol dependency seven years previously and had had an affair with a local woman, which ended when Joan discovered it.

Joan had been diagnosed with a serious life-threatening condition some four years previously, which required regular medical follow-up. She walked with a stick and was sometimes in great pain. For all that she remained positive about herself and cheerful. She would get angry and distressed recalling Malcolm's affair, and berated him for this and the fact that he never finished DIY jobs around their home, finding every pretext to be out cycling or watching soccer with his friends. Both expressed affection for each other and for their two children and grandchildren; however, as you will see below, there were many caveats. The interlocking 'knots' of the assumptive scripts of their different positions emerged as follows:

Malcolm declares he loves Jean above all others.
He thinks she does not believe him.

Jean believes Malcolm would not get aggressive with her if he loved her. She believes unless she nagged him to finish tasks he wouldn't do anything.

Malcolm believes he would not get aggressive with Jean if she stopped nagging.
He believes she can't stop nagging him or start trusting him.

Jean believes Malcolm would not go out cycling to avoid her so often if he loved her.
He believes if she had not been so ill he would not have to go out so often.

Jean believes if she had not been so ill and Malcolm really loved her he would not have needed to have had an affair.
He believes she just doesn't understand the effect his mother's death had on him at the age of 5.

Malcolm believes he has always needed a mother.
Jean believes she'd rather be a wife to him than a mother.

Jean does not believe losing his mother as a child excuses his behaviour.
Malcolm is silent but then says exercise, meeting people and loving her is important to him.

Jean believes Malcolm avoids being close to everyone in the family.
He is very relieved he had a diagnosis of early onset of dementia so he can go out cycling regularly as the doctor advised.

Jean is quietly philosophical about her condition and their situation but wants some joy in sharing with Malcolm what remains of her life.
He is quietly rejoicing that now he doesn't have to change anything about himself, it's official!

The opportunity to discuss their differences openly came as a great relief to them. By the end Malcolm was showing Joan more consideration and she was more accepting of his character as it was and made fewer critical comments about him, tempering them with more humour. He used more humour about himself and ceased using self-excusing beliefs. Both seemed more accepting of the nature of their relationship and able to enjoy the parts of it which were mutually companionable. These changes the couple brought about themselves with no behavioural tasks except some chiding humour about Malcolm's ambivalence to DIY around the home. The context of the setting, the exploration and reflections of the different elements in their shared scripts from the therapists and team helped them to change enough of their experience to make a difference. Malcolm went on to join an Alzheimer's support group where he was reported to be an energizing presence with his humour and seeming acceptance of the nature of his medical condition.

The skills required for dialogue, script analysis and co-scripting fresh experiential interchanges are the abilities to: listen accurately and attentively; précis the emotional and belief content of each contribution to the dialogue and feed that back; seek new and unused openings that assist the individuals and the collective family to bring new energy and values of well-being to the experience of distress and adversity; in short, bring hope. The therapy should, through the relationship, be able to provide the core qualities that patients value most: 'being respected, being cared for, being understood' (Miller, Duncan & Hubble, 1997: 124). Attention needs to be paid to the unspoken qualities of the subscript and to non-verbal communication. All this requires constant practice in order to develop your experience. At all times the patients' abilities for autonomous thought, solution-finding and feelings should be validated. They also need to be skilfully challenged at times, to help raise their aspirations and confidence in their own ability to effect change, or a more genuine acceptance of what is beyond agency.

Summary

- The elements of the family script are described – circumstantial, assumptive, delivered and interactional and subscript.
- Examples of different types of questions that establish the *maieutic* circularity of a systemic phenomenological approach are given.
- An exercise is given to help you develop your own questioning, with options given afterwards.
- A direct piece of family dialogue is presented and analysed in terms of the different elements of the script and subscript.
- Five guiding principles to script analysis and commentary are given.
- An exercise is outlined to practise script analysis and commentary based on transcribing an extract from drama or film.
- A second case is described and the interwoven assumptive scripts are presented in the form of a Laingian knot.
- The creation of a good alliance, safe environment and actualizing 'being respected, being cared for, being understood' is emphasized.

9

CHANGE AND THE INFLUENTIAL
ART OF THERAPY

So, when and how is a systemic-based approach helpful?

John Bowlby's contention that 'we see, furthermore, that to attain the end of a secure, contented and co-operative community in which parents can give love and security to their children enabling them to grow up to be stable and contented people, able to sustain and further a just and friendly society, no one point in the circle is more vital than another' (1949: 297) implies a degree of certainty of positive outcome through use of a circular understanding and intervention. Bowlby was privately convinced of its efficacy. So, for example, to the question, 'In what kinds of problematical situations might a family and systemic approach be helpful?', the explicit answer is 'Every one.' Equally, to the question, 'How many of its methods can be used at any one time?', the answer is 'As many or as few as can be applied.' To the question as to whether it has to be carried out with a reflecting team, a one-way mirror and a recording facility, the answer is no. To the question as to whether it is a method of assessment or treatment, the answer is both. To the question as to which agency settings are best suited for its use, health social care and voluntary sector, the answer is all. As the developmental history of family and systemic therapy suggests, taking Bowlby's view of good outcomes at face value does require specific thinking and applied technique of the kind we have sought to demonstrate in this book.

Systemic orientated thinking and intervention has a contribution to make to every aspect of the human services professions; the only limitation is the organization's awareness of its usefulness and support for its staff to develop their skills in using it. Recently the social services department of the London Borough of Hackney embraced systemic informed practice wholesale under the title 'Social Work Reclaimed' (Goodman & Trowler, 2011), to striking effect.

As we have seen, there are many strands to systemic-based interventions, e.g. improved ease of communication, openness to different ideas and perspectives, identifying the area of uncertainty, improving outcomes by establishing trust and confidence in the process by which fresh ideas and resourcefulness emerge. The leadership is more facilitative than directive to a human system that is looking for a different momentum and perspective. Mapping the relationship connections and their mutual effects, whether as an exercise or directly with the people in question, is the starting point of systemic inquiry.

This is a communal event in which collaboration is directed at alleviating the systemically linked, personal and familial distress. It comes from a shared belief that it is better to understand and intervene in the whole relationship context than only treat symptoms or presented difficulties; that it is better to work for more radical longer-term change than merely fixing the immediate. Human systems have a great potentiality for healing, care and other virtues; by convening those most affected by a difficulty, solutions often emerge from unexpected quarters (kindness, warmth and empathy can surface where none seemed to exist). With close human interaction there is always the possibility of benign surprise at an outcome where the adverse response is anticipated.

Unless there is serious risk of harm to someone, the desire and ownership for change is always the prerogative of the patient. The therapeutic art is to clear away obstructions to change from the accumulated legacy of different scripts and then look for openings to influence change. These can be behaviourally based, even encouraging absurd or paradoxical strategies; temporary intensification of tension and system unbalancing; creating dialogue enactments; reframing and positive connotation; reinterpreting perspectives where only constructions of adversity and victimhood are manifest; releasing new energies systemically through the clarification of shared experiences and their attendant *catharsis*.

Change and what is possible can have different meaning for different members of the same family and therapy team members. It is always on a continuum from the acceptance of living with the unchangeable, to activating the paradox of personal growth through relationships. In balanced family systems sacrifices are generously made for the sake of one another and returned over time, sometimes in a different form. In less well-orientated families, the desire for well-being can be brought into sufficient life to overcome the fears and anxieties of adversity, a difficult but possible accomplishment. The sense of attachment to a community that also prizes difference and belonging is what every individual seeks to create for their family, if only in wishing. To have genuine influence over difficult family processes the therapy system has to believe in the possibility of change, from their practice experience as well as research evidence.

Being clear about what kind of change is sought by the family and how a therapeutic dialogue works is essential. Once the assessment process is completed and agreement reached on further work, then the dialogue about relationships and what emerges and how this is thought about differently and collectively are the main vehicles for influence and change. It is also about creating the **core conditions** identified in research (Miller, Duncan & Hubble, 1997) of 'being respected, being cared for, being understood' experientially through relationships.

There are other influences on relationships at the community level (schools, hospitals, agencies with particular resources for addiction, vocational advice, social care, etc.) which are hidden persuaders through their powers of attribution. They are also open to being influenced by informed work. A systemic view sees that all systems have an influence in shaping the definition of a situation. Like the eight blind men with the elephant, each has its perspective and a capacity to define whatever enters their institutional orbit. A dialogue with other systems is essential, since a therapy system is just one of the eight 'blind' perspectives.

The therapist as shaman and 'magical healer'

The original Greek term *therapeutes*, from which the terms 'therapy' and 'therapeutic' are derived, referred to the attendants in religious healing rituals. From the elaboration of these rituals emerged the early Greek forms of drama. The dramatic arts have a long lineage in social and communal healing rituals, a provenance that can be used and appreciated in their modern variations, of which family systemic work is one.

All cultures evolve their own healing rituals and some knowledge of them is essential when working with cultures different to your own. Some of these forms are preserved in the rituals and beliefs of immigrants to the UK from Africa, Asia and the West Indies. Many people feel more comfortable with healing rituals with which they are familiar than relying on the positive scientific paradigm of Western-derived medicine. Many Westerners also feel more comfortable with the 'alternative' holistic focus of Eastern practices, whether Chinese medicine, acupuncture or the Hindu spiritual system of yoga. Certain Christian churches have rituals for purification and exorcism of 'darker spirits' and recognise the special powers of relics or holy places for healing. These are important culturally specific resources, systems of meaning and healing which have sustained their communities for centuries.

There is an example, cited in *An Introduction to Psychodynamic Counselling* (Spurling, 2004), a companion book in this series, of a modern interpretation of an ancient practice. I have added brief thoughts and questions a family and systemic therapist might pose alongside the extract below, as well as elements of parallel process.

An example of a ritual healer at work in an African tribal society is given in a celebrated study by the anthropologist, Victor Turner (1967).

The healer's therapy draws on cultural assumptions of the members of that society in particular the traditional belief that pain and distress can be caused by the tooth, *ihamba*, of an angry shade which has buried itself in the body and needs to be removed [the externalizing of the pain and its undesired influence over the sufferer; the metaphorical symbolization of the cutting ability of 'angry shade']. Turner observed a healer called in to treat a villager suffering from a variety of complaints, from pains in his body to a general sense of grievance and unhappiness [depression, irritable hostility, existential distress and anomie]. The healer first made a careful investigation of the patient's kin relationship, noting in particular the current tensions in the network [genogram work]. Each significant figure in this network including the patient was then assigned a ritual task, for example the collection of ritual medicines which would be used in the ritual performance where the healing will take place ['homework' between sessions].

Finally the healer gathered together all the relevant figures from the sick man's kin and village [family systemic and community networking]. A series of rites then followed, with intensive drumming and singing, followed by a series of cupping horns attached to the patient's body. If one of these horns fell off during the performance, the healer stopped the proceedings and looked to see whether there was anything in the horn:

If he finds nothing in them he makes a statement to the congregation about why the *ihamba* has not 'come out', which usually entails a fairly detailed account of the patient's life story and of the group's inter-relations [takes a 'no-change' strategic position]. Then he invokes the shade, urging it to 'come quickly' and finally invites village members to come, in order of sex and seniority, to the improvised hunter's shrine set up in the shade and confess any secret ill-feeling they may have toward the patient. The patient himself may be invited as well [encouraging the expression of the conflicting, negative feelings]. (Turner, 1967: 388)

The ceremony started again until another horn fell off [follow-up session], the same ritual of confession of grudges was gone through again and then the drumming and singing continued. In the ritual performance observed by Turner this went on for many hours until all the participants were exhausted [change by dissipation]. Finally when yet another horn dropped off the patient's body, the healer announced that he had found a tooth under the cup [**positive connotation**, experiential affirmation]. Everyone was happy and relieved that the cause of the patient's illness had now been identified and got rid of [relief of 'explanation' through network participation and catharsis]. Turner reports that the patient himself was very affected by the whole process and started to get better after the performance. When Turner visited him again some months after the ritual performance the patient continued to be free from pain and was living a happier life. (Spurling, 2004: 10)

Within a communal ritual there is someone of recognized authority and experience who facilitates the ceremony, the Shamanic figure who commands respect through a profound understanding of the ritual. This has been learned from direct observation and practice, as an apprentice from an experienced master. The ritual involves the active involvement of the community, metaphorical and symbolic use of language and an invocation of the forces of nature, the 'supernatural', especially the forces of the spirit. There is a collective acceptance of a mystery in which the participants take part through their witness, and occasional active contribution.

As with a fever, a climax or critical point is reached. Known by the ancient Greeks as *cairos,* this is where health and illness/life and death, are in the balance. Dis-ease is exactly that, a loss of harmony of the whole being. The sufferer may be aware that the work of the Shaman as well as the witnesses is orientated towards recovery and health; the sharply oppositional forces are usually symbolized in some object or animal that is sacrificed to placate or seek the grace of whatever invisible force field in the universe moves the drama towards health.

Modern psychotherapy is unable to use these resources in such exotic ways, though it may have the same kind of emotional intensity. The family crucible is full of overspilling passion, accusation, counter-accusation, truth and contradicted truth, conciliation and flight from illusion or settled relationships. In a well-managed, containing family systemic psychotherapy session there is scope and safety for the kind of change that comes through reflected openness and catharsis of the kind familiar to the shaman.

Some core factors in change and influence

If change does come, compelling though it may be to observe it, the change does not always hold. It is usually termed 'first-order change'. The psychotherapy industry is notorious for creating its own mythologies, 'new' methods and charismatic 'superstars' whose appeal often burns out as rapidly as a supernova. However, trust in the practitioner, their perceived competence and their concern to help promote well-being is essential. If a physiotherapist behaves attentively in a knowledgeable and authoritative manner then the patient is more likely to trust that he or she has their best interests at heart, which will influence their recovery. Influence is a circular, relational process; the patient in part wants to be persuaded and is open to it; the therapist wants to facilitate change for them in as many ways as are possible.

Psychotherapists and counsellors operate in a highly competitive marketplace and must present themselves as confident in their good outcomes as part of their professional ethos. The development of 'evidence-based practice' to evaluate the efficacy of different therapeutic models of working is an attempt to introduce some rationality into the process of choosing between their competing claims, though cynics often redesignate it 'politics-based evidence'. However, the therapeutic art of promoting well-being involves persuasion and is heavily reliant on factors within the non-conscious; the non-rational and unquantifiable (rather like the subjective, influential effects that music can have).

In their influential book, *Escape from Babel: Towards A Unifying Theory for Psychotherapy Practice* (Miller, Duncan & Hubble, 1997) the authors identify the simultaneous operation of four common curative factors facilitating change in psychotherapy: extra-therapeutic factors (life events outside therapy), 40 per cent; the therapeutic relationship, 30 per cent; approaches and techniques, 15 per cent; hope expectancy and the placebo effect, 15 per cent. Though it is not clear how the fine precision of such factors has been computed, the authors contend that therapy has more beneficial effects than a placebo or no intervention at all. These seemly invariant operational factors, independent of personal characteristics, are drawn from one-to-one therapy and are a helpful antidote to the primacy claims of any single psychotherapy model.

It is important for well-being to have a regular, peaceful space for personal reflection and meditation, though therapists can lose sight of the fact that they may only feature for a few hours a month in a person's life for a relatively short period. Though these hours do have a significant, anchoring influence, especially in the desire for health, recovery and well-being, they are a tiny proportion of a person's waking life. Life, as the psychoanalyst Karen Horney was apt to remark, is the greatest therapist; sometimes responsive, sometimes persecutory.

Let us look briefly at a case study considerably helped by collaborative, reflective teamwork and the use of wider systems.

CASE STUDY 9.1: FRANK AND MARIAN

Frank (62) came with his third wife Marian (52) who was partially disabled. He had a long-standing depression that had not responded to medication, counselling or various forms of psychotherapeutic work. For practically the whole of the first session, Frank sobbed as Marion recounted the story of his sexual abuse in childhood, abandonment by his first wife, violence from his second wife, the placement of his second son in local authority care without his knowledge (from whence he reclaimed and cared for him); his identified concern for his 15-year-old granddaughter Elisa who had been raped by a taxi driver and a feeling that his father-in-law was too intrusive, dominating his wife and marginalizing Frank. Amidst this world of disappointment and failure, a member of the team noticed right at the end of the session that Frank used to play the guitar and liked playing Blues music. He was immediately invited to resume playing between sessions on the basis that the Blues spoke of life experience almost as inconsolable as Frank's. He seemed to brighten up at this, shook hands and left.

At the follow-up session he seemed a little brighter. This time the focus was on Marian, whose life history was in many ways as full of tragedy and rejection as Frank's. She was her father's carer, though he had not been particularly caring; indeed, he had rejected her for much of her life. However, she felt she ought to care for him out of a sense of duty and

→

guilt. Frank, encouraged by a member of the team, began to challenge Marian's helpless submissiveness towards her father. Frank said that though he liked his father-in-law, he wished Marian would assert herself more and that so should he.

At the third session Frank reported that he had written an emotional letter to his son, who he complained had excluded him, pleading to be allowed to support his assaulted granddaughter. The son had replied, saying that Frank's highly emotional reactions made it impossible for him to be open with him, and this added to his already anxious burden about his daughter.

By the fourth and final session, some eight weeks after the first, Frank's manner and Marian's were transformed. Both had challenged the father-in-law and negotiated a better boundary. They were pleased with his response, which had not led to relationship breakdown. They said they had spoken endlessly, rowed some of the time, but realized in making-up how much they loved one another and how they were intending to re-prioritize their lives and let go of many beliefs. One was to declare themselves bankrupt. Having accumulated many debts he was never going to be able to pay, Frank saw this step as regrettable but inevitable. This had given the couple and their families greater peace of mind. Frank said he was going to play the Blues more regularly, to which he received the reply 'rather than live them'.

In this case the team provided a context of thoughtful encouragement and, through their reflections, sought to disentangle the overlapping levels of intergenerational conflict and to persuade Frank to reconnect with an important musical skill and to use it to step outside the sorrowful blues of his own life. The gentle unbalancing of Marian's relationship with her father and the strengthening of the couple's relationship encouraged them to have a more honest dialogue about themselves and how to tackle their lives. Both consulted the Citizen's Advice Bureau and used what they learned to decide to declare themselves bankrupt. They gained confidence using their own resources to take control of their lives and the disruptive emotions that had prevented them finding a solution, so gaining a better balance between thinking and feeling.

At the outset none of the team had expected any favourable change. This was entirely the couple's achievement and they were complimented on it. Though their lives still had its troubles there was a difference in the assumptive script and their ability to communicate and reduce some of the difficult tensions in the subscript.

Other core factors to influence change are:

1. The engagement and encouragement of the collective empathic imagination of the team is as important as it is in individual work. The transformative power of imagination is particularly active in poetry, with its rich use of language and multiple symbolic interpretations. Wordsworth said that with this ability we 'see into the life of things'; while for Coleridge our imagination has a 'shaping power' of that 'dark groundwork'. This use of imagination matters no less for the therapist, as well as an articulate use of imagistic and metaphorical language to associate and connect.

2. Traditionally, family and systemic psychotherapy has used teams as part of its approach, though the way the team has been used has changed over time. The early offering from the strategic and early Milan models used oracular utterances by the therapist, delivered from clipboard notes and then reinforced in letter form as a means of persuasion. The openly democratic and unrehearsed team protocol introduced by Tom Andersen (1987) involved the team and family changing places and witnessing the other's dialogue. The early work of Jay Haley (1963), the Milan Associates (1978), Brian Cade (Cade & O'Hanlon, 1993) and others was very much influenced by Milton Erickson's use of paradox and other strategic challenges to problematical behaviour. This still has a freshness of imaginative irreverence with playful challenges to distressing and disruptive behaviour, and is a welcome difference to the solemn pieties of many other approaches. It is best used in conjunction with an empathic connection to the strong, distressed feelings aired in a whole-family consultation.

   As described in Chapter 2, training mental health staff, who have no previous background in family and systemic therapy, to act as the 'Greek chorus' to a family-therapy team encounter brought a different experience both to the family and the team members and also revealed some confusion and tentativeness about working in this way. It was used to good effect with Marian and Frank, encouraging spontaneous empathic responses in the reflections. The therapy team spoke positively of its capacity to enrich and empower their understanding and use of self in their other mental health roles and a number of the team have gone on to train in systemic psychotherapy. The capacity for imaginative 'shaping power' is an innate and therapeutic characteristic of human psychology often insufficiently recognized in those who work in the mental health field.

3. Periodic reflection and tracking feedback about the accuracy of the therapist/team's attempts to understand and be helpful should include dialogue about background differences between the family's

culture and those apparent in the team (Burnham, 2011): 'You may think from observing us that we rather come from different backgrounds and may not be able to understand yours. Do you think that's possible? You must let us know when it does for we shall check from time to time.'

It is vital and part of most therapy training to be aware of and competent about the culture of other ethnic groups, of other differences to your own. A 'not-knowing' position comes from having enough knowledge to know what you do not know. Families will then be less bothered about differences in background if the work of respectful, accurate connection is present. Otherwise the experiential differences of the GRRAACCEESS can easily result in a failed disconnection of empathy.

4. Offering a different interpretation to a described experience is done through reframing; by connoting and connecting the experience in a different way. Sufficient experiential understanding, however, is necessary for the reframing to be effective. Otherwise, the family may experience the reframe, however technically ingenious, as perplexing. It may have a Zen-like therapeutic intention but they may not be able to take the next step, and accept the invitation to a new possibility. As Carl Rogers maintained, 'being real' is an important condition in all therapy. If you can't experience their distress, even in a small way, keep looking. Faking authenticity is one paradox too far.

It is always essential to look for the virtues of well-being which coexist with the adversities. These are the qualities on which to base a reframe, often acknowledging that they are concealed beneath the stress and distress, like the sun beyond the rain clouds. When you are shown evidence of love and care, thoughtfulness, empathic understanding, functional boundary-making or misconstrued good intention, highlight them almost immediately. They can be re-presented in any later reflection, or in a therapeutic letter. Empowerment develops from the small and recollected evidence of accomplishment and virtue. Fixed recollection of repeated adversity continues patterns of disempowerment and victimhood. In family interactional therapy there is always one or more member eager for some change. They are your temporary allies because they are looking for a better experience. Highlight and affirm their positions, particularly when reflecting back to the family.

5. Securely attached relationships at all stages of life are at the heart of care, comfortable identity, individuation without guilt, freedom to be adventurous, and the satisfied longing to belong. It is the royal road to well-being, to being free. All the existential conditions of

alienation besides poverty (detachment, aloneness, meaninglessness and dependencies) come from deeply held disappointment at not being cared about. 'Good-enough' secure attachment is a hard-won prize in the face of adversities. It is an unconditional good in itself, for it frees the person to explore the fullness of the world and their individuality whilst keeping them connected and belonging.

Attachment bonds (which apply universally to human relationships, as with friends or colleagues) were the basis of a series of lectures by John Bowlby (1988). He maintained that the therapist forms a temporary attachment with the patient (the therapeutic alliance). This permits exploration from a secure base, enabling the patient to experience a personal validation they had previously found elusive, from which they could examine and find corrective experiences to their disrupted attachment patterns. In this model, it can be seen that the 'family of therapists', the therapists and team, provide a symbolic extended family that holds and contains the problem-distressed system by providing space to think, feel and express. They must hold all members of the system in mind and direct their reflective feedback inclusively, with neither fear nor favour.

From this experiential base, persuasion and influence are possible in modelling acceptance, informed and accurate listening, and personal interest in prizing their struggle for better living. This sets the context for change if they can be sufficiently held to sustain the process. The influence of accurate understanding, a good alliance and encouraging the family to experiment with changing strategies is often enough to hold the family (in mind, if not all in situ) in the work. It is difficult for those who bring an assumptive script of deficit through poor nurturance, abuse, neglect and disconfirmed identity to believe anything different is possible. They convince themselves that current relationships have not achieved the wished-for reparation (and seem to have managed to reproduce earlier patterns of familial relationships), so that the subscript is beyond correction and that relief from the most immediately pressing difficulty would be sufficient. They may be beyond influencing for anything more far-reaching than this and it is essential that thought is given to realistic possibilities for change and discussed early in therapy. It is for them to determine.

Anxiety and unpredictability of outcome

Novels and drama can authentically convey the human relational experience, being imaginatively constructed test beds for the lived experience. Through the many tribulations and relational exchanges of the characters who inhabit the narratives there may be an outcome which was not predicted or desired by the reader/audience. Human existence is different. We do not know the outcome of many of the choices we make or their long-term consequences. With risk-taking behaviour the outcomes may be more obvious, e.g. driving a car without regard for speed or conditions, or using addictive substances. These are all in the domain of good sense (sometimes called 'common sense': it may be understood commonly, but is often acted upon uncommonly).

Not knowing the outcome of a job change, a choice of partner, the decision to have a child, electing to have surgery, take medication, join in a revolutionary protest, and so on, is the bittersweet, anxious exhilaration of human freedom. Fortunately, we are not given to read the book or the script of our life, unlike the suicidally depressed character of George Bailey in the 1946 film *It's a Wonderful Life* who, seeing the effect of his never having existed, is led to a transformed view of himself in the Hollywood requirement of a happy ending. We can and do, if we so wish, transform our lives by close re-examination of its script and narrative and correcting for ourself and others whatever seems right to do so. This too is a precious freedom.

The shaman in Laurence Spurling's example had no idea of the outcome of his ministrations but he knew evidentially from custom and practice that if he followed the ritual closely and with conviction this would help create the conditions for the patient's recovery, and so it proved. This was in every sense a persuasive ritual which, like the so-called placebo effect, invokes the deep desire in the human psyche for recovery and well-being.

The search for an oracular statement about future outcomes is deeply embedded in the human psyche, a need satisfied by a huge market in horoscopes. We can guess at fate; we can hope and petition 'it'; we can seek out prophecies and forecasting; for they give us the option to alter the outcome from the one 'predicted'. Oedipus sought desperately to deflect the prophecy of a man who would murder his father and marry his mother, though fate and his relationship system did not permit it. At the end he is left having 'found himself', but at a tragic cost.

In the early development of directed feedback to the family in Strategic and Milan Associates therapy (Milan Associates, 1978), the communication would frequently seek a balance between optimism and pessimism. This was meant to create thoughtful perturbation in the family system, but frequently caused confusion. This now seems predictable in its persuasive attempts, though ingenious in its linkages between different elements of the family experience and playful in its use of paradoxical meaning. Developments since Andersen onwards have tended to a more direct empathic feedback, leaving the predictive outcomes firmly to the gods. The different possible outcomes are sometimes reflected upon in the presence of the family, but the whole tenor is much more towards an experiential realism and confident encouragement to the family to raise their level of consciousness and communication towards one another, and to be able to act with greater effect to achieve their desired outcome.

Written influence: therapeutic letters

In the Narrative Therapy work of White and Epston (1990), the genre of letter writing became almost as literary and artistic a skill as a therapeutic one. However, since Michael White started his career as a family therapist, family systemic therapy laid the groundwork for using powerful, written communications between the family and the therapist team. These work well, as already described, especially for 'older adults' to whom letter writing is still familiar. They require careful thought, evenhandedness, and a balance between positive connotation of intentions and openness about the realistic effects of distressed misunderstandings. Therapeutic change is neither miracle nor magic but is based on a communicated, accurate apprehension of the background adversities envisioned by the capacity of the human psyche. Written communications constructed with care and an empathic sensibility still have the potency to reach down into reservoir of well-being.

CASE STUDY 9.2: DAPHNE

Daphne (67) had suffered acute debilitating bouts of depression at various times in her life. She was told secrets about her birth, rather as Oedipus was in Sophocles' drama, by children at school at the age of 13. The woman she had thought to be her mother was in truth her grandmother (Nan). When she remonstrated with her Nan, an aunt rushed in to accuse her of being a 'foul-mouthed little bitch' for distressing her grandmother. Daphne shook with anger as she told the story to the team, 54 years later. An uncle sexually abused her, a fact she had only ever divulged to her three grown-up children after some counselling ten years before. Recently she had been hospitalized after a further depressive

→

episode accompanied by some distressing psychotic features of penises hanging on the ceiling, and general flashbacks.

At the suggestion of a psychodynamic psychotherapist who had seen her for individual sessions she came for a family consultation with two of her three children (the third, Emily, attended the second session after we wrote to her), her half-sister (who in childhood she had thought of as an aunt), her sister-in-law and her niece, who was a mental health worker in London. Her eldest daughter, Margaret, travelled from the West Country for the session and all the following ones. A genogram with all present finally sorted out the complicated relationships and their secrets, pretences and cover-ups. Daphne's son found it truly illuminating. Daphne had a twin brother, Brian, who she had turned to immediately for support after the playground disclosure. She felt they had a special bond, beyond just twinship, that came from their shared secret. His health had been very fragile lately and this seemed to have triggered the emergence of her psychosis.

We later wrote:

Dear Daphne,

We were pleased to meet you and the many members of your family, who showed us their care and concern for you. We hope you found their presence supportive and helpful. We learnt a lot from our conversations with everyone and hope you did the same. Since then a number of thoughts have remained in our minds.

Firstly, it seemed helpful for you and your family to untangle the complicated sets of relationships in the family, some of which came as a revelation to David [her son from her second marriage].

Secondly, it helped us and others to understand just how important having your twin brother Brian is for you. You clearly said it was important in the confusion of family relationships to have one person who you are close to and whose position in the family was clear and constant.

We were able to understand how it unsettled you when Brian became ill and maybe re-activated your concerns for your own health. We took seriously your worries, echoed by family members that the facial movements [probably the side effects of her medication] make you feel self-conscious and prevent you from going out and meeting people; we promised to look into this and have informed the wider team [the psycho-geriatrician and colleagues] of your concerns. We have also copied them into this letter.

We were very struck that at key stages of your life, you have overcome periods of great distress and depression; Margaret [elder daughter from first marriage] and David gave us a sense of you as a capable and strong mother, a view confirmed by your niece Lisa's description of you as her Aunt. We understand that you feel you have lost your strength to recover this time and noticed that you seem to have been left deflated by your worries about Brian's health coming as it did after a period of great concern for your London daughter's severe distress and attempt on her life.

We would like to see you all again on the ....

Yours sincerely
(names given)
Family Therapy Team

However, recover Daphne did, and with her three children around her, shared with the team the sense of accomplishment at ending the work. The family had always been very open with one another. The therapeutic work built on that and gave them confidence that together the debilitation of the period of mental distress could be overcome, the medication regime changed to a better level and their mutuality as a unit could give them faith in one another's well-being in the future.

Over five sessions, other members of the family system fell away, leaving just Daphne and her three children. Her medication was reduced. She brought family photos in of her and her first husband that, Emily quipped, looked like a marriage between Amy Winehouse and Charlie Kray. The atmosphere in the family had eased considerably, with many humorous anecdotes about how the children's friend went in fear of Daphne's authority. Their united ability to show active care for their mother and one another was marked. Although Daphne had to return to hospital briefly, the changed system around her remained a caring one.

CASE STUDY 9.3: JACK AND JILL

Jack and Jill have been married for over 35 years. Jack, now retired, had been a high-earning engineer working abroad for much of his life, and had a 33-year history of depression. Over the years he had received a great deal of input from psychiatrists and psychotherapy but he and his wife had never been seen as a couple until they received our invitation. To be invited pleased Jill, a plain-speaking, feisty woman. Their relationship had become a complex, stale, conflicted, depression-activated system. Jill recounted that a (male) psychiatrist told her, at least 25 years previously, that if she couldn't stand the 'heat in the kitchen' of their relationship then she should be prepared for the consequences to her husband of leaving. Jill interpreted this as a threat that he could kill himself and had felt trapped and paralysed by this double bind, for she never felt able enough to love him through his depression, nor to leave him (a fact she had considered many times).

Their relationship was dire, and many of the early sessions were filled with heated exchanges of accusation and blame. When they had lived abroad Jill had felt very isolated. In the session, she recounted being raped on one occasion, an event Jack passed over without comment or any response. They had separated for eight years, with him living and working in London and becoming increasingly alcohol-addicted. Jack had returned to the matrimonial home sounding helpless and lost. He claimed to love Jill, wanted to be with her and feared disintegrating into alcoholism if he had to live alone in his last years. Some members of the team felt Jack had used his 'depression' in part to control Jill and prevent her leaving him, as part of a dependency 'game plan'. She allowed him back home and refused to be the one to initiate divorce; she wanted the decision to be his, not hers. We hypothesized that this might be some legacy of the over-developed sense of responsibility for her husband's condition that the psychiatrist had instilled in her, or else some complex dance of intimacy, a test in which he was challenged to show love and change in the face of her abundant hostility from years of accumulating feelings of being used.

We did not expect them to continue attending, and they seemed to look to the team to produce some kind of change for them while having constructed an elaborate knot holding them together in ways neither took responsibility for disentangling. We reflected back in the session and in therapeutic letters what they brought to the position of 'stalemate' into which they had locked themselves

We wrote:

Dear Jack and Jill,

We are writing to see where things are for you at present and whether anything has changed since our meeting on the 8th December. We were struck by the fact that the two of you seemed to be in very different places and wanting different things from the situation. You, Jill, seemed to us to have given a lot of yourself to the relationship and were unsure whether giving any more would lead to a change or whether it might make no significant difference. We were struck by the conviction with which you expressed how you had made the decision to *not* be the one making the decision about your relationship and had left it to Jack. You, Jack, expressed to us that what you brought to the relationship was not valued or recognized and that you were really hoping to find a companionship now that seemed to have escaped you over the years. We were struck by the frustration and disappointment that the two of you had experienced over a great many years from the impact of depression and absorption in work and how this had impacted on your ability to communicate with each other and to feel valued in the relationship. We can see how you were uncertain that you could retrieve a satisfactory relationship and that you have different attitudes of hopelessness towards the situation. This seems to have left you in a stuck position and feeling unwilling and unable to risk making changes.

We can see that coming as a couple to work with us has huge risks for you and we admire the honesty with which you told us of your situation. We feel there is room to help build on your openness with each other without any of us knowing how the situation between you will resolve. We would be pleased to see you again on …. Please let us know within the next week whether you wish to work with us a little bit more.

Our best wishes
FAMILY THERAPY TEAM

We had three more sessions after that during which the couple continued to engage each other in mutual recrimination and blame. Jill stuck to her belief that she should not take the initiative in ending the relationship; Jack expressed his fear of being alone and reverting to serious depression and alcoholism. Jill made it clear that she accepted no

responsibility for what he did to himself. He seemed to lack any awareness of her expressed need for some indication of care for her.

Dear Jack and Jill,

We have continued to think very fully about the dilemmas of your
life and relationship the more we have got to know you, and your
individual strengths and different characters and how over time
these have caused each of you unhappiness from the other.

We hope, as you both said, that our work has at least enabled you
to see the nature and depth of the hurt that has been accumulating
on each side down the years – and the things said in the past and
the actions done which cannot easily be unsaid or undone.

There are small glimmers for us (but not perhaps for you who
are both so close to the dismay and the destructive effects of accumulated bad feeling) of some care that still exists in the relationship; that a part of each of you has remained involved in the
relationship despite the hurts and conflicts.

We are struck that there may be a solution close to hand by
buying up the adjoining property and building a home which will
give you enough room to be as much together or separate as you
feel is best, at any one time.

We would like to arrange one more ending session with you at
the end of the summer just to see whether through it all something of benefit to you both has continued to emerge. It struck us
that you both were very actively involved in line dancing over the
years and that this must be a good metaphor for the future.

We could see you finally on ....
Yours sincerely
Family Therapy Team

At that final session both seemed to have softened to one another. The
atmosphere had eased considerably. They had even shared a hotel room
when they went away to visit old schoolfriends. Their son had warned
them that he would stop contact with their grandchild if they continued their set-tos in front of his family. Being held to account in a reversal of generational authority (parents spoken to as children by their
child) seemed very chastening. There seemed to be almost a sense of
sadness to be losing the involvement of the team. However, we felt we
had accomplished as much through the 'temporary attachment' of the
collaborative therapeutic work as we could. So we wrote finally

Dear Jack and Jill,

We felt you were disappointed to be ending the other week and we are writing, among other things, to remind you of the changes we feel you have made during our work together.

Jack, you seemed much less depressed and more active than you were, with meeting old friends and playing golf. You seemed to have reduced your drinking and were able to listen more and were not negatively reacting to Jill.

Jill, although disappointed at the loss of much of the opportunity of the marriage, you seemed more accepting and at ease with yourself.

We were struck that at our last meeting you were really listening and communicating more respectfully and we thought that the two of you were beginning to understand, as Jack put it, that when you listen for a kick, you hear it. We wondered if this applied to a habit in how you relate to each other that had become rather entrenched. As you said there are grounds for hope that change may be possible for you in the years to come, although how or what that will be is your responsibility. Based on our experience of you in action, we know you both have the skills in articulating ideas and feelings clearly and honesty, this seems to us to give you a good basis for finding a more hopeful way of sharing your life together in future years.

Yours sincerely
Family Therapy Team

Somewhere within their experience families have the seeds of well-being, and an empathic care for one another that is unmistakably therapeutic. It is inconceivable that the human race would have survived thus far were that not the case. However, besides all the important groundwork and core conditions which have been stressed in this book so far, the systemic therapist needs to feel convinced of the efficacy of the method's approach and techniques. This comes from the collaboration of custom and practice, observed learning, and, importantly in an age desirous of evidence, from research. Testing out the method, with suitable guidance, will demonstrate the practice-based evidence. All these elements are firmly in place but this approach to therapy is still not at present sufficiently mainstream to be widely available.

A method that emphasizes inclusivity, collaboration, integration of differences and attention to what patients say distresses them has many strengths. It is flexible enough to incorporate techniques from more individualistic-based therapies but not sufficiently competitive to be perturbed if invitations to collaborate are declined. It can be an extraordinarily potent way of seeing the world and meeting the challenges to living in the world as it is given to us; for finding the ideas, attitudinal stance and persuasive vocabulary to change at least small aspects of that world. If it is possible to make a small difference to the ecology of each family with troubles in their experience of living, then that has to give hope that wider more lasting social, systemic change and harmony may not be such a forlorn dream.

Summary

- The comprehensive nature of the application of the systemic modality is emphasized.
- Parallels between the work of a shaman and systemic therapist are examined.
- Findings from research about common curative, influential factors are discussed, and a case where these elements were influential is examined.
- Other core factors which influence change in systemic work are discussed.
- The ability to connect to transcend difference is developed.
- Bowlby's model of therapy as temporary attachment for 'the royal road of influence to well-being' is discussed.
- The three different existential possibilities of outcome as a source of influence on the family outcome view are explained.
- Two case examples of the use of written influence in the form of therapeutic letters are given.

Appendix: Genograms

A 'family tree', usually known as a genogram, is a pictorial representation of something wholly organic, the 'who's who' of the active present and recent past of the family community. It is usual to consider it over at least three generations in order to get a fuller grasp of the contextual patterns and recurrent themes. It is a highly flexible and potentially infinite container for the information stream that is the family's reservoir of recalled experience and operational attitudes. However, its value is only as measurable as the level of attentive curiosity that has gone into its delineation. This is itself a factor of the quality of joining and engagement arising from the developing relationship alliance between the family system and the therapeutic system.

Usage

- Because it has multiple uses it helps individual therapists of all modalities to orientate themselves to the whole context of the person.
- It helps family therapists, with or without a team, to orientate themselves to the context of the family.
- It identifies the main themes and issues to be explored in therapeutic work by identifying the background distresses and strengths.
- It does not require the person, part or whole set of family relationships to be present in the session.
- It acts as a guiding template for open dialogue if used live and directly with a person, a relationship subsystem or the whole family system.

Factual Information about changes through renewal and loss in the family life cycle and social situation (circumstantial script)

- Illness, including addictions.
- Additions through birth/surrogacy or IVF treatment/adoptions/ fostering/kinship care/enduring partnership (marriage, civil, or cohabitational)
- Divorce/separation.
- Deaths through disease/age-related factors/miscarriage/stillbirth/ termination.
- Migrations (leaving and returning).
- Missing or stigmatized family members
- Employment.
- Income.
- Education.

Since some of these areas of information are extremely personal, often attended with guilt, shame, secrecy or unknowingness, they should be managed with extreme sensitivity and mindfulness in gauging the replies from the respondents. If necessary, they should be set aside until there is a further opening or initiation from the respondents' narrative. This is part of the intuitive area of work with the subscript and the assumptive scripts.

The interpretative frame-beliefs and emotional attitudes (assumptive and identity scripts)

Differing personal attitudes and emotional responses to:

- life experiences, circumstances and situations
- one another's different character identity, attitudes and actions/ reactions (behaviour) and generational perspectives
- differing ethical beliefs
- differing cultural beliefs about ethnicity, class, faith, gender, sexual orientation, intelligence and (dis) ability
- areas of shared beliefs on all these themes and issues.

The areas of shared beliefs may appear covert in the context of an open family dialogue lest they are believed to aggravate further family group disruption and dissent. They are more likely to emerge in individual sessions, along with family secrets. However, their value to enhancing the understanding of the whole family system thereby may be lost. This is also an area for sensitive mindfulness through exploring the subscript.

Patterns of attachment, alliance, triangulation and problem definition (structural problem-solving script)

- Who seems closer to whom (described individually by the family or observed by the therapist(s))?
- The historical evolution of the patterns of closeness/distance and their linkages to life events and experiences (e.g. loss, domestic violence, addictive behaviour or disablement of significant family member(s)).
- Patterns of conflict and their resolution (or enduringness).
- Patterns of blame and responsibility for difficulties, hardships and adversities.
- Patterns of successful negotiation and a peaceful outcome.

The content and process of communication (delivered script)

- The 'what' expressed in dialogue (as in the attitudinal positions described above) as well as the 'how'.
- The emotional resonances in the delivery (anger, tenderness, conciliatoriness, violent rage, anxiety, frustration, etc.).

'Sensing the vibe' (the subscript)

Feeling intuitively or taking non-verbal sensings that the theme or issue is difficult for one or more family members, often because of

- incidents of active violence in the household or other forms of abuse
- patterns of dominance and the denigration of specific family members
- fear of escalation of difficulty as a result of disclosure, or of family dissolution through institutional care/control or other apprehended risk/catastrophe (suicide, psychotic distress, aggravated self-harm and addictive abuse, estrangement, etc.).

Jenny seeks an initial consultation for depression. She relocated to Glasgow to marry Tam. See if you can work out a narrative for her on the basis of the enclosed genogram information and form some initial questions to ask her about the circumstantial script she might be presenting.

How to draw a genogram

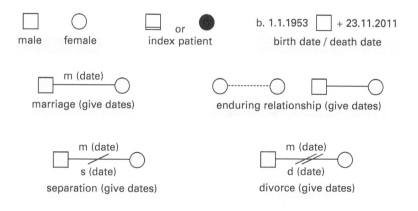

The following symbols are commonly used in the construction of a genogram:

Example: Jenny Brown and family

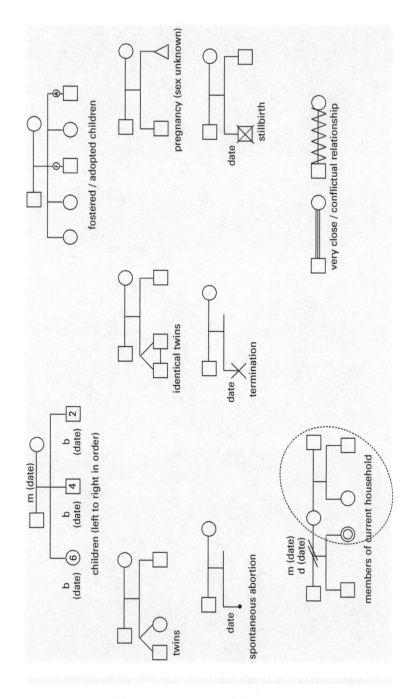

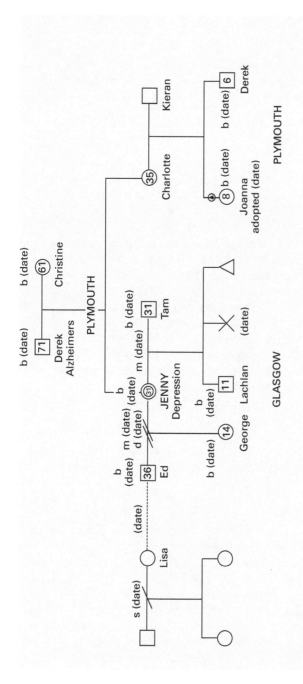

GLOSSARY OF MAIN TERMS

assumptive identity script: The narrative collection reflecting different attitudes and beliefs held towards one another's identity, character and shared heritage within a family network.

assumptive scripts: The narrative sets of different attitudinal beliefs and emotional responses to existential circumstances and events held within a family network.

attachment theory: A theory developed by the child psychiatrist and analyst John Bowlby, in collaboration with Mary Ainsworth and Mary Main, to give object relations theory a clearer grounding in common experience and an observational, empirical basis. Four patterns of attachment were identified: securely attached; anxiously avoidant; anxious-resistant; chaotic–disorganized.

The attachment behaviour of an infant seeks a reliable, dependable figure who is able to assuage anxiety and provide care through a secure relationship. Attachment relationship is a basic building block in forming personal resilience against existential threats to well-being and survival. It is present at many levels, from the daily, comforting familiarity of the presence of supportive others (family members) to the deeper ontological ones in personal experience. Bowlby maintained that the basis for this caring ability lay in early and attuned primary caregivers, though not necessarily the biological parent. Attachment relationships are lifelong in their influence, though they may be temporary ones, such as those with a teacher, nurse, psychotherapist or psychiatrist. Similar comfort may be found in objects which have personal meaning, pets or places of significance.

Attachment-responsive ability is developed experientially through kindness, nurturance and empathic attention to the desire for security innate in the human condition. Examples are the reversal of the caring role during the course of the human life cycle, and the discerning and surrogate care of foster and adoptive parents, who can restore the developmental balance and fulfil a child's ontological needs. Thus the saying: 'blood is thicker than water, but milk is thicker than blood'.

bracketing, or *epoche*: One of key aspects of the phenomenological method in therapy or research: the act of setting aside any personal preconceptions or presuppositions in any inquiry into truth in order for their full, entwined truths to emerge experientially and with best proximity.

catharsis: The release of latent emotions whose effects are freeing and 'purging' (Aristotle). The main passions expressed cathartically are rage, tearfulness, love and laughter and, in private, sexual and orgasmic.

circular questioning: Sometimes called interventive interviewing, this technique was developed by the Milan Associates. It uses a systemic phenomenological method which enables the mindset of a therapist or team to formulate questions that help draw out the latent experience in the family. The emerging information is moved in a circular way, checking and validating the different perceptions and beliefs of everyone in the family system. It is able to clarify confusions, defuse the tensions around the family's differences, increase awareness and free parts of the family's ways of communication.

circumstantial script: The 'objective', shaping events of fortune and misfortune, health and illness, achievement and failure in the family's story which, in the way they tell them to one another, influence the other script elements.

context: The background from which any foreground phenomenon can be better understood. Just as a word whose meaning is not clear discloses its possibilities from its relationship with the sentence around it, so a person discloses themselves more fully from consideration of their whole ontological, living background. Family and systemic therapy is a contextually based psychotherapy par excellence. Therefore, better and unused resources for living emerge from a full exploration of the family context through a therapeutic, open dialogue, since problem formation is often the product of a misunderstood situation or miscommunicated elements in relationships.

It is also the name of a leading publication in the field produced by the UK Association for Family Therapy.

core conditions (for therapy): Patients identified the core experiences for an effective therapeutic relationship as 'being respected, being cared for, being understood' (Miller, Duncan & Hubble, 1997: 23).

cybernetics: The science that studies the process of balance and control in systems. It is derived from the Greek word *cybernetes*, 'steersman', and is similar to the word 'governor', from the Latin *gubernare*. Both can refer to the regulator in an engine or head of a political system. In many ethical systems, well-being derives from balancing between excesses. The balance derived from the cybernetic process is its homeostasis.

delivered script: The text (or discourse) of each participant's contribution to the family dialogue. Within the manifest content of this text are contained other communicated strands of the experiential script, which may be inferred from analysis and reflection on both content and the manner of their expression.

dialogue: From the Greek *dialogos*, 'conversation', and *dialegesthai*, 'to discourse'. Dialogues can be formal forms of philosophical or spiritual exchange, like those of Socrates and of Krishna in the Bhagavad Gita. They are a core form of meaning-imbued human exchange in drama, in lived experience and in the central act of communicational interchange in therapy – the end of which is the easement of mind and feeling and an increased sense of well-being.

distance regulation: A key family process-dynamic where one family member may be recruited non-consciously into a sick or disabled role to protect some other distressed area of the relationship system that cannot be either articulated or resolved. A person who is already sick or disabled may find this role rigidified and their freedoms restricted by others around them acting protectively. Open, effective dialogue is difficult or impossible. This process is akin to triangulation, though whole subsystems can become distant regulators (e.g. children in the midst of domestic violence). Sometimes the distant regulator has to remove themselves from the toxicity of the family dynamic to preserve their own psychic integrity. When retaliatory response occurs, a destructive feedback loop, the vicious circle, is created.

empathy and empathic sensibility: The basic connectivity between persons, in their relational environment, and a major by-product of secure attachment. Experientially perceiving the world through another's experience is a capability, like a muscle, which can be brought into more full, active use. A therapeutic context in which acceptance, interest, understanding and facilitative curiosity are pervasive helps to activate this capability. Empathy arises in our imaginative sensibility (the 'shaping power' of that 'dark groundwork', according to the poet Coleridge) and self-reflection which is also developed through the expressive arts, or in spiritual exploration. A good workplace setting with open, respectful relationships also helps.

enactment: An application from structural therapy which actively promotes a dialogue between key family members about a situation, issue or communication process they seem unable to change. They might be asked to replicate a conflict at home or a related theme such as a life-cycle transition. The therapist can then help co-script the family members into a more productive exchange by affirming constructive openings or reflecting on the obstructing 'emotional ground'. This technique should be frequently practised to assist the therapist in finding experiential confidence and authority in engaging dialogue and re-scripting.

epoche: Like bracketing, the adoption of a sceptical stance of 'what do I know?' in the questioning tradition of Socrates and Montaigne.

experiential: Involves availability to the use of the whole self, balancing its sensory, cognitive, emotional and behavioural aspects with the usually subordinated visceral and spiritual ones. It is also the openness of the person to the full possibilities of their existence which enriches their personal understanding and ability to be a facilitative presence. It involves being discerning about different personal life truths and being able to separate them from each other and from one's own. It is 'whole-life' learning, not solely of an academic kind. Experientially, as family therapists, we use our own family context as a default position. This may assist and guide our appreciation of other systems, but also produces the blind spots that can limit freedom to explore and be a therapeutic presence for someone else's family.

experientialism or personalism: A philosophy that personal, lived experience is the alpha and omega and goal of all philosophy and learning. The Danish existential philosopher Søren Kierkegaard (1974: 178) described its basis as 'truth as subjectivity'.

family crucible: The term given by Carl Whitaker to the emotional matrix and atmosphere of the life of a family and the mixture of passions it may contain. The family is a political system, even if it does not conceptualize itself in this way. Therefore, the patterns of organization and self-governance are crucial in managing the boundaries of aggression, sexuality, the quality of shared respectfulness and the encouragement for individuality and belonging

Discerning authority is used by the leader of the family to provide a holding environment for family members. The purpose of a therapeutic consultation and intervention is to assist the family to negotiate a better means of shared expressiveness and self-governance.

Where the atmosphere in the family crucible is toxic, abuse-activated and with few safeguards to protect members from harm (in the case of vulnerable states of childhood and older adulthood), the assessment of the nature of its governance and the risk and ability to change become an urgent matter of intervention. Such work is therapeutic, but external systems hold the responsibility and protection function for the family, at least temporarily, and use different approaches of challenge and enquiry. Those families directed to using a service express mixed reactions, from relief to deep resentment. Making effective working attachments is paramount.

Sometimes the intensity and mixed passions within the family crucible can overwhelm the individual worker. Teamwork is essential in creating a supportive context for explorative work.

family script: The term comes largely from the work of John Byng Hall. It contains several elements: the circumstantial, assumptive, assumptive identity-structural, problem-solving, delivered script and subscript. Many of these aspects of attitude and response overlap. The different elements of these experiential beliefs are sometimes stated explicitly; at other times they are inferred, and clarification needs to be sought. The basis of scripts and subscripts are discovered through genogram work. Sensitivity is needed in holding the family together through whatever emerges.

family system: The application of systemic analysis and descriptions of the pattern of organization of a family. Families are complex, evolving organizations seeking within their means to find ways of providing 'good enough' care to all their members, effective working boundaries, relationship respect and solidarity in times of change whether through loss, illness or distress. A group of characters in search of a sense of community, families have many different forms, some culturally, religiously and socially constructed. Each family is unique in its own way and is usually a highly protected and protective system, and therefore convening it for the prospect of therapeutic work may be resisted by them, but more especially by therapists. Some family systems can maintain a level of toxicity and dangerousness that subverts the growth of a secure sense of being and well-being of its members.

genogram: A family tree whose organic structure enables many themes and experiences to emerge in the therapy dialogue and for the family to have a deeper grasp of their historical, cultural, ontological and relational roots.

grraacceess: A mnemonic devised by British family therapist John Burnham to delineate the range of personal identity differences (gender, religion, race, age, (dis)ability, culture, class, education, employment, sexuality and spirituality) and which may attract discrimination and social exclusion. These differences can be used to oppress through the projection of negative attribution, and involve depersonalization, through confusing 'the person' with 'the difference'. The genogram helps to reveal beliefs about difference within and without the family at the community interface. The grraacceess is a valuable tool in helping you locate your own differences and any unease about closed ideas towards those differences that are not in experiential contact with self.

holon: A term coined by Arthur Koestler to describe the total systemic, connective structure of our living world, social and natural. All elements comprise parts which are whole in themselves and yet parts of others, like a matryoshka doll. Our world is built from many billions of atomic particles, cells, different levels of assemblies and part assemblies conjoined and organized to make up creation.

homeostasis: The equilibrium or balance that any system or organized structure achieves. The point of equilibrium in a human system may not be conducive to human well-being, e.g. oppressive political regimes where stability is at the expense of human rights, and social equity. Sometimes the homeostasis is freakish, e.g. the leaning Tower of Pisa. In closed family systems the prospect of change in the balance of power and the familiar may be received with apprehension in its homeostatic force field.

human condition: Beneath the personal and interrelational condition is the universal experiential substratum, the human condition, for we exist in a world in which we are transient occupants. In the history of psychotherapy this dimension has been most comprehensively addressed in the existential tradition, especially by Irvin Yalom, who cites the key elements of the human condition as meaninglessness, aloneness, death and freedom. These dimensions are the main sources of distress, fear and anxiety. Spiritual- and humanistic-based philosophies suggest attentive care, co-operation, faith in a higher ideal, conciliation, community, rationally based discourse, work and resilience in living are among the compensating virtues which mitigate the darker elements of the human condition. Literature, the creative arts, philosophy, comparative spirituality and the great contemplative traditions of world spirituality provide the secure base to develop therapeutic insights and knowingness in an area which is otherwise difficult to traverse.

hypothesizing: The process of speculation about what and where the emotional and communication constriction might lie in the family dynamic. Widely conceived as a scientific methodology, this view is best exchanged for one of open engagement with the family's experiential life. Speculation is helpful to identify areas of inquiry. This should not interfere with the *epoche* ('what do I know?'), otherwise key elements of the family's descriptive process will be subjugated by an 'expert' view of what is happening. The family owns the therapy, not the therapist; the therapist owns the methods, techniques and approaches.

intensification: The application of a technique from structural family therapy which, as with unbalancing power relationships, challenges or introduces tension into a situation where difficulties are seen with fatalism or passivity. It reheats the crucible. Where there are high levels of emotional reactivity this can also be used to carry the scenario to absurd limits. An example is the case of a 45-year-old alcoholic diabetic who continued binge drinking, having left his wife and children and moved back in with his parents. His 70-year-old mother had just been discharged from hospital with depression and non-specific stomach pains. All three attended a third session. *Therapist (to son):* 'So, Tony, you're continuing to drink in spite of the advice from the doctors. Really, you're a kamikaze pilot intending to end your life with a bang.' *Tony (triumphantly warming to the description):* 'Yes, a kamikaze pilot – with the cockpit screwed down.' *Therapist:* 'Well, that's helpful for your mother and father, because they now know the game is up, and worrying about you and trying to get you help isn't going anywhere.' *Tony (silent). Therapist to father:* 'It doesn't look as if Tony wants any more help, so perhaps you would be better helping your wife recover her own health than worrying about Tony's.' The father nodded, a little stunned, as was his wife.

inter-experience: A term used by R.D. Laing to describe the interactive process between at least two people who are participant-observers in one another's personal space. A potentially endless feedback loop is created whereby 'I experience you and am experiencing the experience of me experiencing you, and you are experiencing my experience of you', etc. Laing also called it interpersonal perception. His *Knots* (1970) is full of examples of the enfoldingness of such relational interchanges, though the inter-experience process is not inherently problematical or endless.

interrelational phenomenology: Like inter-experience, the relational interactivity in systems, especially the intimacy of family systems. It is the level between personal phenomenology and systemic phenomenology, since it is the living relational exchange between persons in a system. Family systems comprise whole aggregates of such sets of inter-relational experience in its subsystems.

jainist, jainism: Small but influential Indian religion founded between the sixth and ninth centuries BC. Among its many beliefs are non-violence (*ahimsa*), respect for non-absolute thought (*anekantaveda*) and a system of logical reasoning that is paradoxical and inclusive (*sayadavada*). Gandhi was strongly influenced by Jainism.

maieutic: The second part of the phenomenological method with *epoche* in which the stance of the therapist helps the bringing forth of ideas, beliefs and experience, rather as a midwife helps deliver a child.

ontological in/security: A phrase usually attributed to R.D. Laing (from the Greek *ontos*, 'to be', and 'ology', i.e. the knowledge of being). Living in a world that is personally finite and therefore a source of potential fear and anxiety, the starting point of ontology is every person's self-experience. The opening of Hamlet's famous soliloquy – 'To be or not to be ...' – encapsulates the ontological dilemma of personal purpose and suffering. This experience constantly seeks a balance between security and insecurity. Secure attachment helps build the default position early in life, which makes a return to this experience easier to accomplish during times of distress. However, a sense of ontological security can be built from within throughout life.

personal phenomenology: This is the subjectivity of personal experience based on two cognitive elements, conceptions and perceptions (Goethe's 'We only see what we know'). In Bowlby's attachment theory the conceptions are the internalized working models of social-role relationships (of father, mother, or family) and of their experienced behaviour. Where these are secure and good, the perceptions and expectations of interactional response will be also. Where they have been disruptive, the perceptions and expectations are likewise problematical in a child's experience. Sometimes there may be a reaching after archetypical conceptions of the 'good father'/'good mother' through identification with spiritual figures or deities. The family script and subscript contain the working-out of these different experiences, usually with conflict.

phenomenology: The method of deconstructing the conceptions, perceptions, judgements and emotions of subjective experience to reveal their more authentic structure (from the Greek *phainomenon*, 'that which appears'). Though developed by Edmund Husserl (1859–1938), it has its roots in the dialogic encounters of ancient philosophy. The phenomenologist seeks to deepen the description of experience to its truer fullness through the use of bracketing, or *epoche*, and the *maieutic* method. There are three levels of phenomenology: personal, interrelational and systemic.

positive connotation: A description and reinterpretation that seeks to represent the context around distress or conflictual experiences in more productive ways to assist an attitudinal shift within a person, relationship or whole system.

reframing: Like positive connotation, this seeks to set a different context of meaning in which difficulty of attitude or motivation is understood and experienced. Just as reframing a picture highlights its different characteristics, so for a family it points to new possibilities.

research and outcomes: There is a wide and growing international body of evidential research into the efficacy of family and systemic-based therapy. This may be best accessed initially via the UK Association for Family Therapy website, www.aft.org.uk.

script analysis: The process of listening, understanding and reinterpreting the live flow of dialogue in a family therapy session while checking out the accuracy of the apprehended with the subjects. There are a number of different elements that comprise a script.

self-reflection: An allied but slightly different process to self-reflexivity, involving our awareness of our whole ontological position and identity in a finite, changing life process.

self-reflexivity: The incorporation into active consciousness of the values and belief systems that form the relativity and differentiation of personal identity. Our social relationships feed back elements of our identity to us (G.H. Mead).

social constructionism: A sociological and philosophical theory derived from social phenomenology in which meaning and linguistic attribution are products of the social and cultural context. Though a very helpful perspective, therapeutically it can be used unwittingly to take an expert-distancing stance and fail to fully engage experientially, since it neglects to attend to an ontological perspective in its analysis of the ingredients of construction. Empathy as an essential element for effective therapy is likewise neglected.

structural, problem-solving script: The beliefs about family organization; the power, authority, hierarchy, decision-taking and problem resolution on which all families – whatever their size or structure – have to take a position, even if unthinkingly.

subscript: Contains the unspoken beliefs or felt states (which are sometimes non-conscious) of constricted emotions such as desire, need, disappointment, rage, hatred and love; sometimes these emerge into the **delivered script** during the therapeutic dialogue. The subscript is less easy to identify and is layered under the collective and narrative experience of the family in negotiating the pain, stresses and adversities of life. The subscript is often maintained out of an anxiety to protect the imagined unity and security of the family. It is difficult for one person within a turbulent family system to change the pattern of the whole family without high personal cost.

systemic: A 'chameleon word' that can be used in multiple ways, without any unifying principle. It is the pattern of organization of all things organic, inorganic and directed by the human consciousness. To perceive the patterning invites a perspective of a removed observer (e.g. at a sports event or a concert) sharing secondary engagement; or of participant as a member of an interacting human system (e.g. a family, a workplace organization, a professional association). Such a positioning as participant-observer as a member of a system is more challenging, since seeing the pattern is also to be part of the pattern.

The term systemic is derived from the Greek *syn*, 'together', and *histanai*, 'to set', so it means 'to put alongside'. Systems interlock from being 'put alongside' one another. Thus to speak of bio-psycho-social-political-medical dimensions is to an extent redundant from a systemic point of view; they are different but conjoined parts of a unified phenomenon. Systemic thought is naturally interdisciplinary.

The main elements of systems are structure (the interconnection of parts and wholes); function (the goals and objectives of human systems are more complex; natural systems' evolutionary function is to replenish and survive); and process (the communication of information and energy that keeps a sustaining balance to the different elements and levels of the system).

systemic phenomenology: A variation of phenomenological method which deals with the total intersubjectivity of differing perceptions, conceptions and experiences of family membership. It puts alongside one another different descriptions and sets of experience without prejudice, and seeks from continuous clarification and redirection of the dialogue to help different, more helpful meanings to emerge. This is done by moving the dialogue around the family membership, aligning to no one perspective in the family. The therapeutic leadership has to cultivate the *epoche* and maieutic methods in the same way as in personal work. Though the method deepens the family's experience, it is not a long-term therapy. The family's collaboration is sought and confirmed at all stages of the process, which is especially important for the determination of ending.

triangulation: The presence of a third person in a relationship that creates a different, sometimes explosive, dynamic but can also preserve a stable homeostasis. These triangular dynamics are present in many dramatic works, from *Oedipus Rex* (Oedipus is triangulated between his birth family and his adopted family, whom he falsely believes to be his birth one); famously in J.P. Sartre's *Huis Clos* [*No Exit*], where three people are confined to an eternity together, inflicting suffering on one another. The 'drama triangle' (sometimes called the Karpman triangle) articulates the archetypical dynamic of interchangeable role performance in human suffering and conflict between 'victim', 'perpetrator' and 'rescuer' or 'healer'. This is a valuable process analysis for any family systemic therapist to understand, observe and attend to since s/he will be inducted into or unwittingly present themselves in a triangulation role. More vulnerable family members such as children or older adults often get caught up into one of these roles (usually the 'victim' or 'rescuer' archetype).

unbalancing: An active technique of structural family therapy in which the therapists or team make a temporary alliance with a person or subsystem within the family against a different belief or attitude of others in the system. The effect is to disrupt the pattern of power and perception with the intention of empowering a subordinated perspective in the family, or disrupting the lines of resistance in the family power arrangements.

virtues and adversities: The qualities and characteristics of well-being and those of distress and suffering. These are shaped and influenced by external occurrence, but are the interpretations and constructions made by those subject to them and, as such, can be reinterpreted. Reframing, positive connotation and affirmation are all ways of assisting the movement towards a changed consciousness in the family membership.

will to empower: A self- and other-directed drive to release latent human creative potential and resourcefulness, either to enable it to operate with greater effectiveness within the family or within the wider community. It is a necessary attribute in any aspiring therapist. Victor Frankl formulated a similar notional drive: the will to meaning. Cf. **will to power**.

will to power: A phrase first used by Friedrich Nietzsche and taken up by Alfred Adler to denote the drive to dominate and, in the process, deprecate others, usually to cover hidden fears of inadequacy and ontological insecurity. Cf. **will to empower**.

REFERENCES AND RECOMMENDED READING

Note: Recommended reading is graded with an asterisk (* = advised, ** = important and *** = essential).

Ackerman, N. (1958) *The Psychodynamics of Family. Life: Diagnosis and Treatment of Family Relationships*. New York: Basic Books.**

Ackerman, N. (1962) Family Psychotherapy and Psychoanalysis: Implications of Difference. *Family Process* 1(1): 30–43.

Adler, A. (1956) *The Individual Psychology of Alfred Adler*, ed. H. & R. Ansbacher. New York: Harper Torchbooks.

Albee, E. (1962) *Who's Afraid of Virginia Woolf*. London: Penguin.***

Ambler, R. (2001) *Truth of the Heart*. London: Quaker Books.

Andersen, T. (1987) The Reflection Team: Dialogue and Meta-Dialogue in Clinical Work. *Family Process* 26: 415–28.*

Andrews, H. (2007) *Hayley's Story: Using Family Therapy*. Context 94 Warrington: AFT Publishing.

Anon. (c.300 BC) *Dhammapada*. London: Penguin (1975).**

Aristotle (384–322 BC) *The Nicomachean Ethics*. London: Dent (1963).

Aristotle (384–322 BC) *The Politics*. Oxford: Oxford University Press (1995).

Armstrong, K. (2010) *Twelve Steps to a Compassionate Life*. London: Random House.*

Bakewell, S. (2010) *How to Live: A. Life of Montaigne in One Question and Twenty Attempts at an Answer*. London: Chatto & Windus.

Barton Evans, F. (1996) *Harry Stack Sullivan: Interpersonal Theory and Psychotherapy*. London: Routledge.

Bateson, G. (1972) *Steps to an Ecology of Mind*. New York: Ballantine.*

Bateson, G. (1980) *Mind and Nature: A Necessary Unity*. London: Fontana.*

Beckett, S. (1956) *Waiting for Godot*. London: Faber.**

Bell, J.E. (1961) *Family Group Therapy*. Public Health Monograph 64, US Department of Health, Education and Welfare.*

Berg, I.K. (1994) *Family Based Services: A Solution-Focused Approach*. New York: Norton.

Bevan, A. (1952) *In Place of Fear*. London: William Heinemann.

Boal, A. (1992) *Games for Actors and Non-Actors*. Trans. A. Jackson. London: Routledge.

Boal, A. (1998) *Theatre of the Oppressed*. London: Pluto Press.*

Boscolo, L. & Bertrando, P. (1996) *Systemic Therapy with Individuals*. London: Karnac.**

Böszörményi-Nagy, I. & Spark, G. (1973) *Invisible. Loyalties: Reciprocity in Intergenerational Family Therapy*. New York: Harper & Row.**

Bowen, M. (1978) *Family Therapy in Clinical Practice*. Northvale, NJ: Aronson.

Bowlby, J. (1949) The Study and Reduction of Group Tensions in the Family. *Human Relations* 2: 123–8.***

Bowlby, J. (1987) AFT *Newsletter Report on Presentation at Conference on Attachment at the Institute of Psychiatry*. London. Warrington: AFT Publishing.

Bowlby, J. (1988). *Lecture 8: Attachment, Communication and The Therapeutic Process from A Secure Base*. London: Routledge.***

Brown, J. (1997) Circular Questioning: An Introductory Guide. *Australian and New Zealand Journal of Family Therapy* 18(2): 109–14.**

Burnham, J. (2011) Development in Social GRRRAAACCEEESSS: Visible-Invisible and Voiced-Unvoiced. In *Culture, Context, and Therapeutic Reflexivity in Family Therapy*, ed. I-B. Krause. London: Karnac.*

Byng-Hall, J. (1982) Dysfunction of Feeling: Experiential. Life of the Family in A. Bentovim, G. Gorell Barnes & A. Cooklin (eds), *Family Therapy: Complementary Frameworks of Theory and Practice*, Vol. 2. London: Academic Press.

Byng-Hall, J. (1995) *Rewriting Family Scripts*. New York: The Guilford Press.**

Cade, B. & O' Hanlon, W. (1993) *A Brief Guide to Brief Therapy*. New York: Norton.***

Camus, A. (1942) *The Myth of Sisyphus*. London: Penguin (2005).*

Capra, F. (1975) *The Tao of Physics*. Boston, MA: Shambhala.

Carr, A. (1997) *Family Therapy and Systemic Consultation*. Lanham, MD: University Press of America.

Cecchin, G. (1987) Hypothesising, Circularity and Neutrality Revisited: an Invitation to Curiosity. *Family Process* 26(4): 405–13.**

Cockburn, P. and Cockburn, H. (2011) *Henry's Demons*. London/New York: Scribner.***

Cooper, D. (1974) *The Death of the Family*. London: Penguin.

deShazer, S. (1982) *Patterns of Brief Family Therapy: An Ecosystemic Approach*. New York: The Guilford Press.*

Diagnostic and Statistical Manual of Mental Disorders IV (2000) Washington, DC: American Psychiatric Association.

Fallada, H. (1947) *Alone in Berlin*. London: Penguin Classics (2009).

Flaskas, C. & Pocock, D. (eds) (2009) *Systems and Psychoanalysis: Contemporary Integrations in Family Therapy*. London: Karnac.**

Fleuridas, C. et al. (1986) The Evolution of Circular Questions: Training Family Therapists. *Journal of Marital and Family Therapy* 12(2): 113–27.**

Flynn, B. (2010) Using Systemic Reflective Practice to Treat Couples and Families with Alcohol Problems. *Journal of Psychiatric and Mental Health Nursing* 17(7): 583–93.**

Frank, J. (1961) *Persuasion & Healing: A Comparative Study of Psychotherapy.* London: Johns Hopkins University Press.

Frankl, V. (2004) *Man's Search for Meaning.* London: Random House/Rider.*

Freeman, J. (1959) 'Face to Face' interview with Carl Jung (BBC Films).

Freud, S. (1912) Recommendations to Physicians Practising Psycho-Analysis. In the *Standard Edition of the Complete Psychological Works of Sigmund Freud*, Vol. 12, trans. J. Strachey. London: Hogarth Press.

Freud, S. (1916) *Introductory. Lectures in Psychoanalysis.* London: Penguin (1974).

Freud, S. (1923) Two encyclopaedia articles. In the *Standard Edition of the Complete Psychological Works of Sigmund Freud*, Vol. 18, trans. J Strachey. London: Hogarth Press.

Gerhardt, S. (2004) *Why. Love Matters: How Affection Shapes a Baby's Brain.* London: Routledge.

Gibney, P. (2003) *The Pragmatics of Therapeutic Practice.* Melbourne: Psychoz.**

Goodman, S. & Trowler, I. (eds) (2011) *Social Work Reclaimed: Innovative Frameworks for Child And Family Social Work Practice.* London: Jessica Kingsley.

Gorell Barnes, G. (2004) *Family Therapy in Changing Times.* Basingstoke: Palgrave Macmillan.**

Grayling, A. (2003) *What is Good? The Search for the Best Way to. Live.* London: Weidenfeld & Nicolson.

Ha-Joon Chang (2011) *23 Things They Don't Tell You about Capitalism.* London: Penguin.**

Haley, J. (1962) Whither Family Therapy? New York: *Family Process* 1(1): 69–100.

Haley, J. (1963) *Strategies of Psychotherapy.* New York: Grune & Stratton.*

Haley, J. (1973) *Uncommon Therapy: The Psychiatric Techniques of Milton Erickson.* New York: Norton.**

Haley, J. (1975) Why a Mental Health Clinic Should Avoid Family Therapy. *Journal of Marital and Family Therapy* 1: 3–14.***

Haley, J. (1976) *Problem Solving Therapy.* New York: Harper Colophon.***

Hedges, F. (2005) *An Introduction to Systemic Therapy with Individuals.* Basingstoke: Palgrave Macmillan.**

Heidegger, M. (1983 [1962]) *Being and Time.* Oxford: Basil Blackwell.

Hills, J. (2002) *Rescripting Family Experiences.* London: Wiley.

Hills, J. (2004) Irreverence, Curiosity and Circularity: the Systemic Psychotherapy of Gianfranco Cecchin. *The Psychotherapist* 23.

Hills, J. (2005) Holding the Looked After Child Through Reflecting Dialogue. *Context* 78: 18–23. Warrington: AFT Publishing.

James, O. (2007) *Affluenza: How to be Successful and Stay Sane.* London: Vermillion.

James, W. (1983 [1890]) *The Principles of Psychology*, ed. George A Miller. Cambridge, MA: Harvard University Press.

Joyce, J. [1916] (1972) *Portrait of an Artist as a Young Man.* London: Penguin Classics.

Kant, I. (1784) Answering the Question: What is Enlightenment? *Berlinishe Monatsschrift.* Berlin, December.

Karpman, S. (1968) Fairy Tales and Script Drama Analysis. *Transactional Analysis Bulletin* 7(26): 39–43.*

Keats, J. (1817). Letter to his brothers George and Thomas, 21 December.

Kierkegaard, S. (1974 [1843]) *Fear and Trembling* and *Sickness unto Death*. Trans. W. Lowrie, Princeton, NJ: Princeton University Press.

Kierkegaard, S. (1974) *Concluding Unscientific Postscript to the Philosophical Fragments*, trans. David Swenson and Walter Lowrie. Princeton, NJ: Princeton University Press.

Koestler, A. (1975) *The Ghost in the Machine*. London: Picador.*

Koestler, A. (1980) *Bricks to Babel*. London: Picador.*

Laing, R.D. (1967) *The Politics of Experience*. London: Penguin.

Laing, R.D. (1970) *Knots*. London: Penguin.***

Laing, R.D. (2002) Situation, Situation, Situation: The Context of Mental Illness. *Context* 60. Warrington: AFT Publishing.**

Laing, R.D. & Esterson, A. (1964) *Sanity, Madness and the Family*. London: Pelican (1980).***

Lewis, J. (1976) *No Single Thread: Psychological Health in Family Systems*. New York: Brunner/Mazel.*

Lovelock, J. (1979) *Gaia: A New Look at Life on Earth*. Oxford: Oxford University Press.

MacIntyre, A. (1967) *A Short History of Ethics*. London: Routledge & Kegan Paul.

Marx, K. & Engels, F. (2002 [1848]) *The Communist Manifesto*. London: Penguin.

Mead, G. H. (1934) Mind, Self and Society, in A. L. Strauss (ed.), *The Social Psychology of George Herbert Mead*. Chicago: University of Chicago Press (1956).

Milan Associates (Selvini Palazzoli et al.) (1978) *Paradox and Counter Paradox*. New York: Aronson.*

Milan Associates (Selvini Palazzoli et al.) (1980) Hypothesing-Circularity-Neutrality: Three Guidelines for the Conductor of the Session. *Family Process* 19.***

Miller, A. (1949) *Death of a Salesman*. In *Plays: One*. London: Methuen (1988).**

Miller, S., Duncan, B. & Hubble, M. (1997) *Escape from Babel: Towards a Unifying Language for Psychotherapy Practice*. New York: Norton.***

Minuchin, S. (1974) *Families and Family Therapy*. Cambridge MA: Harvard University Press.**

Minuchin, S. & Fishman, H.C. (1981) *Family Therapy Techniques*. Cambridge MA: Harvard University Press.***

Moreno, J. (1987) *The Essential Moreno*, ed Jonathan Fox. New York: Springer.***

O'Leary, C.J. (2011) *The Practice of Person-Centred Couple and Family Therapy*. Basingstoke: Palgrave Macmillan.**

O'Neill, E. (1941). *A Long Day's Journey into Night*. London: Jonathan Cape (1976).***

Paine, T. (1791) *The Rights of Man*. London: Dover (2000).

Papp, P. (1980) The Greek Chorus and Other Techniques of Paradoxical Therapy. *Family Process* 19(1): 45–57.*

Pascal, B. (1670) *Pensées*. London: Penguin (1975).*

Perry, R. (1993) Empathy – Still at the Heart of Therapy: The Interplay of Context and Empathy. *Australian and New Zealand Journal of Family Therapy* 14: 63–74.**

Pinter, H. (1995) Acceptance Speech for the Award of the Nobel Prize for Literature (video, 7 December 2005).

Pirandello, L. (1993) *Six Characters in Search of an Author.* London: Methuen.**

Poole, R. (2008) *Earthrise: How Man First Saw the Earth.* London: Yale University Press.

Ricard, M. (2007) *Motionless Journey From a Hermitage in the Himalayas.* London: Thames & Hudson.

Rogers, C. (1980) *A Way of Being.* Boston: Houghton Mifflin.

Rogers, C. (1986) A Client-Centred/Person Centred Approach to Therapy, in I.L. Kutash and A. Wolf (eds). *Psychotherapist's Casebook.* San Francisco: Jossey-Bass.**

Royston, R. & Humphries, A. (2006) *The Hidden Power of Dreams.* London: Bantam.*

Russell, B. (1930) *The Conquest of Happiness.* London: Liveright (1996).**

Santayana , G. (1905) *Reason in Common Sense: Part of The Life of Reason* (1906). London: Constable. Available online.give link, please

Sartre, J-P. (2000) *Huis Clos and Other Plays.* London: Penguin.***

Satir, V. (1983) *Conjoint Family Therapy.* Palo Alto, CA: Science and Behaviour Books.**

Sayers, J. (2003) *Divine Therapy: Love, Mysticism and Psychoanalysis.* Oxford: Oxford University Press.***

Skynner, R. (1976) *One Flesh: Separate Persons.* London: Constable.**

Skynner, R. & Cleese, J. (1983) *Families and How to Survive Them.* London: Methuen.*

Slator, L. (2010) Systemic Family Therapy within a Secondary Mental Health Service. Unpublished ms.

Sophocles (*c.*429-420 BC) *Plays 1. The Theban Plays.* Trans. Don Taylor. London: Methuen Drama (1998).***

Spinelli, E. (1989) *The Interpreted World: An Introduction to Phenomenological Psychology.* London: Sage.*

Spurling, L. (2004) *An Introduction to Psychodynamic Counselling.* Basingstoke: Palgrave Macmillan.*

Stevens, A. (1991) *On Jung.* London: Penguin.*

Stikker, D. (2005) Investigating Couples/Families Experiences of the Reflecting Team within an Alcohol Treatment Setting. M.Sc. dissertation, Birkbeck College/Institute of Family Therapy, London.

Thoreau, H. (1849) *A Week on the Concord and Merrimack Rivers. Wednesday.* Free web download, Project Gutenberg.

Tillich, P. (1952) *The Courage To Be.* London: Fontana.*

Tolstoy, L. (1869) *War and Peace.* London: Wordsworth Classics (1993).

Tomm, K. (1987a) Interventive Interviewing Part 1: Strategizing as a Fourth Guideline for the Therapist. *Family Process* 26: 3–13.*

Tomm, K. (1987b) Interventive Interviewing Part 11: Reflexive Questioning as a Means to Enabling Self-Healing. *Family Process* 26: 167–83.*

Tomm, K. (1988) Interventive Interviewing Part 111: Intending to Ask. Lineal, Circular, Strategic or Reflexive Questions *Family Process* 27(1): 1–15.**

Traherne, T. (2002) *Poetry and Prose*, ed. Denise Inge. London: SPCK.

Turner, V. (1967) *The Forest of Symbols*. Ithaca, NY: Cornell University Press.

Van de Weyer, R. (2003) *A World Religions Bible*. Alresford, Hampshire: O Books.***

Valle, R. & King, M. (1978) *Existential-Phenomenological Alternatives for Psychology*. New York: Oxford University Press.*

Watzlawick, P., Beavin Bavelas, J. & Jackson, D. (1967) *The Pragmatics of Human Communication*. New York: Norton.**

Watzlawick, P., Weakland, J. & Fisch, R. (1974) *Change, the Principles of Problem Formation and Problem Resolution*. New York: Norton.***

Weil, S. (1986) *Simone Weil: An Anthology*, ed. Sîan Miles. London: Virago.

Whiffen, R. (1981). *Lectures and Tutorials: Sheldon Fellows Family Therapy Training Course*. London: Tavistock Clinic.

Whitaker, C. (1984) *AFT Newsletter*, Spring 1984. Warrington: AFT Publishing.

Whitaker, C. & Napier, A. (1988) *The Family Crucible*. New York: Bantam.***

White, M. & Epston, D. (1990) *Narrative Means to Therapeutic Ends*. New York: Norton.*

Wilkinson, R. & Pickett, K. (2009) *The Spirit Level*. London: Penguin.*

Williams, T. (1955) *Cat on a Hot Tin Roof*. London: Penguin.***

Wittgenstein, L. (1916) Journal entry, 12 October.

Wittgenstein, L. [1921] (1981) *Tractatus Logico-Philosophicus*. London: Routledge & Kegan Paul.

Wittgenstein, L. (1953) *Philosophical Investigations*. Malden: Blackwell.*

Yalom, I. (1980) *Existential Psychotherapy*. New York: Basic Books.**

Yalom, I. (2002) *The Gift Of Therapy*. London: Piatkus.***

Yalom, I. (2009) *Staring at the Sun: Overcoming the Terror of Death*. San Francisco: Jossey-Bass.***

INDEX